VOL

ALIGNING
WITH THE
APOSTOLIC

AN ANTHOLOGY OF APOSTLESHIP

APOSTLES AND APOSTOLIC MOVEMENT
IN THE SEVEN MOUNTAINS OF CULTURE

DR. BRUCE COOK
GENERAL EDITOR

Copyright © 2012 VentureAdvisers.com, Inc. d.b.a. Kingdom House Publishing

First Printing May 2013

ALIGNING WITH THE APOSTOLIC: VOLUME FIVE

Printed in the USA

ISBN: 978-1-939944-04-7

Library of Congress Control Number: 2013905713

Cover Design: Wendy K. Walters with James L. Nesbit

Interior Formatting: Wendy K. Walters

Published By KINGDOM HOUSE PUBLISHING | LAKEBAY, WASHINGTON, USA

To contact the Publisher or General Editor, call 253-858-8929 or text 512-845-3070, or email kingdomhousepublishing@gmail.com, or Skype: wbcook1, or visit:

www.KingdomHouse.net | www.KEYSnetwork.org
www.GloryRealm.net | www.VentureAdvisers.com

DEDICATION

TO THE CHIEF APOSTLE: JESUS, THE ONLY-BEGOTTEN SON OF GOD

(John 3:16-18, John 14:6, Rom. 8:32,
Rom. 10:9-13, 1 John 4:9-15)

*"Therefore, holy brothers, who share in the heavenly calling,
fix your thoughts on Jesus, the apostle and high
priest whom we confess."*
(Heb. 3:1, NIV)

AND TO THE NEXT GENERATION OF APOSTLES –

We Invite You to Stand Upon Our Shoulders

CONTRIBUTING AUTHORS

In Alphabetical Order

LaRue Adkinson
John Anderson, M.B.A.
David Andrade, Ph.D.
Doug Atha, D.S.L.
Ted Baehr, J.D., Hh.D.
Gary Beaton, B.A.
Ken Beaudry
Sharon Billins, B.S., Hh.D.
Laurie Boyd
Gordon Bradshaw, Ph.D., D.D.
Kari Browning
John Burpee, D.Min.
Philip Byler, D.R.E.
Duncan Campbell
Al Caperna, B.S.B.A.
Nick Castellano, Ph.D.
Bob Cathers, Hh.D.
Bruce Cook, Ph.D., Th.D.
Paul Cuny, B.A.
Tony Dale, M.D.
Stan DeKoven, Ph.D., D.Min.
Henry Falany
Tommi Femrite, D.P.M.
Charlie Fisher

Daniel Geraci
Berin Gilfillan, D.Min.
A.L. ("Papa") Gill, Ph.D.
Curtis Gillespie, B.S.B.A.
Max Greiner Jr., B.E.D.
Jon Grieser
Fernando Guillen, M.B.A.
Tim Hamon, Ph.D.
Mark Henderson
Robert Henderson, Hh.D.
Ray Hughes, D.D.
Kent Humphreys, B.A.
Christopher James
Stan Jeffery, M.B.A., D.Tech.
Bill Johnson, Hh.D.
Wende Jones, B.S.B.A.
Rick Joyner, Th.D.
Mark Kauffman, Ph.D.
Stephanie Klinzing
Erik Kudlis, Ph.D.
Candace Long, M.B.A.
Lee Ann Marino, Ph.D., D.D.
Joseph Mattera, D.Min.
Michelle Morrison, J.D.

CONTRIBUTING AUTHORS CONTINUED

John Muratori, D.C.L.

James Nesbit

Alice Patterson

Mark Pfeifer, B.A.

Lloyd Phillips, B.A.

Cal Pierce, B.S.B.A.

Walt Pilcher, M.B.A.

Paula Price, D.Min., Ph.D.

Gayle Rogers, Ph.D.

Morris Ruddick, B.S., M.S.

Michael Scantlebury, D.D.

Axel Sippach, Hh.D.

Kluane Spake, D.Min.

Tim Taylor, B.S.B.A.

Lorne Tebbutt

Ed Turose, B.S.B.A.

Larry Tyler, M.B.A.

Joseph Umidi, D.Min.

Thomas Webb, B.A., B.Th.

Arleen Westerhof, Ph.D.

Dick Westerhof, M.Eng.

Carl White Jr., D.D.

Dennis Wiedrick, B.A.

In addition to the General Editor, this multi-volume anthology was contributed to by 70 authors—almost all apostles and a few apostolic leaders; these are 70 spiritual elders in the body of Christ. Their contribution adds a depth of experience and authority to this historic work.

ADDITIONAL MATERIALS

VOLUME FIVE
ALIGNING WITH THE APOSTOLIC:
AN ANTHOLOGY OF APOSTLESHIP

This five-volume anthology represents an extensive body of work covering a wide range of topics discussing apostles and the apostolic. In order to keep the length of the volumes manageable, the General Editor has chosen to keep certain elements exclusive to Volume One. Each of these elements are an important part of the anthology as a whole, and reading them will provide you with a richer experience. We invite you to reference these materials in Volume One.

AVAILABLE IN VOLUME ONE:

"Whether generals or patriarchs, *nepios, teknion, paidios,* or *pater,* apostles are ambassadors of the Kingdom, duly appointed and commissioned to carry out the duties of their office. They need the strength of their weaponry, and they need to be able to use it effectively in times of warfare and in times of peace, with righteousness, peace, and joy in the Holy Spirit being the operable status of Kingdom relationships."

Dr. Bruce Cook
General Editor of *Aligning With the Apostolic, An Anthology of Apostleship*

CONTENTS

SECTION XI—APOSTOLIC CULTURE

FOREWORD BY
LYNN WILFORD
SCARBOROUGH

It is a great joy to share a few thoughts about the importance of *Aligning with the Apostolic*. When I began reading, it was difficult to stay seated because my spirit was so activated. Often I found myself pacing in the living room praying out loud while processing the new revelations. My feet wanted to do a happy dance while shouting GLORY!

There are many reasons why I believe this anthology and Dr. Bruce Cook's revelatory guidance are so important and critical to the growth and maturing of the Body of Christ in this hour. Specifically, I would like to address the three advantages of dimension, function and creative process.

Dr. Bruce Cook's book on the Apostolic adds multiple dimensions to our understanding of the Apostolic. Every architect knows that the 2-dimensional drawings are only lines on a page and the beginning steps of creating. An architect's job is not done until a structure forms and a building exists where none existed before. The architect takes what was invisible and helps it become a reality. Likewise, our previous understanding of the Apostolic has been like a beginning blueprint—flat and 2-dimensional. The scope and information offered by *Aligning with the Apostolic* takes our flat pictures and transforms them into a sculpted 3-D model. This added dimension gives new weight, form, and depth to our understanding of apostles, apostleship, and the apostolic church, and a new model, identity and place to belong for those individuals and unrecognized apostles who never fit into the previous pictures of the apostolic.

Design principles teach us that function precedes form. This means that the function of a building determines what the form will be. In Christian leadership principles, this translates into "purpose precedes position." Too often in our soulish wisdom, we try to build the form and position of spiritual things before recognizing what the function and purpose of a person, ministry, five-fold calling, spiritual gift or Apostolic was created for by God's wisdom and design. We have to return to what was in the Imagination of the Father, ordained by the Trinity, established by Christ and coached by the Holy Spirit. We often believe that we have a divine grasp, when in fact, we only have a glimpse. Paul reminds us that our glimpse of the eternal only provides a shadowy shape of the future. But, it is wonderful when new light is released from Heaven's window that allows us to see more clearly what the Father's purposes are for us all.

Aligning With the Apostolic gives light and understanding of God's design for His Bride. It helps remind us to return to the basics of function and purpose of the Apostolic in order to discover the form, position and authority that will allow us to be faithful stewards of building and equipping those entrusted to us.

"In the beginning God created..." Creating is the first attribute of the Almighty and one that we share as His sons. When we think about creating, there is difference in the forms used by man and God. Man creates with squares,

rectangles, triangles or boxes which are the building blocks of homes, castles, towers, pyramids and office buildings. Yet, God creates with a simpler form, circles. From the smallest cells to massive galaxies that fill the expanses of heaven, circles are organic living forms that have no beginning or end. Circles represent the covenant and eternal presence.

Unfortunately, for the last several thousand years, the Apostolic has been defined by and patterned after the building blocks of men instead of God's original design. Without the Spirit, man creates systems out of his logic and reason. These squares formed literal blocks that have built walls, established platforms, created denominations, started wars and destroyed faith.

As we consider the Apostolic future, and the current reformation movement, perhaps we should look at what and how we have built. Instead of returning to our denominational boxes, and religious boxes with sharp corners and boundary-defining edges, perhaps we should begin to think about circles of cooperation, fellowship, leadership. A circle is inclusive, flexible, organic at the essence, and can adapt to its environment. In *Aligning with the Apostolic*, Dr. Cook challenges our well-used paradigms and calls us to link hearts, hands and shields with each other. In these circles will be formed the true "band of brothers" and cell groups and networks that are life-giving and nourishing. What will happen when these circles are committed to honoring each other and celebrating the unique redemptive gifts of each person?

For years we have been waiting for a fuller and more complete reflection of what the Father's heart was for church growth. Could it be that when we lay aside our "boxes of religion" and embrace the flow and unity created by circles of community that then we will see the Bride of Christ manifest before our eyes?

Aligning With the Apostolic is a rich river of jewels that provides revelatory and evolutionary guidance for today's church and challenges us all to be transformed by the wisdom of the Father.

Lynn Wilford Scarborough
President, Empower.com & Prep2Bless
Author: *Talk Like Jesus* and *Spiritual Moms*
www.Empower.com.us | www.Prep2Bless.com

FOREWORD BY
DR. JOHN LOUIS
MURATORI

My foreword to Volume Five may seem a little different. However, I believe it is something the Lord has directed me to write as you begin this final installment to what has now become one of the most comprehensive series of books ever written on the exclusive subject of "The Apostolic."

Let me start by sharing something I learned many years ago when speaking to Jewish business leaders on the subjects of economics and commerce. They are not interested in discoursing about the issues or financial calamities; rather, they are invested in finding the root or source of any problem. You might say they want to discover the Genesis or beginnings of all things. Beginnings are vital to every area of life—not just knowing, but understanding them. In Biblical Hermeneutics we apply the interpretive principle of the "Law of First Mention." Whenever a word or concept is first introduced in the scriptures, it contains special significance and holds interpretive secrets for future usages. The first sets the pattern for those that follow.

Isa. 46:10 says, *"Declaring the end from the beginning, and from ancient times the things that are not yet done, saying, My counsel shall stand, and I will do all my pleasure."*

In Judaism, the beginning of a something is more important than the end. This is a reversal to how the church sees and interprets life and scripture. We lean or bend toward the end that usually justifies the means. The church has become rapture driven, waiting and longing for Jesus to rescue His bride. This type of thinking has crippled the body of Christ from occupying 'till He comes. These are two opposing mindsets – "how" can I occupy or "why" would I occupy and infiltrate all spheres of societal influence if I'm waiting to be taken out of this world?

To compound this matter, church leadership has been redefined to accommodate a more cultural acceptance. Senior church leaders are adopting more secular titles such as coaches and motivational speakers. Why am I saying this and what does it have to do with a book series on the Apostolic? I say, "Everything!" The key to the church's function, influence and power today is found in its beginning or genesis. When the Pharisees questioned Jesus concerning a list that qualifies for divorce, He redirected them back to the beginning. Jesus confirmed the original purpose of marriage and reestablished God's commitment to this covenant from the beginning.

The church has suffered from two strategic attacks of the enemy against the office and calling of the Apostle. The first occurred under Constantine with the marriage of church and state. This solidified the titles of cardinals, archbishops, bishops and monsignors. The office "Apostle" was no longer recognized.

The second happened under King James and his commissioning of the English translation of the Bible.

When the King James Bible was published in 1611, it was flawed before it got started. King James in 1604 contacted Archbishop Bancroft to oversee the translation. However, strict guidelines were to be placed upon the translators concerning the original text and the message of this "people's language" translation. The outcome was the 15 rules governing the King James translation.

Archbishop Bancroft, the head of the Anglican Church, set 14 rules of translation to maintain the doctrine and practices of the Anglican Church of England.

Bishop Bancroft and Erasmus were the architects of the King James Version translation and they were far from being saints.

The translators were obligated to fit the translation with the Anglican agenda and beliefs without any conflict between church and state.

One more rule was contributed by King James himself as "head" of the Church of England. He required a translation, which would facilitate his control over the church and the people.

Rule number three instructed the word "Ecclesia" to be translated Church. The English word "church" first appeared in 1560 in the Geneva Bible. The word "church" actually comes from the Greek word kuriakon, pronounced koo-ree-a-kon — which means, pertaining to the Lord.

Kur-i-akon is used only twice in scripture:

- 1 Cor. 11:20 — The "Lords (kuriakon) supper"
- Rev. 1:10 — The "Lords (kuriakon) day"

The translators were required to produce a translation without any conflict between church and state. Basically, King James was stripping the church from its Ecclesiastical Power and Authority. The church should only be engaged with such things that pertain to the Lord. Believers should go to church and fellowship, pray, worship and sing – that's it!! Do not let the people discover that the church is actually a congress, legislation, government, kingdom and an army.

Considering the office of Apostle had been previously removed – the church was now minimalized to effect change upon the mountains of societal influence. As a result, the church has become believer centered. Church leaders are compelled to fashion their services to cater to seekers and meet the ever-growing needs of believers.

The Apostles in the book of Acts resisted this mindset and committed themselves to the mandate and purpose Christ had commissioned them with.

Acts 6:1-8 says, *"And in those days, when the number of the disciples was multiplied, there arose a murmuring of the Grecians against the Hebrews, because their widows were neglected in the daily ministration. Then the twelve called the multitude of the disciples unto them, and said, It is not reason that we should leave the word of God, and serve tables. Wherefore, brethren, look ye out among you seven men of honest report, full of the Holy Ghost and wisdom, whom we may appoint over this business. But we will give ourselves continually to prayer, and to the ministry of the word. And the saying pleased the whole multitude: and they chose Stephen, a man full of faith and of the Holy Ghost, and Philip, and Prochorus, and Nicanor, and Timon, and Parmenas, and Nicolas a proselyte of Antioch: Whom they set before the apostles: and when they had prayed, they laid their hands on them. And the word of God increased; and the number of the disciples multiplied in Jerusalem greatly; and a great company of the priests were obedient to the faith. And Stephen, full of faith and power, did great wonders and miracles among the people."*

The early Apostles understood the difference between revival and reformation, family and government, fellowship and Ecclesia, feeling the presence and demonstrating the power, having anointing and being authorized, having compassion for sheep and commanding an army, healing people and healing nations, delivering the possessed person and pulling down principalities, powers and rulers of the darkness.

In the wake of current and ensuing global debt and conflict, our society and world await the end-time Apostolic Movement, comprised of and led by men and women who have obeyed the call, been tried in the fires of maturity, and have been commissioned as Apostles to bring order where there is chaos.

Let the pastors nurture, protect, gather and pray – but release the Apostles to decree, commission, send and demand risk.

With excitement I have read the manuscripts of these five books on the Apostolic that take the reader from the genesis of the Apostolic to the current strategy that churches and leaders can implement to see cultural transformation.

Dr. Cook has connected leaders from all over the world to contribute to this *tour-de-force* series. The vision Bruce received for this project is the Tipping Point to what I pray is the last Great Apostolic Awakening and Reformation.

Dr. John Louis Muratori
President, John Muratori Ministries
Author: *Money by Design®, Rich Church Poor Church,*
and *Seven Women Shall Take Hold of One Man*
www.johnmuratori.org

APOSTOLIC MULTIPLICATION & WEALTH

CHAPTER SIXTY-TWO

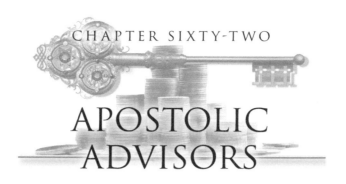

APOSTOLIC ADVISORS

DR. JOHN LOUIS MURATORI

INTRODUCTION

Have you ever wondered, *"What in the world is going on?"* Well, I have and I've come to the conclusion that the world is a mess! Yes, a mess. I searched for a better word to describe the situation we're in; however, mess defines it perfectly. This word means chaos, confusion, disarray, and disorder.

Please, don't listen to the propaganda of the liberal media or government. They would have us believe that elections, politicians and government can solve our problems. In reality, that's exactly who has spawned, what I believe is, the worst global economic crisis in world history.

As a business owner, international consultant, economics instructor and a member of an emerging generation of apostolic leaders—I'm dismayed at the "business-as-usual" mindset and the actions of both church and secular leadership. As in the days of Noah, we are inundated with the affairs of life so much so that we don't see or heed the signs or warnings of impending disaster.

We are living on the verge of a cataclysmic shift in our institutions, social structures and geography. The significance of the time we are in can't be overstated.

Let me describe the three contributing factors affecting our current global crisis.

MARKET MANIPULATORS

The first is "Market Manipulators." We are witnessing what I call "Money Manipulators" who are profiting from an unstable economy. The stock market should never experience 300-point swings in either direction – almost daily. Wall Street speculators are using new practices to control and drive the markets for greedy gain at the expense of taxpayers. I believe these types of swings violate insider trader laws; yet, no one is policing their dealings. Consider this: in January 2008 the stock market fell into the 6,000-point range. That number was a reflection of the poor health of our publically-traded companies, global markets and economies. Four years later we are approaching 14,000. You would naturally think that is the result of a booming economy with a strong housing market, low unemployment and growing GDP.

Here is the scam; since 2008 we have increased the national debt by five trillion dollars. That number is truly unthinkable and incomprehensible. We've maintained above 8.2% unemployment and hit as high as 12%. Serious economists will tell you that the number is much higher when you factor in those who have given up looking for work. We've lost on average 500,000 jobs per month over four years tallying over 26 million Americans unemployed. For every one job the government claims they've created

– we've lost five. The subprime housing market crash has pillaged the wealth of the middle class.

In the past four years, more than 3.7 million homes have been lost to foreclosure, according to market research firm CoreLogic. There's no end in sight, considering 20% of Americans are upside down in their mortgages—meaning the value of their home is less than the amount of their loan! Speaking of foreclosures – over 150 U.S. cities have filed for bankruptcy, now a growing trend. Considering the overwhelming data, how do we reconcile the outrageous market highs with the pitiful economic lows? The lack of common sense is resulting in trillions lost.[1]

INCALCULABLE NUMBERS

The second factor is incalculable numbers. It's not that we've lost sight of the enormity of our debt; rather, we can't comprehend it. We are experiencing a new level in human comprehension. I compare this to the 4-minute mile. It was once believed that running a mile in under four minutes was physically impossible... until Roger Bannister did it on May 6, 1954. We now know the 4-minute barrier was not physical – rather, it was psychological. Two months after Bannister broke the barrier, two other runners followed suit. Once people could comprehend it, they could achieve it. Similarly, *because we cannot comprehend the debt, we cannot constrain it.*

U.S. and world debt is at an incomprehensible amount. The numbers are so staggering they appear make believe. Even calculator manufacturers don't produce calculators that work in the trillions. They consider it unnecessary and, for most, unfathomable. Here's a little exercise to help wrap your head around the numbers.

How much is "a trillion" dollars? Well, if you had gone into business on the day Jesus was born, and your business lost a million dollars *each day*, 365 days a year, *it would take you until October 2737 to lose $1 trillion*. One trillion $10 bills, taped end to end, would wrap around the Earth more than 380 times. You could spend $10 million a day and it would still take you 273 years to spend $1 trillion.

We are now playing with Monopoly money – except no one goes to jail, and the few that do have a "get out of jail free" card!

People say "time" has a way of healing and putting things in perspective. So, let's use time to understand a trillion dollars. If every second were a dollar then a million seconds (dollars) would calculate to 12 days. A billion seconds or dollars would equate to 32 years. And a trillion seconds or dollars would be 31,688 years.

Because we can't comprehend our current debt crisis, we cannot even start to devise a plan to correct the problem.

NORMALCY BIAS

I've often wondered, "Why are people not outraged at what is happening in our nation, and the world economies?" Could it be the frog in the frying pan syndrome or something more? In my quest for understanding, I came across a psychological condition called Normalcy Bias.[2] This is a mental state people enter when facing a horrific or unthinkable disaster. According to research, Normalcy Bias causes people to *underestimate* both the *possibility* of a disaster occurring and its *possible effects*. People fail to adequately prepare for a disaster. The *assumption* of *Normalcy Bias* is that since a disaster has never occurred, then it never will occur. Normalcy Bias reflects the *inability of people to cope* or react adequately to something they've not experienced before. So then, Americans are denying the warning signs and just believing things are going to be all right. Maybe that's why they voted for a President who runs his campaign on "hope" rather than his policies and record.

CHURCH SHAKE

Where will the church be in five years? That discussion needs to happen now. With the rapid change in the world around us, the church must present new methodologies anchored in our core kingdom message. If you are a Pastor or church leader, you must accept that the economic recession, job loss and social apathy will affect your congregation. Currently 350 churches per month are closing their doors.[3] You have an opportunity to position your church ahead of this curve. It begins by learning to lead from an *apostolic mandate* rather than from a pastoral care-giver paradigm and position. This is very different than the current status quo.

For the most part the church has responded to these social challenges with a business-as-usual approach. We hide ourselves under our prayer blankets and hope the government will solve our problems or the rapture happens soon. Part of the dilemma is most church leaders have not been adequately trained to deal with such economic and social structure issues. However, this is an opportunity for the church to move to the forefront, and a time to open our sanctuaries to become centers for job-training where our communities hear God's plan and receive His provision for their families. Churches are the places where faith conquers fear and God's people advance through the valleys of life.

This is not just a novel concept; rather, it's a reality that's gaining momentum as you read this. For starters, our *Money by Design*™ curriculum (MBD) is now being used in colleges and churches around the world. It has initiated business startups, released an entrepreneurial spirit, created economic relief and new jobs on an international level. This is just the beginning as we confront these economic issues head on. God is raising a new breed of entrepreneurs called and anointed to create wealth.

Our church leadership came to the realization that our great grandmother's envelope system is not biblical theology. With 26 million people out of a job and numerous industries gone for good, where do you get the money to put in the envelope? I submit to you that jobs should be a priority in Christian Theology. Genesis reveals God as the Almighty job creator. Creation Design shows God created a job for Adam before he was formed. These verses declare the rain neither descended nor the plants grew *UNTIL* man was placed in his position.

Gen. 2:5 *"And every plant of the field before it was in the earth, and every herb of the field before it grew: for the LORD God had not caused it to rain upon the earth, and there was not a man to till the ground."*

Gen. 2:8 *"And the LORD God planted a garden eastward in Eden; and there he put the man whom he had formed."*

Gen. 2:15 *"And the LORD God took the man, and put him into the Garden of Eden to dress it and to keep it."*

Fruit and prosperity was the result of man finding and fulfilling his job. Imagine this: 26 million unemployed Americans storm our churches to find wisdom, knowledge and God's will for their careers and family. We then offer them training built upon the biblical principles for wealth creation, management and distribution – principles, transferable to every nation, that work best in difficult and turbulent economic times. My friend, it's happening! Churches are being transformed into Apostolic Houses of City transformation. This transformation speaks of the various methodologies being used to minister the correct antidote to each social and personal deficiency.

APOSTOLIC ADVISORS

There is an emerging company of Apostolic Advisors who are providing kingdom strategies for governments, corporations, institutions and churches. You may liken them to Joseph who provided Pharaoh with a multi-year strategic plan to save the known world from famine. Joseph wasn't just a dreamer – he was an unmatched strategist. It wasn't his interpretation of the dream that caused his promotion. It was his plan of survival and divine instruction to Pharaoh that triggered his *prison to power* and *rags to riches* story.

"'Now therefore let Pharaoh look out for a man discreet and wise, and set him over the land of Egypt. Let Pharaoh do this, and let him appoint officers over the land, and take up the fifth part of the land of Egypt in the seven plenteous years. And let them gather all the food of those good years that come, and lay up corn under the hand of Pharaoh, and let them keep food in the cities. And that food shall be for store to the land against the seven years of famine, which shall be in the land of Egypt; that the land perish not through the famine.' And the thing was good in the eyes of Pharaoh, and in the eyes of all his servants. And Pharaoh said unto his servants, 'Can we find such a one as this is, a man in whom the Spirit of God is?' And Pharaoh said unto Joseph, 'Forasmuch as God hath shewed thee all this, there is none

so discreet and wise as thou art: Thou shalt be over my house, and according unto thy word shall all my people be ruled: only in the throne will I be greater than thou.' And Pharaoh said unto Joseph, 'See, I have set thee over all the land of Egypt'" (Gen. 41:33-41).

The 21st Century church would do well to function in a similar manner to its biblical counterpart. The Apostles mingled, ministered and gave ear to kings, princes, governors, senators, merchants, militaries, bankers, lenders, business and world leaders. They were recognized as Kingdom Authorities. You might say they were Apostolic Ambassadors, Advisors, Strategists and Economists.

APOSTOLIC GRACE

In the book of Acts we see that the Apostles were not just conscientious in spreading the gospel message. Over the years I've been told more times than I can count, "just preach." It is said as if preaching is the "end all" of personal, social and human difficulties. In addition, I've been criticized for consulting with politicians and government agencies, owning businesses and developing multiple streams of income for personal and kingdom purposes.

These verses show us the apostles became responsible for Kingdom Capital. The equivalent of millions of dollars was put at the apostles' feet.

*"Neither was there any among them that lacked: for as many as were possessors of lands or houses sold them, and brought the prices of the things that were sold, And **laid them down at the apostles' feet**: and **distribution was made** unto every man according as he had need. And Joses, who by the apostles was surnamed Barnabas, (which is, being interpreted, The son of consolation,) a Levite, and of the country of Cyprus, Having land,*

*sold it, and brought the money, and **laid it at the apostles'
feet***" (Acts 4:34-37, author's emphasis).

So, the apostles were then and are now faced with a
unique problem. People were selling their properties and
making an investment in the mission of the Kingdom. At
first glance you could be thinking, "What's the problem?"
The fact is not all five-fold leaders can handle finances—
therein lies the problem. In fact, large amounts of money
carry the potential to bring lots of trouble. In over two and
a half decades of ministry, I've traveled the world assisting
churches, ministries and ministers with numerous matters.
Finance has consistently topped the list. I've learned
ministers and ministries are in serious need of economic
advice and guidance.

Like the Jerusalem church in the New Testament, many
current pastors are facing an economic downturn that has
the potential to devastate their congregations. So, how did
the first Apostles handle persecution, poverty and hostile
government policies while still engaging in church planting,
meeting needs and growing disciples?

The answer is found in the preceding verse, which says,
"Great grace was given to them" (Acts 4:33, author's
emphasis). Certain apostles were given a particular grace
— you might say a mantle to understand and administer
(govern) wealth for Kingdom purposes. This isn't "saving
grace," considering the apostles were already believers;
rather, it was an additional portion of grace given to confront
the issues the church was facing.

Great grace was made available to help them deal with
what they lacked in capacity and wisdom. Though they had
just been filled with the spirit, they still needed additional

strategies, policies, structures and governance. I believe *the church is in this same condition today.*

Fortunately, I see many apostolic leaders who have an anointing to raise, collect, invest, and oversee large amounts of Kingdom resources. They have the ability and the understanding to handle and leverage millions of dollars for Kingdom expansion.

The church planter, pastor, teacher or evangelist may have been given the grace to gather people and teach, yet may not have the grace to raise capital, finance spiritual ventures or distribute wealth. The missionary may have the specific grace to explain the Cross of Christ and start the process of discipleship. The pastor may have the particular grace to shepherd and care for the sheep. However, they NEED apostolic strategies and advice. This is reminiscent of Paul's instruction that the church must operate with all the parts of the body executing specific functions. Each one of them is important. The synergy of collaboration produces the greatest success.

So, a main function of the apostle is to develop strategies to govern and guide prosperity—not just in the church but in the societies it reaches.

"For unto us a child is born, unto us a son is given: and the government shall be upon his shoulder: and his name shall be called Wonderful, Counselor, the mighty God, The everlasting Father, and the Prince of Peace. Of the increase of his government and peace there shall be no end…" (Isa. 9:6-7).

I suggest that a major component of the kingdom mandate to reach the world is also to disciple nations. This means assisting international governments to establish righteous laws and policies.

"When the righteous are in authority, the people rejoice: but when the wicked beareth rule, the people mourn" (Prov. 29:2).

Early in ministry I received a call from a member of my congregation looking to bounce some ideas off of me. I met with him, expecting he would ask a series of biblical questions or maybe the great money question, *"When to tithe, and when not to tithe."* However, his questions were concerning his decision to expand his business and his need for a new management model. He said, while in prayer, the Lord had prompted him to seek my counsel. I went on to assist him and his business with Spirit-birthed solutions that I didn't learn in formal ministry training.

That meeting, more than 20 years ago, changed my perspective regarding my calling and position. Since then, I've consulted for the U.S. Department of Homeland Security, and political candidates and corporations, to name just a few. I've also been called in to consult with international governments and universities. I was asked by the U.S. Department of Mental Health to come to Washington and speak to a gathering of hundreds of Non-Profits on the subject of creating businesses and income streams to fund their organizations.

Today, our consulting firm, *City Ink* ™ has a global initiative to work with social, economic and political arenas that build and sustain wealth, justice and morality. In addition, we collaborate on projects with education product developers, election campaigns, publishers, brand managers and media production for TV and film.

In addition, I still pastor a growing church that has expanded to two campuses. One is located in Dallas, Tex. and the other in Cheshire, Conn.

APOSTOLIC LAW AND POLICY

I mentioned earlier the idea of Government (apostles) setting policy and supporting organizations (churches, ministers) with management, wealth distribution and aid.

How important is it to have representation and input into legislation and policy making? Laws and policies are structural components of society and government. They help maintain order and safety while establishing cultural priorities. In essence, they shape the political and social fabric of communities at every level—from towns and cities to states and the nation.

Laws establish a system of rules and regulations that govern private citizens, organizations, institutions, companies and organized groups. The judicial system, executive branch, law enforcement and, at times, the military are authorized and empowered to enforce agreed-upon laws.

Policies are principles and procedures formulated to accomplish long-term results to provide resolution to particular problems. Policies can be hindered or enhanced by the law. Policy influences laws just as laws influence policy.

Notice how policy is always changing? Policy is created to establish a desired outcome. It is either reinforced by the old law or creates a need to establish a new law. Jesus shared a message concerning a Kingdom. I believe the church was established for God to partner with man in the establishment of policies and procedures for His kingdom to function on this earth. His intention was not to replace the old law but to establish a new law under grace. Policy is required for governance.

Apostolic leaders must influence policy makers to secure positive change and create laws that promote justice, freedom and morality. I was hosting and moderating a political forum on the condition of our nation and elections with former campaign strategist, best-selling author and Fox contributor Dick Morris. During our private conversations, he stated that the church has always been the catalyst for social change. I was stunned at his fluid knowledge of church history dating back hundreds of years. He said, *"John, the church must engage the political and cultural agendas or our nation is doomed."*

Mr. Morris encouraged me to influence the political landscape, while churches in the area, criticized me for mingling church and state, politics and ministry. Maybe we should just wait until free speech isn't free anymore and then say something. Wake up church! I pray, as you read this chapter, you are moved to connect to apostolic leaders who are creating and influencing policy. It's time to release our congregations to influence every aspect of society.

APOSTOLIC SETBACKS

I must admit there are many apostles who are talkers and not walkers. They are titled leaders who carry no influence because they have ignored their responsibility to lead and guide beyond their narrow interests. They haven't built anything that would put the church in its rightful position of authority. This has frustrated the apostolic movement. This issue dates back to the New Testament church where Paul is clarifying his apostolic calling.

*"Truly the **signs** of an **apostle** were wrought among you in all patience, in **signs,** and **wonders,** and **mighty deeds"** (2 Cor. 12:12, author's emphasis).

He warns the church to beware of false apostles. That warning applies to every church - governing position, including pastors, elders, deacons and so on...

*"For such are **false apostles**, deceitful workers, transforming themselves into the apostles of Christ"* (2 Cor. 11:13, author's emphasis).

This is why many leaders and churches don't go to the apostles for resources and strategy. They are missing out on all the benefits the government officials (apostles) have labored to establish for the people (church). God has given the true apostles wisdom and understanding that would immensely benefit the church.

One of the problems I've seen is that the 21st century leader wants to be an apostle, a teacher, a pastor, a prophet, an administrator... so on and so on. However, the reality is God may not have given them this grace. Sure, you can probably do all of those things, but you are not maximizing the grace God has given for your particular assignment and calling. The result is frustration in the life of others and in your own life.

On the flip side, many apostles have been so busy playing secretary (taking phone calls and responding to emails) that they don't have time to write policy and develop strategy with other leaders. They get bogged down in details and miss the opportunity to be a voice in the circles of power and influence. The bottom line is the church is losing out because of it.

To sum up all of this, the apostle has been given the grace and gifting to, among other things, develop strategies that impact the political and cultural outcomes of our time.

Jethro gave Moses a multilevel strategy to govern and adjudicate every possible social concern that would arise. As you can imagine, there were many in the transition from two million plus unorganized slaves to a well-ordered nation. Included was a multi-level management structure that today's rabbis teach and is in use in most Fortune 500 companies.

This apostolic mandate included the strategy to create, gather, accumulate and distribute wealth. It would seem that these are the main roles of the 21st Century apostles. Therefore, true apostles should be sought out for guidance and direction in handling the many-faceted finances and resources God wants to put at the church's disposal.

"But thou shalt remember the LORD thy God: for it is He that giveth thee power to get wealth..." (Deut. 8:18).

In my experience, consulting with struggling organizations, all lack is the result of four potential failures.

- **FAILED POLICY**: This constitutes the laws that businesses and entrepreneurs rely upon.
- **FAILED PROCEDURE:** methodologies and processes used in wealth creation and distribution.
- **FAILED PERSONNEL**: misguided, incompetent or mismanaged leaders.
- **FAILED PRAYER:** lack of prayer, the wrong kind of prayer, misguided prayer, ineffective prayer, or prayer that is not governmental in nature (without authority).

APOSTOLIC TEAMS

This brings me to what I call apostolic teams. There is safety, increased authority and wisdom in numbers. I write about this extensively in *Money by Design.*

*"Where no counsel is, the people fall: but in the **multitude of counselors** there is safety"* (Prov. 11:14, author's emphasis).

Here is the concept of an Apostolic Finance Team. In corporations we have a progression, from Bookkeeper to Accounting Clerk to Controller to Chief Financial Officer. Then we have outside Auditors, Accountants, CPAs, etc. I think apostles of finance and governance do well to emulate this as much as possible – the difference being that each of those functions must be handled with God's wisdom and grace. We can then share the load, just as Moses had Bezalel and others help him with the tabernacle, and David had Asaph to help him with 24-7 worship. Large amounts of money are too tempting and too seductive for any one person to manage by himself. Having a financial team or council in place promotes accountability and godly stewardship. In my opinion, there is great wisdom in having financial and accounting safeguards and controls built into the management process.

One must understand the full spectrum or cycle of wealth—from creation or inheritance, multiplication or management, and distribution or generational investment.

APOSTOLIC ROOTS

It is important to clarify that the apostolic movement was birthed on the shoulders of Judaism. What I mean is, what we have learned or been taught about the apostles and the first century church they pioneered is from a post apostle —Christian worldview. You must understand that most believers have a Christian worldview that originates *after* Constantine. The First Council of Nicaea in 325 A.D. was the final break between Christianity and Judaism.

One may think, "How is that important?" It is important because this event completed the exodus of Christianity from their Jewish roots. The church would eventually embrace replacement theology and declare it is the New Jerusalem. Simultaneously, this marriage of church and state through Constantine would open the church to pagan gods, festivals and practices. They don't call it the "Dark Ages" for no reason.

Let me focus on what I believe is the key to understanding the Apostolic spheres of influence. Jesus was a Jewish Rabbi who chose 12 male Jews to establish the Church. Their message was the New Covenant, which can only be understood by those who had in-depth knowledge of the previous covenants. Their assignment flowed from His assignment. Jews were equipped and empowered by the Torah and Talmud to be the head and not the tail – meaning, to occupy positions of authority and engage in every sphere of social influence.

God instructed the Jews to be lenders and not borrowers. The Talmud gave instruction to use honest interest rates and forbade usury. Modern-day credit card companies charge outrageous interest rates. That practice would have been condemned as usurious (Deut. 28:12-13). Rabbis had to know not only ritual observances but commercial regulations as well. Rabbis were also responsible for setting the interest rates on Gentile loans.

I chronicle the history of the Jews through three chapters in *Money By Design*, connecting God, Judaism and Christianity. I also trace Modern Capitalism to its roots in the Talmud. Do you know that 90% of all global wealth is controlled by 3% of the populace? That 3% is the Jewish people.

So then, Jesus' teaching about a Messiah Kingdom and Meshiach was accepted and understood by the apostles. Judaism had prepared the apostles for Kingdom rule. All they needed was power and authority, which Jesus declared He has after His resurrection.

"And Jesus came and spake unto them, saying, 'All power is given unto me in heaven and in earth'" (Matt. 28:18, author's emphasis).

You might say this chapter is built upon our apostolic forefathers Abraham, Moses, David, Solomon, Zerubbabel, Nehemiah and Daniel. These Jewish heroes laid the foundation for New Testament and 21st century Apostles.

The church would do well to identify and listen to those apostles who have the calling and the understanding to develop strategies for kingdom resources.

ENDNOTES

1. http://www.foxbusiness.com/government/2012/09/05/what-foreclosure-crisis-means-for-election/

2. Finding Something to Do: the Disaster Continuity Care Model http://en.wikipedia.org/wiki/Normalcy_bias

3. http://www.keepgodinamerica.com/statistics.asp

ABOUT THE AUTHOR

Dr. John Louis Muratori is Author of the Best-Selling book and multi-media curriculum *Money by Design,* and Founder and CEO of City Ink Consulting, a New England-based brand consulting and marketing firm. With his international ministry, John Muratori Ministries (JMM), John has been consulting with CEOs, pastors, and government leaders across the globe for over 20 years. He is also a frequent keynote speaker at conferences, and serves as senior pastor and apostolic overseer of Calvary Life Family Worship Center. John holds a Doctor of Christian Leadership degree (D.C.L.) from Christian Leadership University. For more information or to contact him, visit his web sites www.johnmuratori.com or www.moneybydesign.tv or www.calvarylife.us.

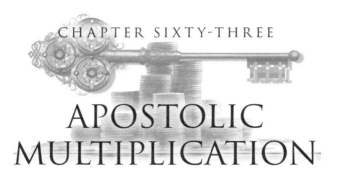

CHAPTER SIXTY-THREE

APOSTOLIC MULTIPLICATION

JON R. GRIESER

INTRODUCTION

At 1:45 a.m. Eastern time, September 15, 2008, the investment bank Lehman Brothers filed for bankruptcy. CNBC had broken into their regular broadcast schedule the evening before to bring live coverage of Lehman Brothers employees arriving to clean out their desks while many of their colleagues were already leaving the building carrying boxes containing personal items. CNBC commentators had the "deer in the headlights" stare as the financial markets were in crisis and panic was prevalent on trading floors during the late summer and autumn of 2008. Many were wondering what direness the future months would bring as the financial markets appeared to be seizing up.

The last decade or so has been very interesting to say the least for anyone managing their investments. Since 2000, there are times when it has been relatively easy to multiply assets, and there have been other times, such as the last half of 2008, where it has proven to be a challenge.

The primary purpose of a financial advisor is merging the vision of the client with prudent investment selection in order to multiply the resources under the client's stewardship. While each advisor may have different methods to accomplish this, a very general strategy may be similar to the following: 1) assess the needs, goals, risk tolerance, and time horizons of the client; 2) formulate an asset allocation based on that assessment; 3) choose specific investments for the portfolio; and 4) continue to monitor the portfolio, making changes as conditions warrant. The goal is to multiply the client's assets. While markets fluctuate and there have been some very challenging times in the last 10 to 12 years, if there is no increase in a client's portfolio, then chances are it is only a matter of time before the client will probably be hunting for a new advisor!

MULTIPLICATION: A SIGN OF COVENANT AND A KINGDOM MANDATE

Just as a client expects his portfolio to grow under the stewardship of the financial advisor, it is God's expectation that His sons and daughters increase and multiply in every area. In fact, multiplication is a sign of covenant blessing. God told Abram in Gen. 12:2-3:

"I will make you a great nation; I will bless you; And make your name great; And you shall be a blessing. I will bless those who bless you, And I will curse him who curses you; And in you all the families of the earth shall be blessed."

In Gen. 15:5 He said, *"Look now toward heaven, and count the stars if you are able to number them ... So shall your descendants be."* Then in Genesis chapter 17, God said:

"I am Almighty God; walk before Me and be blameless. And I will make My covenant between Me and you, and will multiply

you exceedingly." And later in the same chapter, as a sign of that covenant, He said, *"No longer shall your name be called Abram, but your name shall be Abraham; for I have made you a father of many nations. I will make you exceedingly fruitful; and I will make nations of you, and kings shall come from you. And I will establish My covenant between Me and you and your descendants after you in their generations, for an everlasting covenant, to be God to you and your descendants after you."*

God is a God of increase and multiplication! It is part of His covenant with Abraham into which we are grafted.

Multiplication is also one of the primary mandates of Kingdom operations. We are commanded to *"Go therefore and make disciples of all the nations, baptizing them in the name of the Father and of the Son and of the Holy Spirit, teaching them to observe all things that I have commanded you"* (Matt. 28: 19-20). In Matthew's account of the parable of the talents (Matt. 25:14-30), each slave who multiplied the portion given him, no matter how small to begin with, was told, *"Well done, good and faithful servant; you have been faithful over a few things, I will make you ruler over many things. Enter into the joy of your lord."*

The servant who wasted the opportunity and did nothing with the talent he was given so infuriated his master, that the talent was taken away and he was thrown out after being called worthless. In this parable, Jesus gives us a vivid image of Kingdom stewardship (verse 29): *"To those who use well what they are given, even more will be given, and they will have an abundance. But from those who do nothing, even what little they have will be taken away"* (NLT).

God gives us the power to multiply. Deut. 8:18 states:

"And you shall remember the Lord your God, for it is He who gives you the power to get wealth that He may establish His covenant which He swore to your fathers, as it is this day."

We also see the promise of *"all these blessings shall come upon you and overtake you, because you obey the voice of the LORD your God"* listed in the first 14 verses of Deut. 28. We read of how God, through the Prophet Elijah, caused the widow's flour to not run out until the famine ended, and then, through the Prophet Elisha, caused the oil to last until every borrowed pot and jar was filled so the widow and her sons could sell the oil, pay off her debts and live off the rest.

Imagine with me for a moment the widow and her son, after beginning to experience God's faithfulness at her flour not running out, and seeing the need of others, opening up a bakery to sell her cakes. Thus, not only did the flour care for her and her son, but for her customers as well, and she made enough selling her cakes to live off of for the rest of her life. Of course, I have no Biblical proof of this, but if God imparted the miracle, He very well would have also imparted the wisdom to best steward that miracle.

THE DIVINE EXCHANGE

God prospers us, blesses us and gives us the power to multiply and increase. God is a God of giving. Does He prosper us and give us the power to multiply just so we can store it up for ourselves and hold onto it with a tight-fisted grip? Of course not! However, this is exactly how many operate. Whether it is admitted or not, there is still a pervasive fear of lack that causes the appearance of one's circumstances to override the Truth of the Word of God. It is not so much with outright stinginess, since we all know intellectually that we are to be a generous people, but what we must come to understand is that we are already a prosperous people! Jesus Christ ushered in a new dimension of God blessing His people so we in turn could be a blessing. Jesus bore our sin so we could have redemption. By His stripes we have been healed. And He also bore our poverty so that we are rich! Paul writes in 2 Cor. 8:9:

"For you know the grace of our Lord Jesus Christ, that though He was rich, yet for your sakes He became poor, that you through His poverty might become rich."

That means we are rich in every way – eternally, spiritually and naturally— including tangible resources: assets, finances, goods, etc. As Tommi Femrite states in her book, *Invading the Seven Mountains with Intercession:*

"What a divine exchange! After centuries of pursuing His people to bless them so that they in turn could bless all the nations of the world, God established a permanent means—His only Son—to accomplish the task. Jesus' poverty forever opened the door to our eternal riches. Now that's good news!"[1]

These riches are not just earthly riches meant only for our own earthly use. Nor are these riches limited to only spiritual blessing. God has opened up His storehouse of treasure for us and there is no reason not to be generous on any occasion. We lack for nothing. Yet, for some reason, there are many of us that have yet to embrace all that Jesus has accomplished. We still try to earn our way to a position of prosperity through our giving rather than be generous givers BECAUSE of our position of prosperity. It's as though we are continually trying to enter a room that we are already in! We continue to chase after things because of the fear of lack, the fear of never having enough that has clouded our mind to the truth of 2 Cor. 8:9. In fact, if we are truthful with ourselves, there have been times when we have even given out of fear in order to get God "to move on our behalf." Let's face it; sometimes God is treated more like the lottery commission than El Shaddai! Seed given in faith is tremendously different than seed given in fear. As our minds are renewed to the truth that Jesus bore the curse of poverty and in doing so, brought us into a place of wealth, we can then focus on our true cause, His Kingdom.

Jesus addresses this very point in Luke 12:29-31 when he said, *"And do not seek what you should eat or what you should drink, nor have an anxious mind. For all these things the nations of the world seek after, and your Father knows that you need these things. But seek the kingdom of God, and all these things shall be added to you."* Fear Sells! Madison Avenue knows it, Wall Street knows it, Media knows it, and the Government knows it. (And its counterpart, Greed, works pretty well, too!). But, for something to sell, there has to be a buyer, and in the case of Fear and Greed, that is our carnal nature, which we are commanded to put to death.

Jesus continues in verse 32, saying, *"Do not fear, little flock, for it is your Father's good pleasure to give you the kingdom."* Incredible! As we seek the Kingdom, all the things the world seeks after are added unto us AND it is the Father's pleasure to give us the Kingdom! We can focus on His Kingdom and have no worry about needs. As we pursue what He has called us to do, we lack for nothing. Now this brings up an interesting question. If God has called us to do something, then why doesn't there seem to be the necessary resources in many cases to complete the task? Some may even ask, where are the resources to begin the task? There are many with incredible, God-given visions but no resources.

ACCESS DEMONSTRATED

The Lord Jesus never lacked for anything as He did what the Father told Him to do. In fact, according to Jesus, neither should we. He makes an incredible statement in Matthew 13 to that effect. This chapter finds Jesus first speaking to a crowd of people, then speaking to the disciples in front of the crowd. Finally, sending the crowd away, He continues speaking with the disciples. Jesus first addresses the crowd with the parable of the sower:

"Behold, a sower went out to sow. And as he sowed, some seed fell by the wayside; and the birds came and devoured them. Some fell on stony places, where they did not have much earth; and they immediately sprang up because they had no depth of earth. But when the sun was up they were scorched, and because they had no root they withered away. And some fell among thorns, and the thorns sprang up and choked them. But others fell on good ground and yielded a crop: some a hundredfold, some sixty, some thirty. He who has ears to hear, let him hear!"

He continues as He explains the parable to the disciples in verses 18-23:

"Therefore hear the parable of the sower: When anyone hears the word of the kingdom, and does not understand it, then the wicked one comes and snatches away what was sown in his heart. This is he who received seed by the wayside. But he who received the seed on stony places, this is he who hears the word and immediately receives it with joy; yet he has no root in himself, but endures only for a while. For when tribulation or persecution arises because of the word, immediately he stumbles. Now he who received seed among the thorns is he who hears the word, and the cares of this world and the deceitfulness of riches choke the word, and he becomes unfruitful. But he who received seed on the good ground

is he who hears the word and understands it, who indeed bears
fruit and produces: some a hundredfold, some sixty, some thirty."

Notice that he who hears the word of the Kingdom and
understands it and activates it in his life is one who produces,
multiplies, thirty, sixty or a hundredfold. Understanding
the word, not just on an intellectual basis, but as a heartfelt
belief, brings about a multiplication.

As encouraging as this is, Jesus went on to say something
incredible. Jesus, after explaining the parable of the sower,
began to unlock revelation of the Kingdom. Six times
in verses 24-49, He started His illustrations with *"The
Kingdom of Heaven is like."* He spoke three parables to the
crowd regarding the Kingdom of Heaven, the first with
it being like the wheat and the tares, the second like the
mustard seed and the third as the leaven. He then sent
the crowd away and spoke to the disciples alone. First,
he explained the parable of the wheat and the tares and
then added three more examples of what the Kingdom of
Heaven is like: the treasure hidden in a field, the pearl of
great price and the dragnet. Thus ended a "crash course"
on the Kingdom of Heaven.

Upon finishing, like the good Teacher He is, He asked the
disciples, *"Have you understood all these things?"* Think about
it for a moment. They had been with Jesus for some time,
seen some incredible miracles, and heard some powerful
messages. He had just given them multiple examples of
what the Kingdom of Heaven is like, even explaining one
of them in detail. All of this came within the span of a few
minutes. Whether they really had a grasp on it or not, they
replied, *"Yes Lord."*

Then Jesus revealed an incredible piece of Apostolic
Kingdom operations. He replied to the disciples (verse 52):

"Therefore every teacher and interpreter of the Sacred Writings who has been instructed about and trained for the kingdom of heaven and has become a disciple is like a householder who brings forth out of his storehouse treasure that is new and [treasure that is] old [the fresh as well as the familiar]" (AMP).

THE MESSAGE BIBLE PUTS IT THIS WAY

"Then you see how every student well-trained in God's kingdom is like the owner of a general store who can put his hands on anything you need, old or new, exactly when you need it" (MSG).

Earlier we have seen that we are already in a place of prosperity because of the divine exchange through Jesus, and we lack for nothing as we focus on the Kingdom and His righteousness. Now Jesus states that those well instructed, trained and discipled now have access to that provision whenever needed. Revelation, understanding, resources, are all available when needed. It's needed now; it's here. Now. Efficiently. Whatever is necessary to fulfill the need. Even when it looks like there isn't any possibility, Jesus says access to the necessary resources is not only available, but immediate! So, even if there are only five loaves and two fish, an entire community can be fed.

Do you recognize a set up when you see one? Shortly after saying in Matthew 13 that those well trained in and disciples of the Kingdom have access to whatever is needed, whenever it is needed, 5,000 people are fed with the aforementioned five loaves and two fish (Matt. 14). Let's look at John's account of it in John chapter 6.

Imagine Jesus sitting with the disciples on a mountainside and looking up, seeing a crowd the size of a small community coming toward them. They were well away from any town or city where these folks could go get dinner. Jesus turned to Philip and asked him, *"Where shall we buy bread that these may eat?"* John then writes something very interesting. *"But this He said to test him, for He Himself knew what He would do."* Interesting...because He was testing Philip. Jesus had recently stated those well trained in the Kingdom could access what was needed. Philip could have tapped into that revelation, but didn't. He was perceiving the situation by the circumstances at hand.

This statement is also interesting in the fact that Jesus already knew what He was going to do.

Jesus did only what the Father told Him to do and said what the Father told Him to say. According to Jesus, He and the Father are one. Thus, Jesus had already gotten the strategy from Heaven and already knew what He was going to do before he posed that question to Philip. He didn't act out of presumption, thinking that was what the Father would want done in order to glorify His name. No, He already knew what the Father wished done. Had the Father not said to use the loaves and fish to feed the crowd, Jesus wouldn't have done it.

SEEING CLEARLY THROUGH THE MIND'S EYE

Not only had Jesus gotten the strategy from Heaven before His question to Philip, but the word knew used here is the Greek word *eido* meaning to see, perceive, know, "with the fullness of knowledge"; to see with the mind's eye and signifies a clear and purely mental perception.[2] Jesus saw in His mind's eye, His imagination, what the Father instructed Him to do. He saw Himself giving thanks and breaking those loaves and fish into pieces and having more than enough to feed the crowd and disciples. He heard the strategy from Heaven, and He then saw it in his imagination. Then it became a reality as He gave thanks, broke the loaves and fish, people ate their fill and 12 baskets were left over. He was using His spiritual eyes, if you will, to see Himself being used by the Father to supernaturally multiply food for the crowd. And He did not stagger at the thought. Unlike Philip, Jesus perceived the situation from His positional authority.

Imagination is defined as "the image making power of the mind; the power to reconstruct or recombine the materials furnished by direct apprehension; the complex faculty usually termed the creative power; the power to recombine the materials furnished by experience or memory for the accomplishment of an elevated purpose."[3]

Our imaginations are a powerful seedbed. Think of a young child lying in bed at night. The room is dark and a shadow from the window is cast on the open closet door. "Dad! Come here! There's a monster in the closet!" Of course there isn't, but to the child, the reality is that there is a monster in the closet. Why? It's a creation of her imagination based on how she perceived the shadow. Until Dad turns on the light to prove otherwise, it's a truth to her.

After turning on the light and showing her there is no monster in the closet, Dad says something like, "It's only your imagination!" And thus, the imagination has a negative reputation. We equate imagination with fantasy or daydreaming. The enemy has us deceived in believing that if it has anything to do with the imagination, it is fiction. And even though the monster was fiction, to the child it was such a truth; she was tormented by fear, unable to sleep and desperate to get that thing OUT!

This illustration gives us an indication to the power of our imagination. If false imaginations bring that strong of convictions, how much more powerful can having our minds staid upon truth be! Imagining the Word in action. Seeing the effect of the Word in our mind's eye. As we see the strategy of Heaven in our mind's eye, as Jesus did, it emboldens our faith. Then when we put our voices to that strategy with that emboldened faith, there is nothing that can stand in the way of those words accomplishing what they are intended to do!

Our imaginations are powerful. Otherwise, why would Paul be adamant that we become transformed by the renewing of our mind, casting down every vain imagination? The enemy knows that as long as there are areas in our minds that haven't been renewed to the truth of the word of God, then we will not walk in the fullness of one who is instructed, well trained and a disciple of the Kingdom. In other words, we will be unable to access what is needed when it is needed.

We will be perceiving through current circumstance, our emotions, or previous experience rather than His Truth. To perceive means to become aware of, know, or identify by means of the senses; and to recognize, discern, envision or understand. One can perceive circumstances through natural sight, sound, experiences, traditions, culture, etc. Or one can perceive through the Word of God. Perceiving through anything but the Word of God causes the imagination, or the seeing through the mind's eye, to be tainted by old wounds, traumas, opinions, deception of the enemy, lack, poverty, greed, pride, presumption, etc.

Jesus already knew what He was going to do on that mountain. Remember, the word *knew* in that verse means to see, perceive and know with the fullness of knowledge. As He heard the strategy from Heaven, He perceived it as the voice of the Father – therefore as Truth – and then saw it in His mind's eye as He carried out that strategy. There was no perceiving amiss with Jesus; otherwise, He couldn't say as Judas and the detachment approached Him in the garden, *"Here comes the devil and he has nothing in me."*

How we perceive is critical to how we are seeing in our mind's eye. For example, imagine for a moment that it is you on that mountain seated next to Philip. What is the first thought that comes to your mind when the download from Heaven comes, giving you the instruction for the five loaves and two fish? Is it "What if it doesn't work?" Did you feel a twinge of fear? Or was it, "Why me, Lord?" Or is your answer, "No problem! Let's do it!" while grabbing the loaves and fish and then beginning to decree and declare that they multiply in Jesus' name? (Remember, Jesus gave thanks, broke them, and then distributed.)

While decrees and declarations are an integral part of our Kingdom arsenal, perceiving through pride and presumption is a subtle and insidious (sometimes not so subtle and insidious!) stumbling block that has sidelined many God-ordained visions. God hates pride, and presumption always places us out of His timing or His ways of accomplishing what He wants us to do. How often have we presumed what God wanted done and moved ahead, only to fail or struggle. Sure, there is going to be warfare over things, but all too often we are our biggest enemy due to presumption. Praise God we can repent of our presumption and get in alignment with what He wishes done!

Hopefully you see yourself in your mind's eye as God sees you: one who is walking in humility, one who is well trained and discipled in the Kingdom, and one He is using to accomplish this for His glory!

Supernatural multiplication is part of an Apostolic Kingdom lifestyle. We already are a wealthy people in every area. We, being well trained in and a disciple of the Kingdom, have access to whatever is needed whenever it is needed. We are no longer swayed by current circumstances but stand in our positional authority. Getting the strategy from Holy Spirit, seeing it in our mind's eye and speaking what is seen into the situation, cannot fail.

ENDNOTES

1. Tommi Femrite, *Invading the Seven Mountains with Intercession*, p. 197. Lake Mary, FL: Creation House, 2011.
2. Blue Letter Bible. "Dictionary and Word Search for eidō (Strong's 1492)". Blue Letter Bible. 1996-2012. 1 Sep 2012. <http:// www.blueletterbible.org/lang/lexicon/lexicon.cfm? See also Strongs=G1492&t=KJV>
3. "Public Reference Tools - The ARTFL Project." Public Reference Tools - The ARTFL Project. N.p., n.d. Web. 01 Sept. 2012. <http:// machaut.uchicago.edu/?action=search>.

ABOUT THE AUTHOR

For over 30 years Jon Grieser has been involved in the financial services industry and holds several industry licenses. Over that time he has assisted clients in various capacities in formulating and implementing financial strategies.

Jon is the Intercession Coordinator for the Kingdom Economic Yearly Summit and K.E.Y.S. Network, overseeing each Summit's intercessory campaign. Jon is also a founding partner of The Paga Group, a team of experienced intercessory leaders and licensed ministers. They minister freedom and wholeness to business leaders and their families, and through that process, help bring strategic success to their businesses and organizations, and expansion to the borders of their Kingdom destiny and legacy.

Commissioned as an Apostle in 2003, Jon serves as an Apostle to the marketplace and as an elder at Believers Church International in Defiance, Ohio under the oversight of Apostle O. Michael and Pastor Beverly Smith. Jon and his wife Jan reside in Wauseon, Ohio and have two married daughters. He can be reached at jon.grieser@gmail.com.

CHAPTER SIXTY-FOUR

APOSTLES OF THE BUSINESS AS MISSION MOVEMENT

THOMAS WEBB & AL CAPERNA

OUR MANDATE

"...fill the earth and subdue it" (Gen. 1:28).

GOD'S COVENANT WITH ABRAHAM

"I will make you into a great nation, and I will bless you; I will make your name great, and you will be a blessing...; and all peoples on earth will be blessed through you" (Gen. 12:2-3).

THE GREAT COMMISSION

Jesus said, "go and make disciples of all nations..." (Matt. 28:19).

BUSINESS AND THE COVENANT

"But remember the LORD your God, for it is he who gives you the ability to produce wealth, and so confirms his covenant..." (Deut. 8:18).

INTRODUCTION

Our mandate, in obedience with the covenant God made with Abraham, is to subdue the earth, produce wealth and be a blessing to all "nations" or "peoples," meaning every linguistic, cultural group of people. When this happens, we see the Church restored, culture reformed, nations transformed, and the Kingdom of God advance. A new generation of apostles is doing this through the Business As Mission (BAM) movement. They are building business, commerce and trade focused on four bottom lines: producing wealth, benefiting society, caring for the creation, and proclaiming the gospel. The BAM apostles are taking this marketplace Kingdom restoration out into the "nations."

AUTHORS' NOTE: *The BAM movement has many practitioners, pioneers and advocates globally. We look to the Bible for the founders of BAM. For this essay we will use the term Business As Mission or BAM, because it is most widely recognized and came into usage around the late 1990s[1] and early 2000s[2]. However, it should be known that **most apostles in this movement, especially Kingdom practitioners working in restricted access countries, would prefer the term Business for Transformation (B4T).** These apostolic business leaders today agree we do not need any new term to describe this kingdom work. We just need to redeem business for the purpose it was meant for— to be a witness bringing glory to God by being "a blessing to every nation."*

THE POOR NEED
AN ECONOMIC OPPORTUNITY

As business leaders, we should understand the signs of the times and know how to respond. In order to respond and make informed decisions, accurate information about these signs is needed. Some of these signs include the global economic changes that are currently in progress. Do we see these as opportunities that God has provided for business leaders?

One of these Global economic changes, is that four billion of the over seven billion people on earth, at what economists call the "bottom of the pyramid," are emerging with new opportunities. Their income of between $2 and $5 U.S. dollars a day is rapidly increasing and for the first time in history, will provide some disposable income.

Global wealth numbers include the following:[3]

- 1% of the world's population makes over $65,000 USD/year

- 4% of the world's population makes between $35,000- $65,000/year

- 12% of the world's population makes between $20,000- $35,000/year

- 22% of the world's population makes between $3000- $20,000/year

- 46% of the world's population makes between $500- $3000/year (Bottom of the Pyramid[4])

- 15% of the world's population makes less than $500 USD/year (Bottom of the Pyramid[5])

Additionally, the current advances of technology will change the world more than the Industrial Revolution. For example, many remote people groups now have cell phones connecting them for the first time to local, regional and international markets. Also, the fact that the global population has doubled in the last 50 years will cause the largest growth of cities and businesses in the history of the world. We will see more businesses started in this next season of development than the total of businesses that have been started in all of history. This is a bold statement but business development is and will be a major focus for all companies and markets for the next several decades. As believers we have a few choices: watch what is happening, follow this market development, or lead it. I believe we have sound business principles that need to be communicated and this next season of business and marketplace needs our leadership and involvement to purpose it. It is time for us to take on our responsibilities as local and global marketplace leaders seriously. Will you join us?

OUR MANDATES: CLOSING THE SACRED/SECULAR DIVIDE

The separation we have had between the sacred and the secular is on a repair track; the dividing walls of separation are quickly coming down. Apostles in the religious sphere and apostles in the business sphere are reaching out to each other, building strong bridges that provide the way for many to engage their business gifting directly in fulfilling the covenant to be a blessing. More people are integrating their faith and mission into their work in the business world. Some of the many books written on the marketplace during the last three decades with the title *Thank God It's Monday* are an example of this.

Over the centuries we saw some great movements fully integrating work and worship. Such groups took seriously all the mandates—to rule over and subdue and cultivate the earth; to take care of creation; to produce wealth, goods and services for the betterment of mankind; and to proclaim the saving knowledge of Jesus to fulfill the Great Commission.

BAM APOSTLES: HISTORICAL EXAMPLES

Through sending teams of one monk with one trader, the reach of the Nestorian Church in the East went much further and over a longer time than the Roman roads and Greek language took the Church to the West. Nestorian Christianity had a 1,400-year history of nation transformation and kingdom of God advance all over Asia and China.

Count Zinzendorf and the Moravians rode on the power of a 24-hour continuous prayer movement that went on for 100 years. In community they built businesses and preached the gospel of the kingdom to the ends of the earth. These unordained, "lay" folk had great, far-reaching success as they stayed in deep communion with God and daily accountability with each other. They shared their wealth generously and saw no class division. The best BAM apostles in our modern times are also protected by community accountability and marked by strong relational connections with God and man.

BEER AND THE GOSPEL

Guinness & Co.® has been in continuous business for 250 years, and is recognized as having been part of the solution to the problems of poverty and drunkenness in British society during the late 16th century and into the 17th century. At that time there was no understanding of microorganisms and how disease was spread. People knew they were dying from drinking water for some reason, so they took to making and drinking alcohol (hard liquor). Many houses advertised: "Drunk for a penny, dead drunk for two pennies."[6] Poverty and crime were everywhere.

When John Wesley came to St. Patrick's Cathedral in Dublin, Arthur Guinness heard Wesley's usual message to the entrepreneurial folk: "Earn all you can, save all you can, give all you can." Wesley himself was among the wealthiest in all of Europe at that time. He would say, "Your wealth is evidence of a calling from God, so use your abundance for the good of mankind."[7] Guinness developed beer as a weaker alternative to strong alcohol, which helped reduce drunkenness and crime among the people. Arthur Guinness also supported Hudson Taylor's mission work and Bible school in China. Guinness & Co. continues to be involved in socially-minded endeavors.

THE MISSIONARY WHO WAS A BUSINESSMAN

William Carey, the famous British missionary, went to India and is called the founder of the modern missions movement. Most don't realize that he was also an industrialist, economist, reformer, media pioneer, educator, and botanist. Carey found several business models that worked to advance his evangelical calling and impact his community.

Another, Robert Moffatt, became known as the King's Gardener in Africa. He used his agricultural gifting to turn the desert of South Africa into lush gardens.

As he worked, he would say about his gardens that they are symbolic and this spiritual desert will blossom into a garden for God. Moffatt's purpose was lived out; he planted physical gardens and gardens in the souls of men.

THE RELIGIOUS SPHERE AND BAM

Church teaching should confirm, affirm and empower God's people for works of service to build up the body in unity of faith.

> *"Christ himself gave apostles, prophets, evangelists, pastors and teachers, to equip his people for works of service, so that the body of Christ may be built up until we all reach unity in the faith..."* (Eph. 4:11-13).

Missionaries often quote the covenant God made with Abraham. As they talk about taking the blessings (according to Gen. 12:1-3) to the world, they are learning that the vehicles of those blessings are not limited to those in religious professions. Often the blessings are in the hands of those who create wealth in business. When we develop in the nations the ability to create jobs and wealth, along with proclaiming Jesus Christ, we see the coming of the whole gospel of the kingdom. This blessing through wealth is not just about the businessperson giving the missionary financial support. Rather, the businessperson engages the skill, gifting, or training he or she uses in the business sphere and takes that out into the nations. The business entrepreneur is doing this in consultation with and often in partnership with the missionary.

The relationship between the religious sphere and the business world has some unresolved tensions. Several reasons account for this tug-of-war. As the business community responds to the call to move into the nations, directly engaging the great commission with the covenant to be a blessing to every nation, the traditional church structures are wondering what is happening and what their response should be.

With most of the church still living in the framework of a secular/spiritual divide, seeking to understand BAM raises many areas of uncertainty, or potential conflict:

- volunteer vs. employee;
- material profit vs. souls being saved;
- using the cover of a half-hearted "business" as a platform for getting into a country to evangelize, vs. a real business that is both aiming to make a profit and working out the gospel of salvation in the thick of the marketplace.

Then there are more practical issues:

- What happens with support money vs. profit from the business?
- If a missionary sets up a company, who owns the company? Does the voluntary agency he or she may be connected with own it, or do those who set up and run the business own it? Things like this need good communication, clarification and hearts focused on building up toward unity of the faith and seeking first the Kingdom of God.

PRAYER AND THE BAM MOVEMENT

As we know from the Moravian movement, BAM success is born and sustained out of relationship between God and man through prayer. At a recent Call2Business gathering in Kansas City, Mo., this was evident as apostles leading prayer initiatives and those leading the BAM projects covered the Chinese "Back to Jerusalem" movement with prayer. God has plans for business blessings to flow to the ends of the earth. The Back to Jerusalem movement is poised to release what may become the largest missionary force of all history. Businesses are key in gaining physical and relational access to cultures all along the Silk Road.

THE WORLD FINANCIAL CRISIS AND THE GREAT COMMISSION

Knowing that God works all things together for good, what is he doing through the financial crisis? Many missionaries who raise financial support have come off of the field due to a drop in traditional giving. So, what do the mission agencies do now? The Great Commission has not changed. At the same time a glorious revelation is coming into the understanding of the Christian business community. God is interested in using more than their money—he wants their lives. So, we are seeing more merging and integration between business and missions.

Why is God moving the missionaries and business people out into the nations together? The nations need food, jobs, market access, and coaching/mentoring. The missionaries need the "DNA" God has put in the business sphere. The business people need the missionary for local knowledge, language, contacts, cultural understanding, and gospel-sharing experience.

For a time I (Tom) served a British power generation company as a forward marketing man in Central Asia. Using the local relationships and knowledge I had gained during my mission work on the field, I saved them spending larger amounts to relocate one of their engineers.

ARAB REVOLUTIONS AND AGRICULTURAL BAM OPPORTUNITIES

Revolutionary leaders in Egypt and other Arab countries have recently used the high prices of food, along with a call to end corruption, to mobilize the masses to support the revolutions.

The world food crisis is pushing many to search for BAM opportunities. Agricultural best practice and technology transfer is an essential area. The increasing price of staples in poor countries, combined with huge unemployment, is causing growing unrest. This is an opportunity to work out the gospel of the kingdom through meeting people at their point of need. For example, a Christian agricultural expert from Asia is one of a group invited a second time to Oman to help work out a government-to-government contract, where Southeast Asia would provide Oman with a regular assured delivery of staples like rice and fish.

SLAVERY/HUMAN TRAFFICKING AND BAM INVESTMENT

High-profile media groups CNN and Al Jazeera have partnered with advocacy groups like Not for Sale which are focusing attention on human trafficking and slavery. The new social media phenomenon is quickly building awareness and a global response to correct these wrongs. Kingdom companies are finding ways to address the economic root of this issue. By providing income alternatives, businesses can effect long-term cultural change. One wealthy evangelical from Australia is ready to invest $1 million in businesses that are working in communities to prevent human trafficking before it happens, for example by providing work for the impoverished in high-risk areas. He knows it is possible for the entrepreneurially gifted to rise to this challenge and he expects a return on his investment, both financially and in changed lives.

SOCIAL ENTREPRENEURSHIP AND THE BAM APOSTLES

It has been reported that marketing personnel from a giant retail chain have asked a leading missions organization for a supply of products that are produced by the poorest 1.5 billion of the world's population, who live on less than $1 a day. It looks good for company image if they can sell with labels saying, "By buying this product you are improving the lives of the poor." There are BAMers who are coordinating locally-produced items coming from small-scale business among the poor, but there is a great need to scale up. An association of these kingdom companies is in the partnership-building stage.

SIR RICHARD BRANSON

The world is looking for leaders. In his book *Screw Business as Usual*, Sir Richard Branson, founder and chairman of the Virgin Group®, outlines his vision for nothing less than global transformation. He asks, "Can we bring more meaning to our lives and help change the world at the same time...a whole new way of doing things, solving major problems and turning our working into something we both love and are proud of?" His proposed solution is a new way of doing business. "It is time to...shift our values, to switch from a profit focus to caring for people, communities and the planet," he added.[8] Sometimes God uses prophets and kings from outside the Church to proclaim His heart and accomplish His purposes! Just look at Cyrus (Isa. 45).

The apostles of the BAM movement are asking: are we going to leave it up to the Richard Bransons in the world to lead, or will we listen to the voice of God leading us into building spiritual, bottom-line businesses? Will we empower God's business people to take the blessings of the marketplace to restore the church, reform culture, transform peoples and nations and see the kingdom of God advance?

EXAMPLES FROM TODAY

Who are the Apostles of the BAM movement today? What sort of kingdom work do they do? The following are real BAM initiatives in the form of Kingdom businesses: They are often in restricted-access countries that don't allow open gospel witness, so names and locations are withheld.

In the service industry, some are building a chain of successful hotels, leading employees to faith and teaching them to work and live a kingdom witness as they serve the hotel customers.

After being expelled for proselytizing among university students, one group later returned to the same country and opened a coffee shop business. They found their evangelism efforts more successful and they were making money. The whole coffee industry—from growing, roasting, and trading to coffee shops—is one of the fastest - growing BAM opportunities in the world. Also:

1. Owners of companies in the oil and gas industry are placing workers, trading, building infrastructure

and maintaining successful business in places where traditional missionary workers are being kicked out. From their place of work, a church, school and community organization benefiting the local society have been built.

2. Producing and trading furniture and household items from Asia to Europe, a BAM practitioner sets an example of ethical business, and by refusing to operate under the cultural norm of bribery, has changed government policy and made credible witness to a righteous God.

3. *Time* magazine highlighted the work of a major church group coming into an African country with $1 billion in aid. Their work through the church basically failed. Others came to the same country with businessmen and worked with government and local business. They have seen success and the country is growing away from dependency. Businessmen and politicians go on prayer retreats and seek God for their country.

4. An elderly woman followed God's call to move from the West to a country in Asia and start a factory employing land-mine victims who are shunned by society. She also addresses their spiritual and housing needs.

5. Many small businesses are producing high-end products, have secured buying partners and are providing jobs for populations that are vulnerable to human trafficking.

6. There seems to be a race on to build reproducible aquaponics (symbiotic fish and vegetable farming systems) and natural farming businesses that have a positive impact on environment and health by developing organic food production. God is

answering the cry for food and jobs from Siberia to the South Pacific.

7. Impact investors, coaches and mentors are directly partnering with Kingdom businesses in developing and closed-door nations to advance the Kingdom and reproduce their impact.

8. Some in the successful micro loans programs around the world are finding a need to pull together micro-enterprise entities into larger business groups. Those in micro business usually see their goods and services revolve only around the lower socio-economic levels of their society. There are BAM Apostles who have helped some groups move into the middle class.

9. A serial entrepreneur started an international business focused on the poor. With the tag line "charity has not ended poverty; opportunity will" and an exciting international fast growth trajectory, we are seeing both the missions and business workers affirmed and empowered.

IN MEMORY OF A BAM CHAMPION

We just lost one of our best BAM leaders—Ken Crowell, owner of Galtronics in Tiberius, Israel.

God gives us the ability to produce wealth (Deut. 8:18). He is showing his people 'disruptive technologies,' potentially world-changing inventions. Ken Crowell was one to whom God gave a world-changing technology. He helped invent the aerial for cell phones. His electronics company Galtronics® in Israel employs many, and he and his associates have started a number of messianic churches. Galtronics' cutting-edge technology has given rise to several organizations like

MegaVoice® that sends the spoken electronic Word of God around the world in hundreds of languages.

GO THEREFORE AND JOIN THE BUSINESS HARVEST

There are different roles within BAM—not everyone has to be an entrepreneur. Every entrepreneur who builds a company needs an army of support. Find one of the many BAM practitioners building a for-profit company among the poor. Many of those poor have been, up 'till now, out of reach of the gospel. Learn and join the movement. Find a businessperson who leads out of a strong relationship with the One who gives him or her the power to create wealth. Look for the kingdom company that is striving with excellence to make money and live out biblical values, morals and ethics. Find those whose lives proclaim a witness, drawing those within reach of the company to the King of Kings and Lord of Lords.

ENDNOTES

1. Personal correspondence of 11/27/12 with Dr. Steven Rundle. See essay on pp. 66-79 of the following link by Dr. Rundle. http://www.cbfa.org/JBIBVol15No1.pdf.

2. Personal correspondence of 11/30/12 and 12/08/12 with Mats Tunehag, in which he references a Lausanne BAM paper prepared in fall 2004. http://www.matstunehag.com/wp-content/uploads/2011/04/BAM-LOP-June-05.pdf. Mats also founded the BAM Think Tank in 2002.

3. Information taken from IFC International Financial Corporation, World Bank Group 2007. Estimates also obtained from www.globalrichlist.com.

4. Ibid.

5. Ibid.

6. http://www.relevantmagazine.com/god/mission/features/20993-god-and-guinness

7. Ibid.

8. http://www.instantapostle.com/blog/the-prophet-richard/

ABOUT THE AUTHOR

Thomas Webb, B.A., B.Th., is an Australian with over 26 years of experience living and working overseas. He has built partnerships with mission agencies and business people, and worked in recruiting, missions, and in marketing for the oil and gas industry. Having been to more than 60 countries, Thomas promotes and catalyzes several diverse BAM projects. He enjoys developing relationships and connecting people all over the world with a special focus in Asia.

Al Caperna made a personal commitment to Jesus Christ as his Lord and Savior in 1974 on the campus of Bowling Green State University. Al does not believe faith in Jesus should be restricted to Sunday. This belief, coupled with a management style that helps encourage strong business ethics, innovation, achievement and selective risk taking, has helped Al achieve success in starting and developing businesses. Starting his own business in 1980, he now has five businesses with 300 employees and has been recognized nationally as a business leader.

Al is the Chairman of CMC Group, an association of companies that has been selling to retail and industrial customers in the U.S. and internationally for over 32 years. Al's main goal is "to embody the Christian life in business practices." Out of this goal birthed the vision for Affirm Global Development, which exists to empower entrepreneurs globally in setting up businesses and helping to end economic poverty. Al is a member of the call2all Executive Team, where he is serving to bring awareness to the role business has in the completion of the Great Commission. Happily married for 36 years, Al and Kathy have three married daughters and three grandchildren.

Helpful web sites for those who want to learn more about the BAM movement include the following:

- http://bamthinktank.org/
- http://c2bevents.com/
- http://www.affirmglobal.com/
- http://www.partnersworldwide.org
- http://www.businessasmission.com/
- http://www.businessasmissionnetwork.com/
- https://www.wikibam.com/wiki/Main_Page
- http://bammatch.com/

CHAPTER SIXTY-FIVE

APOSTOLIC ALIGNMENT FOR DIVINE MULTIPLICATION

LARUE ADKINSON

We are living in an hour of human history in which all things are being restored and fulfilled in the Body of Christ. In particular, the church is entering a season in which the end-time Apostolic Government will be brought to full age, demonstrating the immeasurable grace of God to all nations. Moreover, we are witnessing the rise and establishment of marketplace kings, gospel entrepreneurs and business leaders, who are being aligned to function within the emerging Apostolic King-Priest Government.

Within this chapter, we will discover the source of the interconnected blessing of generational inheritance that rested upon Abraham, Isaac, Jacob, Caleb and King David. Furthermore, we will witness the power of divine multiplication that originates from that blessing and discover God's alignment process to receive it.

CHRIST THE APPOINTED HEIR

Hebrews declares the Father appointed Jesus heir of all things both in heaven and earth, having set Him as the reigning King over all the earth and its resources.

"God, who at sundry times and in divers manners spake in time past unto the fathers by the prophets, Hath in these last days spoken unto us by his Son, whom he hath appointed heir of all things, by whom also he made the worlds" (Heb. 1:1-2).

Isaiah prophetically spoke of Christ receiving the inheritance of the Father's mountains:

"I will bring forth a seed out of Jacob, and out of Judah an inheritor of my mountains: and mine elect shall inherit it, and my servants shall dwell there" (Isa. 65:9).

Christ, being both the seed to come out of the lineage of Abraham, and King to rise out of Judah, has become the sole inheritor of all the Father's mountains. These mountains in times past represented a natural inheritance, but now they have been transformed into a spiritual inheritance of which we all are partakers as joint-heirs.

MT. HEBRON AND THE PATRIARCHS

Within this chapter we will explore the inheritance of one particular mountain located in the land of Judah - Mt. Hebron. Judah represented the royal lineage from which the Old Testament kings were brought forth, from which Christ, the Lion of the Tribe of Judah, was born. Throughout the Bible, Mt. Hebron was a significant location in the lives of some of the greatest men of God to walk the face of the earth. Since it would require an entire book to capture the complete historical precedence of this mountain, we will focus, at this time, exclusively upon the significance it played in the lives of Abraham, Isaac, Jacob, Caleb and King David, for they were the marketplace kings of their generation.

It is important to recognize that Mt. Hebron is no ordinary mountain. From its conception, it was ordained of God to be the mountain of generational inheritance. The blessing that descended upon this mountain has its origin with Abraham, Isaac and Jacob. These early patriarchs all received the blessing of increase and divine multiplication directly from God, and walked in the manifestation of that blessing the whole of their lifetime. We clearly see within scripture the origins of the Abrahamic Blessing:

"I will make thee exceeding fruitful, and I will make nations of thee, and kings shall come out of thee" (Gen. 17:6).

"That in blessing I will bless thee, and in multiplying I will multiply thy seed as the stars of the heaven, and as the sand which is upon the sea shore; and thy seed shall possess the gate of his enemies; And in thy seed shall all the nations of the earth be blessed; because thou hast obeyed my voice" (Gen. 22:17-18).

The blessing of generational inheritance that rested within Abraham, Isaac and Jacob continued long after their natural lives, as God had something greater in mind. God in His infinite wisdom divinely orchestrated that the early patriarchs and their wives, were to be buried in Mt. Hebron.

"And after this, Abraham buried Sarah his wife in the cave of the field of Machpelah before Mamre: the same is Hebron in the land of Canaan" (Gen. 23:19).

"In the cave that is in the field of Machpelah, which is before Mamre, in the land of Canaan, which Abraham bought with the field of Ephron the Hittite for a possession of a burial place. There

they buried Abraham and Sarah his wife; there they buried Isaac and Rebekah his wife; and there I buried Leah" (Gen. 49:30-31).

The blessing of Abraham that produced such fruitfulness and abundance in the course of their lives, was strategically planted in Mt. Hebron. In the same manner that Elisha's bones retained the anointing to raise the dead Moabite, the blessing of generational inheritance that rested within these early patriarchs was planted within the soil of God's chosen mountain.

"And it came to pass, as they were burying a man, that, behold, they spied a band of men; and they cast the man into the sepulchre of Elisha: and when the man was let down, and touched the bones of Elisha, he revived, and stood up on his feet" (2 Kings 13:21).

THE PROMISE LAND OF MT. HEBRON

Four hundred years later, we see very clear evidence that the blessing was alive and well during the time of Moses. In the Book of Numbers, Moses instructed the 12 spies to bring some of the fruit of the land back to the camp. On their journey, they immediately came to Hebron, where the giants, the descendants of Anak, dwelt. From there they came to the brook of Eshcol located in the valley of Mt. Hebron, where they cut down a branch with one cluster of grapes so enormous that it required two men to carry it on a pole. This was, without a doubt, a result of the blessing that God had been strategically planted into this mountain, and it was now due season to reap the rewards.

"So they went up, and searched the land from the wilderness of Zin unto Rehob, as men come to Hamath. And they ascended by the south, and came unto Hebron; where Ahiman, Sheshai, and Talmai, the children of Anak, were. (Now Hebron was built

seven years before Zoan in Egypt.) And they came unto the brook of Eshcol, and cut down from thence a branch with one cluster of grapes, and they bare it between two upon a staff; and they brought of the pomegranates, and of the figs" (Num. 13:21-23).

Why else would Caleb at 85 years of age ask Joshua for this specific mountain above all others? Joshua and Caleb were the only two remaining spies of the original twelve that were allowed to enter the Promise Land. Caleb was a first-hand witness of the abundant riches of the Promise Land. Although he was forced to wonder in the desert for another 40 years because of the unbelief of the children of Israel, he never lost sight of the prized possession of the Promise Land. After standing in faith for 45 years, Caleb received the inheritance of Mt. Hebron.

"Behold, the LORD hath kept me alive, these forty and five years, even since the LORD spake this word unto Moses, while the children of Israel wandered in the wilderness: and now, lo, I am this day fourscore and five years old. As yet I am as strong this day as I was in the day that Moses sent me: as my strength was then, even so is my strength now, for war, both to go out, and to come in. Now therefore give me this mountain, whereof the LORD spake in that day; for thou heardest in that day how the Anakims were there, and that the cities were great and fenced: if so be the LORD will be with me, then I shall be able to drive them out, as the LORD said. And Joshua blessed him, and gave unto Caleb the son of Jephunneh Hebron for an inheritance" (Josh. 14:10-13).

You may ask, what does this have to with the apostolic alignment of marketplace kings? Well, this was only a foretaste of the generational treasures coming forth from this mountain. As we will see in the life of David, God divinely orchestrated that He would be first crowned king in Mt. Hebron, and at the time of His coronation, He would receive one of the greatest blessings of divine multiplication ever recorded in the Bible. This event would transpire during the most difficult trial of his life, as His transition to Mt. Hebron did not come without price. Divine alignment in many instances is a very painful process, because it involves the uprooting of our lives from the place of rest that we have chosen, to the place of rest that God has chosen. Sometimes this requires a geographical transition and at other times, it requires a spiritual transition. This is exactly what happened to David to prepare him for the Throne.

THE BLESSING OF DIVINE MULTIPLICATION

Before David's coronation in Hebron, he had chosen Ziklag as his place of rest along with his family and band of 600 men. Ziklag was given to David to dwell in by King Achish of the Philistines. You may ask, why was David dwelling in a city belonging to Philistines, especially after he slayed their champion Goliath? This was a result of the relentless pursuit of King Saul over many years to kill him during his wilderness afflictions. David decided to flee to the land of the Philistines rather than perish by the sword of Saul. In doing so, he was granted favor with his very own enemies. So much so that when King Achish was ready to go to war against Saul and the host of Israel, David wanted to join him. As you could imagine, the Philistine lords rejected his ambitions and sent David home to Ziklag. As David returns to Ziklag, he finds his city of rest burned to the ground and his wives and children taken by the Amalekites.

"And it came to pass, when David and his men were come to Ziklag on the third day, that the Amalekites had invaded the south, and Ziklag, and smitten Ziklag, and burned it with fire;

And had taken the women captives, that were therein: they slew not any, either great or small, but carried them away, and went on their way. So David and his men came to the city, and, behold, it was burned with fire; and their wives, and their sons, and their daughters, were taken captives. Then David and the people that were with him lifted up their voice and wept, until they had no more power to weep" (1 Sam. 30:1-4).

This was without a doubt the absolute lowest place that David had ever been. The once champion of Israel, was broken spiritually, physically and emotionally. His own men wanted to stone him. David fell on his face and began to worship God in the midst of the most excruciating trial of his life, and little did he know that he was within days of his coronation. You may ask, why would God allow Ziklag to burn to the ground? Ziklag was never ordained to be the resting place for David, as God had something better in store for him. Oftentimes God allows a baptism of fire in the process of Apostolic alignment, in order to move us to the place of rest that He has chosen for us.

The Hand of God was at work on many fronts, as the Philistines were about to defeat Saul and his entire army in battle, setting the stage for David's ascension to the Throne of Israel. There are many Apostolic marketplace kings hidden in caves and dens awaiting their word from God to 'come forth' from the chains or limitations that have held them captive. Spiritual transition will oftentimes require the process of divine alignment.

As a result, David and his 600 men recovered all that was stolen. It was now time for David to receive his coronation in Mt. Hebron, the place of generational inheritance. Throughout the time of David's wanderings, his army remained at a maximum of 600 men. Sometimes it feels that way in our own lives. We do all we know to do, serving God day and night with all of our might, only to find ourselves in the same place year after year.

However, God is orchestrating an alignment to those who are following Him with all of their heart, and once again, He is calling for the release of the inheritance of His mountains. As a result of divine alignment, David was now in position to be crowned King in Mt. Hebron. Upon his coronation, the supernatural inheritance within this mountain immediately released, multiplying King David's army of 600 men to over 348,000.

1 CHRONICLES 12:23-39

"And these are the numbers of the bands that were ready armed to the war, and came to David to Hebron, to turn the kingdom of Saul to him, according to the word of the LORD.

*"**Children of Judah**—6,800 men that bare shield and sword.*

*"**Children of Simeon**—7,100 mighty men of valor for war.*

*"**Children of Levi**—4,600 men.*

*"**Jehoiada the leader of the Aaronites**—3700 men.*

*"**Zadok**—22 Captains from his father's house.*

*"**Children of Benjamin**—3000 the house of Saul.*

*"**Children of Ephraim**—28,000 famed mighty men of valor.*

*"**Half tribe of Manasseh**—18,000 men.*

*"**Children of Issachar**—200 men that had understanding of the times.*

"Tribe Of Zebulun—50,000 expert in war,
men that kept rank.

"Tribe of Naphtali—1000 captains and
37,000 that bare shield and spear.

"Tribe of Danites—28,600 expert in war.

"Tribe of Asher—40,000 expert in war.

"The Reubenites, Gadites, and half of Manasseh—
120,000 men of war

*"All these men of war, that could keep rank,
came with a perfect heart to Hebron, to make David
king over all Israel: and all the rest also of Israel were
of one heart to make David king.*

*"And there they were with David three days, eating and
drinking: for their brethren had prepared for them."*

David's coronation at Mt. Hebron transformed an army of 600 distressed, indebted and discontented men, into an army of over 348,000 mighty men of valor, expert in war, who would not break rank. The Mt. Hebron inheritance continued throughout the reign of King David and Solomon, establishing one of the wealthiest and most prosperous kingdoms to have ever existed in the history of humanity.

JOINT-HEIRS OF THE INHERITANCE

In His ascension into the Right Hand of God, Christ received the inheritance of this mountain. Furthermore, Jesus strategically positioned this inheritance in heavenly places so that no thief may ever break through or steal it. In His great mercy, God has positioned us as Joint-Heirs with

Christ, granting access to the continuous inheritance that emanates from this mountain.

Several years ago a man approached me in my church and asked if he could share something with me. He said after listening to the Mt. Hebron teaching series, he began to pray for God to grant him oil contracts for a special drilling mud that his company had been storing in a warehouse. He had several years of backlogged product that had not sold, while at the same time having to pay burdensome monthly inventory expenses. As he listened to the teachings, he said faith and confidence began to rise up within his spirit as he daily contended for the blessing of generational inheritance to be released in his life.

In a matter weeks, he was contacted by an oil company in Mexico that purchased the entire inventory that had been stored and issued a 12-month contract for additional product. I will never forget the look on his face, when he reached into his suit pocket and pulled out a check from the oil company for $92,000.

I have also personally experienced the favor associated with this mountain. Before receiving the revelation of Mt. Hebron, I was continually trapped in a state of frustration and striving, endeavoring to build a church, ministry and business through my own works and human sufficiency. During that season of my life, God spoke the following word to my heart, "I have many of My sons that walk with Me and I have many of My sons that run for Me, but I have only few that are willing to sit with Me. I want to teach you how to transfer wealth from a seated position of authority." It was at that point that the Holy Spirit led me into the understanding of the Mt. Hebron Inheritance and the Right Hand of God.

Since receiving the revelation of the Mt. Hebron Inheritance, the Holy Spirit strategically positioned me within an international partnership responsible for the brokering of historical antiquities, bonds and precious metals. Access to such clientele would normally require many years of specialized networking within elite circles of influence; however, the Holy Spirit orchestrated the divine connections associated with this partnership within a matter of months.

Our partnership has recently witnessed the favor of God in an extraordinary manner, as one of our foremost clients was officially approved in an historic international bond offering. Our client was one of only three candidates out of more than 300 applicants to be accepted. This was truly a miracle in and of itself, as only 1% of all international participants were chosen. However, this testimony is a work in progress, as we are currently awaiting the final process of funding for the bonds. We are presently standing at the door of a significant breakthrough of generational inheritance for the Kingdom of God.

Today, there is a clarion call sounding out from the Right Hand of God, calling the end-time marketplace kings and business leaders to once again lay hold of the generational inheritance of Mt. Hebron, in order to advance the Kingdom of God throughout the earth.

ABOUT THE AUTHOR

LaRue Adkinson presides as the Founder and Apostle of Houston Revival Center, an apostolic equipping center located in Houston, Texas. He and his wife, Anna, have ministered alongside national and international ministries, leaders and businessmen around the world.

Through his unique gifting and cutting-edge revelation, LaRue delivers apostolic truth that captivates, transforms and equips believers throughout the Body of Christ to move into the fullness of their inheritance in Christ.

The Framing Your World website was established as a global media outreach dedicated to equipping, establishing and maturing believers to walk in the fullness of the emerging apostolic king-priest government. In depth discipleship is accomplished through the unique "One on One" teaching library made available free of charge. For specific revelation on The Right Hand of God, visit this link: http://www.framingyourworld.com/righthandofgod.

Contained within the "One on One" library is a masterful collection of Signature series interwoven with doctrinal integrity, providing master keys in unlocking the power and demonstration of the emerging apostolic age. Series such as "The Right Hand of God," "Authentic Apostolic Government," "Mt. Hebron Inheritance," "The Capernaum Inheritance," "The Melchisedec Government," "Spiritual Constitution," "Unlocking the Inheritance of the Kingdom Within," "The Blessing is in the Water" and "The Throne of Grace."

LaRue and Anna Adkinson reside in Houston, Texas along with their two children Karson and Victoria. For more information concerning this ministry, please visit their website or contact them at: www.framingyourworld.com.

CHAPTER SIXTY-SIX

APOSTLES AS CO-CREATORS: IMITATING THE WORKS OF THE FATHER

LAURIE L. BOYD

INTRODUCTION

The time has come for the uncompromising gospel to be demonstrated in power and authority in the earth. Our ministry should not have to rely on *"persuasive words of human wisdom, but in demonstration of the Spirit and of power, that the faith of the people should not be in the wisdom of men but in the power of God"* (1 Cor. 2:4-5).

One of the most powerful revelations of the cry of this age was spoken by Christ Jesus as He sat reclining with the apostles in the upper room after they had eaten their last Passover meal together. Earlier He had humbled Himself to wash their feet as an example of their conduct toward one another. Then He had spoken revelation and final instruction as He prepared them for His departure and exhorted them to continue the work of the gospel. Phillip had said, *"Lord, show us the Father, and it is sufficient for us."*

Jesus replied, *"Have I been with you so long and yet you have not known Me? He who has seen Me has seen the Father...I am sending you a Helper who will abide with you forever...when the Helper comes, whom I shall send to you from the Father, the Spirit of truth who proceeds from the Father, He will testify of Me"* (John 14:8-9, 16; 15:26).

We have a whole world out there, from our brothers and sisters of the Jewish faith to the kids in the clubs and streets of America to the orphans in India to the followers of Islam crying out: "Show us the Father, and it is enough for us!"

Why did Christ pray to the Father that we would understand this revelation, *"I do not pray for these alone, but also for those who will believe in Me through their word; and the glory which You gave Me I have given them, that they may be one just as We are one: I in them, and You in Me; that they may be made perfect in one..."*? It is for this purpose which He spoke in the next verse, *"and that the world may know that You [Father] have sent Me, and have loved them as You have loved Me"* (John 17:20, 22-23). The Father has heard this powerful declaration of His Son Christ Jesus as He set divine order and succession of His Word becoming our Word. Through our Word, Our Father is daily answering the cry of "Show us the Father!" in the world supernaturally through His servants in one accord and in one place with Him.

Until Christ returns to rule and reign, we have an important assignment to execute in the earth through the power of the Holy Spirit. Not only must we conduct ourselves in the demonstration of the Spirit and of power so that the faith of the people is in the power of God and in His Son, their only Savior Christ Jesus, but as He has commissioned us as His apostles, we represent the Father in the earth as Christ did. As Fathers, our hearts are to be turned to the children just as His heart is turned toward the children, and the hearts of the children will be turned toward the Father and their cry will be answered.

Once they are reconciled to the Father through Christ Jesus by the Holy Spirit, only then will their eyes be opened that they are turned from darkness to light, from the power of satan to God, that they may receive forgiveness of sins and an inheritance among those who are sanctified by faith in Him (1 Cor. 2:4-5, Mal. 4:6, Acts 26:18).

The world must see the Father through us. Christ, our example, said it best: *"Most assuredly, I say to you, the Son can do nothing of Himself, but what He sees the Father do; for whatever He does, the Son also does in like manner"* (John 5:19).

BECOMING IMITATORS OF THE FATHER: THE "WHY"

Through the Holy Spirit revelation, we start to comprehend not only the Who, What, Where, and When of the Word of God, but also the Why and the How.

The "why" of God is simple and must be revealed, examined, and imparted before we talk about and walk in the 'how' of God. Why has God the Father or Christ Jesus said anything He has said or done anything that He has done? Because He is Love, everything He does is because of Love—perfect Love which casts out fear, which lays one's life down for even an enemy, which restores, reconciles, heals, and delivers. Everything recorded, every miracle, sign, or wonder was and is because He demonstrates His love toward us. The pursuit of love takes us from glory to glory in Him.

Paul exhorts in Eph. that we are to "be imitators of God as dear children. And walk in love, as Christ also has loved us and given Himself for us..." (Eph. 5:1-2). Understanding love and walking in that love is the absolute foundation principle as we seek to be imitators of God and co-creators in the earth.

Love is the key to all miracles; it is the catalyst which moves the heart to awakening, speaking the Word, and taking the action of faith. It is the fourth dimension, described by Paul in Eph. 3:18-19 as the fullness of God, the love of Christ Jesus which passes knowledge, and is comprehended by the width and length and depth and height.

This fourth dimension can be described in mathematical terms. (All true science and mathematics always agree with the Word of God; unbelievers simply lack the interpretation since they do not yet have the Holy Spirit.) The fourth dimension is called a *'Tesseract'* in geometry. A *tesseract* is loosely defined as two parallel cubes which have connected in another dimension to become a 'hypercube'. The two cubes of the hypercube simultaneously occupy the space within one another and around one another. You can find an animation of how this works in the *Tesseract* article on Wikipedia. This is a representation of the dimension called

'on earth as it is in heaven': and of us dwelling in Him as He dwells in us! We know this fourth dimension according to the Word is Perfect Love, and it's a great mystery revealed in Eph. 1:10; that in the dispensation of the fullness of the times He might

Figure 5. Tesseract
(Source: Wikipedia. Image is in the public domain.) Created by Dnm.
http://en.wikipedia.org/wiki/File:Tesseract2.svg[11/27/2012 9:44:18 AM]

gather together in one all things in Christ, both which are in heaven and which are on earth—in Him. It is so awesome, and so much the mind of Christ, that even when you "unfold" a representation of a tesseract or hypercube, you see this:

The dimension of Perfect Love, the fourth dimension, the joining of heaven and earth in Christ...is the CROSS! (Col. 1:19-20).

I know you have to have faith. I know you have to speak the Word. I know you have to take action in obedience. But these are only three 'dimensions'. The Lord wants to quicken your spirit and impart this revelation in you so that you can be an imitator of God in the earth, as you are in heaven! In Perfect Love, you are seated with Christ in heavenly places, as you are walking in love on the earth.

Figure 5. Unfolded Tesseract or Hypercube (Source: Wikipedia. Image in the Public Domain.) Created by Jason Hise. http://en.wikipedia.org/wiki/File:8-cell-simple.gif[11/27/2012 9:46:38 AM]

This is possible in the fourth dimension! Understanding the fourth dimension changes things!

Perfect Love precedes all faith. Or even faith will do nothing, because you must first have faith in His love. Every miracle, sign, and wonder is first evidence of the LOVE of Christ, then His faith, then His Word, then His action. When we understand perfect love, we have faith and know His answer is always 'yes' and in Him 'amen'. If we know His love, we know He will not refuse us when we ask. When we do not ask in love, we ask amiss. Abiding in Him means abiding, living in the fourth dimension, the dimension of Perfect Love.

Love is the soil that the seed of faith grows in, that covers and activates the word of faith. The Word says that Christ dwells in our hearts through faith and that we are rooted and grounded in love (Eph. 3:17). If we do not have love, we are not love, and we are nothing. With no love we are ineffective and are not true imitators of the Father (1 Cor. 13).

Perfect Love is the motivation for serving God and one another. If we do not do what we do because of love, we do it for the wrong reasons. Evangelism, or fulfilling the Great Commission, is simply finding ways to tell people that He loves them. Every gift is a different manifestation and mantle of His Perfect Love demonstrated.

Perfect Love is the place, the fourth dimension that is represented by the fourth row of stones on the breastplate of Aaron. It is the realm that satan cannot enter. Remember, even when he occupied his position as Lucifer, son of the morning, his breastplate had only three rows. He was on the holy mountain of God, but he never entered the glory! He never entered the glory that was given us, so that we would all be one, just as Christ and the Father are one. Just think, when we are in the glory, when we have come boldly to the throne of grace through the veil of His flesh, it is not even possible for the enemy to enter in.

Perfect Love is the difference between a divided kingdom or divided house in the third dimension and a double portion-double kingdom in the fourth dimension! Perfect Love is the house that the thief cannot break into. If a house is occupied by the 'strong man', Perfect Love is the one who is stronger that the strongman who comes upon him and overcomes him, taking from him all his armor in which he trusted, and dividing his spoils. Love is what occupies the house so that when the unclean spirit tries to return, it cannot come in. Perfect Love is the REAL occupy movement; we OCCUPY until He comes (Luke 11:14-26, 19:13, KJV).

Perfect Love is everything. It is the 'Why' of creation, the consummation of covenant, and the continuance of all life and power! We are in Him; we are part of Him; therefore, we are like Him. Does a part of your body belong to someone else, or is it identifiable as you? He is Perfect Love, so we are perfect love. God is love, and he who abides in love abides in God, and God in him. As He is, so are we in the world (1 John 4:16-17).

Therefore, as apostles and other ministers, let us walk in the fourth dimension of Perfect Love and be true imitators of the Father in heaven so that we can be co-creators on earth.

BEING IMITATORS OF THE FATHER: THE "HOW"

Now that we know that Perfect Love is why the Father and Christ Jesus say or do anything, and that it's the motivation behind every miracle, sign, and wonder in the earth, we can look at how these acts of love were done, that we through the power of the Holy Spirit might imitate these works of love.

When studying the acts of the earthly ministry of Christ Jesus, the Lord showed me what He calls the 'Creation Process'. As we examine this process, let us keep in mind the impartation of the revelation we received earlier that the FOURTH DIMENSION, PERFECT LOVE, on earth as it is in heaven, is the catalyst for all things in the third dimension. Let us continue to allow our hearts to be encouraged, being knit together in love, and attaining to all riches of the full assurance of understanding, to the knowledge of the mystery of God, both of the Father and of Christ, in whom are hidden all the treasures of wisdom and knowledge (Col. 2:2).

Although there are more than four dimensions in creation, getting the Body the revelation to understanding the dimensions beyond our common three is an important first step as we execute the co-creation process in Christ. After all, His will is that in Him we would *"make all see what is the fellowship of the mystery, which from the beginning of the ages has been hidden in God who created all things through Jesus Christ; to the intent that now the manifold [multi-dimensional] wisdom of God might be made known by the church to the principalities and powers in the heavenly places, according to the eternal purpose which He accomplished in Christ Jesus our Lord."*

Therefore, it is His will that we understand His mysteries in every dimension so that according to His purpose, we can make them known to the principalities and powers (Eph. 3:9-11). This is part of the blessing and the first commandment issued to mankind in Gen. 1:28, where we are to *"be fruitful, multiply, take dominion, and subdue the earth."* As this is done on earth in Christ, it is accomplished and made known to the principalities and powers in heavenly places!

The CREATION PROCESS can be briefly described as follows:

1. Faith in the heart
2. Word in the mouth/thanksgiving; blessing
3. Action: Breaking/dividing

GIVING/DISTRIBUTING

And "it" shall multiply after its own kind. These represent the three dimensions of faith rooted and grounded in love. If faith is not rooted and grounded in love, in this creation process you can wrongly put faith in something that manifests fear and eventual death through the same three dimensions.

FAITH IN THE HEART

The Word of God is very clear in Heb. 11:1 and 3: *"Now faith is the substance of things hoped for, the evidence of things not seen. ... By faith we understand that the worlds were framed by the word of God, so that the things which are seen were not made of things which are visible."*

If you can see it with your natural eyes, no faith is required because it already exists. So NOT SEEING something, or something not existing, is a REQUIREMENT of the situation where you must do something with the WORD OF FAITH 'in your heart out of your mouth'. (FAITH is/equals the substance, or the 'manifestation/existence' of whatever you are hoping for.) Remember, faith is the seed planted in the soil of Perfect Love in the process of creation.

"FAITH IN THE HEART" BECOMES "WORD IN THE MOUTH"

Your confession by faith made your salvation a reality. As a person thinks in his heart, so is he. Your word (that you believe in your heart) is the catalyst that creates the vision, idea, or the declaration you just made. God said, *"Let there be,"* and then it was. So, your word in your

mouth becomes the EVIDENCE of THINGS NOT SEEN...
that means it happens.

"WORD IN THE MOUTH" BECOMES "ACTION"

We are coming to an unprecedented season in the end of this
age where as apostles and fathers we must be able to look at
a multitude through the eyes of perfect love and meet their
needs according to the will of God. We must have faith that
they will be reconciled back to our heavenly Father, speak
the Word of the gospel, and in the demonstration of the
Spirit and of power do mighty miracles, signs and wonders,
and deliverances pointing to Christ as their only way, truth,
and life.

Our understanding of these mysteries has never been
more important, which is why the Holy Spirit is imparting
into us His revelation knowledge for our instruction. We
know by observation and discernment of the times that in
these current governments and an economy worldwide that
is increasingly out of our control, we must be able to execute
His supernatural measures in the earth, being in the world
but not of it.

We know the counterfeit Christ, the lawless one, is waiting
in the wings to deceive even if possible the very elect with
all power, signs, and lying wonders (2 Thess. 2:9). We must
have understanding of how to do the actions that are the
result of the faith in our heart and Word in our mouth. The
Lord performs His Word (Jer. 1:12). When our word is His
Word mixed with our faith, and rooted and grounded in
the fourth dimension of Perfect Love, He performs "our"
word as well.

Specifically, let's look at the mystery of the miracle of the loaves and the fish in Matt. 14:14-21 as a sign and wonder revealing the creation process. This work must be part of our ability in Christ now and in the times ahead.

"And when Jesus went out He saw a great multitude; and He was moved with compassion for them, and healed their sick. When it was evening, His disciples came to Him, saying, "This is a deserted place, and the hour is already late. Send the multitudes away, that they may go into the villages and buy themselves food."

"But Jesus said to them, 'They do not need to go away. You give them something to eat.'

"And they said to Him, 'We have here only five loaves and two fish.'

"He said, 'Bring them here to Me.' Then He commanded the multitudes to sit down on the grass. And He took the five loaves and the two fish, and looking up to heaven, He blessed and broke and gave the loaves to the disciples; and the disciples gave to the multitudes. So they all ate and were filled, and they took up twelve baskets full of the fragments that remained. Now those who had eaten were about five thousand men, besides women and children."

Christ Jesus wants us to walk in the same love, authority, and power that He demonstrated and do even greater exploits in the kingdom on earth as it is in heaven. He told the apostles, *"You do it. You give them something to eat."* It's the same thing He told Simon Peter as He prepared breakfast for them after His resurrection. *"You feed my sheep."* He is saying to us to answer the cry of *"Show us the Father!"* from a lost and dying world by doing His works.

When they brought Him what they had in their hand, the loaves and fish, He said, *"Give them to me; I'll get this process started for you."* They obeyed Him, and He ACTIVATED

THE CREATION PROCESS in the loaves and fish by thanksgiving, blessing, and breaking. And He put it back into THEIR hands.

They continued to offer thanksgiving/blessing; they broke it, and they gave it, which caused a chain reaction among the companies of people sitting. Thanksgiving/ Blessing, breaking, and giving is the pattern, like ripples in a lake.

Truly this passage demonstrates the creation process. We know by this passage that Christ was moved by Perfect Love for the multitude. He was always walking in the fourth dimension. He had faith that all of the people would be fed. The Word in His mouth was blessing and thanksgiving. His actions were in two parts: breaking/ dividing the bread and loaves and fish, then giving/ distributing it to the apostles.

ACTION: BREAKING/DIVIDING ... WHAT HAPPENS?

The miracle of the loaves and fish was not just multiplication, but replication. When the Lord was imparting this revelation to me, He showed me a cell getting ready to replicate—first it makes copies of all of its components, then it breaks in half, and you have two new whole cells. Jesus gave thanks and broke the bread and fish. How does this happen biologically? Does this happen at all?

Yes! Let the Holy Spirit increase your faith. On the following page, examine this diagram for the biological process of cell replication called MITOSIS.

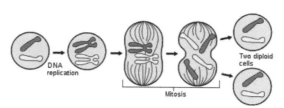

Figure 7. Major Events in Mitosis
(Source: Wikipedia. Image is in the Public Domain.)
Created by Mysid. http://en.wikipedia.org/wiki/File:Major_
events_in_mitosis.svg[11/27/2012 9:48:43 AM]

Mitosis is only one part of how a parent cell replicates itself into two identical 'daughter' cells. But this should quicken your spirit man to see how this process is occurring all around us. If we will understand how to tap into this revelation of the 'How' of the Word of God, the possibilities for the apostles and the rest of the Body of Christ are unlimited.

Consider how the strongholds of fear and death are conquered in this scenario of the fathers turning their hearts toward the children and in the demonstration of the Spirit and of power, feeding 5,000 men plus women and children with five loaves and two fish! No plan of the enemy to starve humanity or control the world's food supply would succeed for a second.

Let's look deeper into the miracle of the loaves and fish for understanding. The grain and yeast in the bread replicated themselves at one point because they are part of LIVING CREATION, and so did the fish for the same reason. In the hands of Christ, He reactivated them, by His power, His faith, and His Word.

I want to increase your faith even more. If you are saying to yourself, "I can walk in the fourth dimension of Perfect Love, but I don't know if I have enough faith in my heart to speak a word from my mouth that will reactivate the creation process in whatever I have in my hand."

Do you have the faith in God Himself that He will perform His own Word? Here is good news! He said ALREADY to ALL LIVING CREATION "be fruitful and multiply" (He added "take dominion and subdue" to mankind!) So, His Word is already in place! Use His own Word to reactivate what is in your hand.

In the creation process, it is apparent that activation through faith and the Word and then breaking and dividing are keys to how it works. Here are some further examples of the creation process which highlight breaking and dividing as demonstrated throughout the Word:

- The Lord divided the light from the darkness in Gen. 1:4.

- He divided the waters by a firmament in Gen. 1:7.

- He divided the sacrifice into two mirror images, to show us there was a lack and something missing (CHRIST), which is why He passes through the two pieces.

- The fire of the Holy Spirit divided among all in the upper room at Pentecost!

- After Pentecost, people brought things to the apostles, who followed the same process as Christ Jesus. *"Now all who believed were together, and had all things in common, and sold their possessions and goods, and divided them among all, as anyone had need"* (Acts 2:44-45).

- The parable of the talents demonstrated that the Lord's instructions to His servants are

Creation vs. consumption. When their master returned they had replicated the talents, doubling them (Matt. 25:14-30, according to their ability=according to their measure of faith). The one who disobeyed lost his stewardship and the provision.

ACTION: GIVING AND DISTRIBUTING

After Christ Jesus blessed and gave thanks for the bread and fish, reactivating His Word to be fruitful and multiply, the Lord gave the broken pieces, activated to replicate, back to the apostles to distribute from their baskets as a chain reaction in each company of people. The apostles blessed, and broke and distributed among all who had need, and there was no lack. So, they all ate and were filled, and they took up 12 baskets full of the fragments that remained (Matt. 14:20). Clearly they had been activated to replicate until the need was met, and even then 12 full baskets of the continuously-replicating bread and fish remained!

Christ's original commandment to us is "You give them something to eat." The changing of hands, the changing of ownership from Him to us, as well as giving and distribution is part of the creation process.

In the beginning when the creation process was implemented by the Word of God through His power, He said to mankind, *"Be fruitful, multiply, take dominion, and subdue the earth"* (Gen. 1:28). In Ps. 115:16 it says *"The heaven, even the heavens, are the LORD's; But the earth He has given to the children of men."* Therefore, God has already given us the earth and the fullness of the activated creation, now completed in Christ, for us to distribute into the earth!

Where else do we see the evidence of replicated power being given and distributed in the earth? Christ has broken and divided Himself after replicating Himself, in order that He may multiply not only in us, but that we might give of Him to the world! He has given us His Holy Spirit that is being distributed to all who ask of Him, for the same spirit that raised Christ from the dead dwells in us. He has given His gifts to mankind to activate and impart into others. Mankind believes in Him through our word speaking His gospel. He is the fiery torch that lights all others on fire, never diminishing in strength or power, but multiplying as He divides!

OUR DESTINY AND THE WORKS PREPARED BY GOD BEFOREHAND THAT WE SHOULD WALK IN THEM

Our destiny and our calling as apostles is to be sent by the Father into all the earth to be imitators of His works through Christ demonstrated in Spirit and in power. We are called to be His answer to the cry of the world to "Show us the Father!" We are called to be executors in the process of co-creation, dwelling in the fourth dimension of Perfect Love where we are in the secret place of the Most High God, and the true signs and wonders pointing to Perfect Love and glorifying our Lord and Savior, Christ, shall manifest on the earth as it is in heaven!

THE WORD OF MY TESTIMONY AS HIS APOSTLE

Every time I've been sent by the Lord into a land to minister, I have been given a supernatural ability to love those who reside there. This love is the Perfect Love of the Father. It has nothing to do with my capacity to love, because this comes with a power to pierce the darkness of anything that may be manifesting before me to reach in and deliver people out of bondage. It causes me and others with me to occupy the higher realm of being seated with Christ in heavenly places above any principality, power, or spiritual wickedness in high places in the territory or nation. Here is one testimony out of many about the principles I've just described to you in this chapter.

In December 2011, two other apostles and I joined together to go to parts of Kenya, Africa. We were sent by God to minister to the groups of ministers that had been gathered to hear from the fathers, and we also ministered at many ministries, both separately and together. The three of us recognized from the beginning that we were there IN CHRIST and representing CHRIST, not ourselves in any way. We had no agenda but the Lord's and came to advance His Kingdom of Love on earth as it is in heaven, not promote anything else except His will and His love, on earth as it is in heaven! We truly understood that we are CHRIST'S apostles, sent by Him as gifts of grace to His people all over the earth; we poured out everything of Christ in us as the Father and held nothing back, even during the times of the testing each of us were faced with.

The first night we had arrived, after traveling two exhausting days to reach Eldoret, Kenya, I experienced the most intense spiritual battle I had ever experienced before or since. It took the entire night of constant resistance to withstand the physical, mental and spiritual manifestations that came against me. Still in the battle at first light, I then heard the Lord speak to me out of the darkness. He said to me, "Are you in Me?" I answered, "Yes." Quietly He said, "And where am I?" I replied, "Everywhere." Finally He said,

"Because you are in Me, and I am everywhere, everywhere you are is home."

Suddenly the demonic battle ceased and I felt the Lord's presence like a garment fall upon me. I felt Him physically from that time forth until we completed the assignment in the land. I was truly in another dimension, completely unaware of anything except Him and His love pouring out through me to minister to His people. I was above all of the principalities and powers in the land and couldn't even readily see them as I normally do, even though they were being tormented around me. They still tried to attack Christ in me and I did go through other tests, but there is nothing like the effectiveness and fruitfulness that comes from walking in the dimension of Perfect Love, where we are seated with Christ and above all things, yet walking in and demonstrating His Perfect Love in the earth!

God's Perfect Love descended upon all of us because we were sent by Him to answer the cry of 'Show us the Father.' He did not let any of the Word He spoke through us fall to the ground. The ministers received His Word from us and immediately ran with it. There is fruit evident and multiplication even as I write this today! People were healed right before our eyes. Demons manifested only to be bound and cast out to a dry place never to return. People practicing witchcraft were delivered so they could know they are loved by God, and receive salvation. Their eyes were opened to see that their gifts had been robbed and perverted by the enemy to be used for his purposes instead of the purposes of our Creator. Foundations were established and identity was restored so that the saints could be equipped for their works of ministry.

The Lord was constantly multiplying what was entrusted to Him. The food prepared for us fed whole rooms full of people, and although there didn't appear to be enough, people ate until they were full. Between the three of us apostles, we had all things in common: coffee, food, even the Lord's Treasury funds that we had each been sent with. We were always tossing in shillings to get things done; we blessed the ministers in the land, and I know for a fact the money in my envelope MULTIPLIED to meet the need of what the Lord told me I was to distribute. None of us thought anything of it; it was the Lord's money and we did exactly what the Holy Spirit told us to do with it. Because we moved in Perfect Love, the word of faith in our mouths caused the money to multiply. We knew there had to be enough to meet every need, and indeed there was more than enough. I even brought a few dollars home!

The Lord's assignment for us in Africa had many other powerful examples that I don't have space to share here. Everything of His will was accomplished, and quickly, because we walked in the supernatural dimension of His Perfect Love. The Lord began and continued His good work of love in us; He is seeing it through to completion as He answers the cry of His people, 'Show us the Father!' It was a true manifestation of being in one accord and in one place: CHRIST. I'm at a loss to truly describe this. It was as though I was them and they were me, and all of us were CHRIST, the FATHER, the HOLY SPIRIT. It was John 17:23: *"I in them, and You in Me; that they may be made perfect in one, and that the world may know that You have sent Me, and have loved them as You have loved me."*

For those of us who have experienced this new level in Him, a "from glory to glory" transformation by this revelation and immersion in Him, there is no turning back once we have entered the fourth dimension. This is the new standard in the Body of Christ; this is the way and we are walking in it. The world has cried out to see the Father and they will see Him through us. The Lord will fulfill His Word and His precepts in it. For you who are reading this, the waiting is over; now it's your turn! Will you "Come up here" and enter the dimension of Perfect Love? Will you too become an imitator of the Father through Christ Jesus so that the world will know Him?

YOUR IMPARTATION OF THE MYSTERIES

"Father, as one of your apostles in the earth in this hour, one of Your sent ones to the world, I hereby impart this revelation knowledge and understanding to your Servants, as well as the faith to execute Your Word as You have revealed it. May they receive even greater revelation of your mysteries, all of which are hidden in Christ, and may they may truly be rooted and grounded in love and be able to comprehend with all the saints what is the width and length and depth and height, to know the love of Christ which passes knowledge, and that they may be filled with all the fullness of God, as they walk as Co-Creators with Christ and imitators of You. Let it be on earth as it is in heaven. In the Name of Christ Jesus the King of Kings and Lord of Lords, so be it. Amen."

ABOUT THE AUTHOR

Laurie L. Boyd is an ordained apostle of Christ Jesus. She is the founder and president of Dwelling Place Worship &

Prayer Ministries, a Global House of Worship & Prayer and Training Center in Paw Paw, Mich., which she established along with her husband Rick T. Boyd in February 2009. She also facilitates The Council of Fire in Paw Paw, which is a growing apostolic and five-fold ministry network of unity and open forum attended by powerhouse ministers from the tri-state region, and has done this once a month since June of 2011 when the Lord established it through her.

Laurie carries the mantle of both king and priest. She is the owner of Teleios Business Solutions, established in 2006. In April of 2011, she established Tabernacle Treasures, a worship arts company. Her latest business venture, Teleios Enterprises LLC, was established in January 2012 with her husband, and is moving forward to be able to provide the elements of Christian kingship consulting, private equity and seed capital, and property and commercial leasing for which it is designed.

Laurie also carries the mantle of governments and strategic reconnaissance in order to execute the Word of the Lord and build His Kingdom on earth as it is in heaven. She has been given a vision of the Heart of the Father, exposure of the enemy's camp, and many other prolific revelations which she has ministered worldwide as one of the Lord's vessels to birth and bring forth His vision, strategy, and teaching into the earth in this hour so that the Bride will make herself ready. Often with her husband Rick Boyd, they have traveled worldwide individually and also with other apostles on missions to train up ministers and encourage the Lord's end-time army, to declare and decree and expose the camp of the enemy of God and mankind, with signs and wonders following. Laurie has also been gifted in the worship ministry to bring forth the sound from heaven to transform the atmosphere and the people in His presence.

Laurie and Rick and their extended family live in the Paw Paw area. She can be reached at 269-655-4255 or via email at villagecorporate@aim.com. To find out more about their ministry, visit www.dwellingplaceworship.com.

CHAPTER SIXTY-SEVEN

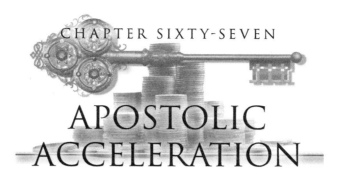

APOSTOLIC ACCELERATION

CHARLIE FISHER

God told Moses that they had circled the mountain long enough, that it was time to go to the land of promise. How many of us have felt that we have gone in circles long enough, but weren't quite sure where to turn? The purpose of this chapter is to help light a fire under us in order to move us beyond where we've been to where we are destined, by embracing Apostolic leaders, mantles, models, and ministry, and reaping the acceleration that accompanies them. I have experienced the fruit of this in my own life, and am excited about sharing that with you here. My own process and spiritual journey has taken me from being a pastor to a bishop to an apostle over many years, and these transitions were foretold and set in motion by prophecies such as this one below.

CORPORATE PROPHECY BY APOSTLE JANA ALCORN

"'I am moving you into a new season,' says the Lord. 'I have something in mind,' says the Lord, 'that will bring forth the **acceleration** *into what I have ordained for you. This is not what man has ordained, or even wanted, but it is what I want,' says the*

Lord, 'and it is what will be. I will not be bound by the mindsets of men; I will not confine your ministry to the imprisonment of religious attitudes,' says the Lord. 'I free you, my called one; I free you from those who do not know the shift that I am taking you through. I have called you and I have ordained you an apostle unto the nations so do not limit Me; Follow Me now and begin to move into this new thing,' says the Lord, 'and do not look back and do not go back.'

"'For I have commanded a blessing in my new move,' says the Lord your God, 'and that is where you will find the fulfillment. Old paths will not fulfill you now and old mindset will no longer appeal to you; For what I do now, shall be a formation of new things and new ways, and new mindsets. Step out in faith and do not worry about the resources,' says the Lord, 'for an **apostolic anointing** to receive shall come upon you and you shall see a hunger in those that I have called and joined to you and it shall come forth, says the Lord!'" (author's emphasis).

As I waited patiently for this and other prophecies to come to pass in my life, the Lord was faithful to prepare and position me and bring new people onto my path and into my life. Are we listening for the new sound of the Spirit? Everywhere I look, I'm witnessing believers who desire a new unveiling of God's glory, new revelations, new songs, new wine and new wineskins.

The apostles Paul and Peter said it like this, respectively:

"...I do not count myself to have apprehended; but one thing I do, forgetting those things which are behind and reaching forward to those things which are ahead, I press toward the goal for the prize of the upward call of God in Christ Jesus" (Phil. 3:13-14, NKJ).

"Most important of all, continue to show deep love for each other, for love covers a multitude of sins" (1 Pet. 4:8).

Okay, we've started; now where are we going? Good question! Answer: "To boldly go where no man has gone before," to quote the mission of Star Trek.

It has been suggested that this quotation was taken from a White House booklet published in 1958. *The Introduction to Outer Space* was produced in an effort to garner support for a national space program in the wake of the Sputnik flight. Today's apostle has been called by God and anointed to go beyond the limits where no one has gone before and to blaze a trail led not by man's limitations but by our counselor and guide, the Holy Spirit.

WE NEED HELP TO SUCCEED

No one can get there by himself. This is why the scripture tells us we need the whole body, and we are not to tell any parts of the body I have no need of you! And the eye cannot say to the hand, *"I have no need of you"; or again the head to the feet, "I have no need of you"* (1 Cor. 12:21).

As a former national champion boxer, I had coaches to help me succeed. I did not get there on my own. If we are to go to the next level as a spouse, parent, business executive, athlete, etc. then we need to associate ourselves with the best coaching, teaching and influence possible. Solomon, the wisest man that ever lived, tells us, *"Plans fail for lack of counsel, but with many advisers they succeed"* (Prov. 15:22). My company, Guiding Business Transitions, is dedicated to hiring the best advisors possible to help our clients. If we don't have them, then we'll get them. There are two vital keys to success: know not only your strengths, but also your weaknesses. Hire the best advisors you can afford.

My friend Ron Kardashian, executive trainer and author of *The Solutionist* says, "The process of acceleration does just not bear with it a Speeding Up but in fact a Stepping Up. I'm constantly reminding my clients.... if one is going to make significant increase and growth, one cannot just stare up the stairs, but one must step up the stairs."

Tom Cruise famously said it right in playing the role of Jerry Maguire, sports agent, when he said "You complete me." We need to see each person in the Body of Christ in the same light; that without them, we are incomplete.

We need to be in the vanguard of Apostolic Acceleration and recognize that the apostolic gift and calling was needed not only in the early church, but also in today's church. We must honor and accept the apostolic as well as we do all of the other spiritual gifts and offices in the church.

The word *Apostle* means one sent. An apostle is one who is sent by God.

The word *Acceleration* means a change in the rate of motion, speed or action.

SUPERNATURAL KEYS TO ACCELERATION

The Apostolic mandate is to empower all the KEYS and GIFTS that God has given us and to assess what is needed to move forward. Several things will take place when there is an increase in apostolic presence. There will be an increase in anointing, an increase in revelation, an increase in authority and an increase in power.

The following are Keys to Supernatural Acceleration:

- Key of David — Rev. 3:6,7; Isa. 22:22

- Key of Knowledge — Luke 11:49-53
- Key of Discernment — Heb. 5:14
- Key of Simplicity — Acts 15:28-29
- Keys of the Kingdom — Matt. 16:19
- Key of Revelation — Matt. 16:15
- Key of Anointing — James 5:14
- Key of Authority — Matt. 28:18
- Key of Power — Luke 10:19
- Key of Vision & Strategy — Acts 2:17

If there is a lack of the above being demonstrated where you are, then increase the apostolic presence!

SUPERNATURAL GIFTS TO ACCELERATION

"And in the church God has appointed first of all apostles, second prophets, third teachers, then workers of miracles, also those having gifts of healing, those able to help others, those with gifts of administration, and those speaking in different kinds of tongues. But eagerly desire the greater gifts. And now I will show you the most excellent way. The way of exercising gifts rightly, namely, by love" (1 Cor. 12:28, 31).

"But now hath God set the members every one of them in the body, as it hath pleased him" (1 Cor. 12:18).

In the natural realm, we may like some foods and dislike others, but in the Kingdom everything God prepares is good and is received with thanksgiving. This isn't a spiritual smorgasbord that we can choose what we like or dislike and expect to get the same results. If we leave out anything on the above list, then we will fall short of God's ultimate design. To do so is to say to that part of the body that "I have no need of you" and to our Savior, "Thanks for these.... but no thank you for those...."

SUPERNATURAL PROPHETIC PRAYER ACCELERATION

I personally have several prophetic intercessors that pray for me. Here is one example of the prophetic words I received recently.

"Hello Charlie!

"I see the Lord narrowing your focus. He is bringing to you a few key people to sow into for a very high return for the Kingdom. He may reduce the quantity, but He is greatly increasing the QUALITY of impact. It is a season to sow into these few and then reap the harvest of your labors later.

"Abba, thank you for Charlie! Thank you that you are giving Him a voice to speak to strategic people for great impact. I declare favor over Charlie in the name of Jesus, divine appointments and connections with these ones who are on your heart. I declare that Charlie sows in peace and reaps a harvest of righteousness. Thank you that Charlie is your pastor wherever you place him. Thank you for your faithful servant. I speak grace to his heart to persevere in Jesus' name. Amen."

Wherever you see lack, call for and increase the presence of God in that area. Need order and organization? Pray for those having the gift of administration. Lacking souls being saved? Pray for evangelists. Need miracles? Pray for God to raise up or bring workers of miracles! Need Healings? Pray for those having gift of healings. Want more

Revelation, power, authority, discernment, strategy, vision, breakthrough and anointing? Pray for Apostles. We then must receive them and release them to do what they're called to do in the body of Christ and Kingdom.

Today's Apostolic Pioneer is not stuck on traditions of man and doesn't regard change as a problem but as a stepping stone for progress. Thank God he has set us as Apostolic Pioneers in the world to blaze new trails of acceleration.

Two things that hinder ministries and businesses from accelerating are:

1. A lack of Apostolic covering: The Apostolic covering increases the scope of what ministry or business should look like.

2. A lack of vision: Without vision, whatever we are doing will end up stagnant and lacking strategy.

George Barna understood vision and in *The Power of Vision* said, "Without God's vision for your ministry, you are simply playing a dangerous game." Barna's word to all Christian leaders is: "Uncovering God's vision for your ministry is not an option." As Barna clearly states, "To minister authentically and authoritatively, you must first clarify your vision, then embrace it and make it the focus of your life's work and the heartbeat of your church. Vision is the insight God provides to instruct and direct our paths, a reflection of what God wants to accomplish through us in building His kingdom. With this clear picture, from Him, of where you are headed, your chances of a successful journey are increased a thousand fold."[1]

APOSTOLIC EMPOWERMENT

"They presented these men to the apostles, who prayed and laid their hands on them. So the word of God spread. The number of disciples in Jerusalem increased rapidly, and a large number of priests became obedient to the faith" (Acts 6:6-7).

There is such an amazing impartation that takes place when apostles pray; it is often accompanied with prophetic words and declarations. These things when combined produce an amazing supernatural acceleration in the lives of the people being prayed for and in the lives of the people they are associated with. Apostles are more focused on building the kingdom of God than focusing on selfish motives or ambitions that would result in building their own kingdoms. God has given the Apostles and the rest of the five-fold ministry to help the body of Christ reach the measure of the stature of the fullness of Christ and without them the church will be crippled and unable to accelerate to her full potential.

Today's apostles are seasoned spiritual fathers whose hearts and gifts are used to release and empower not just the Body of Christ to carry on the work of the ministry, but whatever mountain or sphere they have been called to influence. Apostles constantly look to honor people by giving honor to whom honor is due. Apostles are looking at working themselves out of a job by raising up faithful sons to whom they can hand the batons to. The Gideon organization has been greatly used in distributing Bibles around the world; however, the average age of a Gideon is 70 years old. Many organizations are struggling today, because they have not had a plan of succession. Dr. Gordon E. Bradshaw's book, *The Technology of Apostolic Succession*, is a must read on this subject.

The apostle Paul declared, *"...and my speech and my preaching was not with enticing words of man's wisdom, but in demonstration of the Spirit and of power"* (1 Cor. 2:4).

There is a righteous discontent in the Body of Christ to not settle for the status quo or church as usual and many, while still honoring the past, have taken hold of the future into the greater realms of God's unveiling glory. Worship has gone to a whole new level. People aren't satisfied with just hearing about God, they want to experience him. Apostles facilitate an ushering in of God's presence and power!

On 11/11/11 we hosted the first international K.E.Y.S. (Kingdom Economic Yearly Summit), with Dr. Bruce Cook, entitled "Supernatural Abundance of Favor" in Grande Prairie, Alberta, Canada. What I am about to share not only changed my life, but also the people who attended or viewed the webcast or the DVDs as well.

Before sharing about this K.E.Y.S., let me give you a little background of personal events leading up to this event that made me experience acceleration on a whole new level.

MY JOURNEY BEFORE K.E.Y.S. CANADA

To begin with, I have been a pastor for 25 years and before that was a traveling evangelist. I had been taught that the Apostolic was done away with and that the marketplace was not a place for ministers. Ministry was sacred and making money outside of ministry was secular; sound familiar? Our church model was that of the Levitical priesthood and not after the Order of Melchizedek. God was about to give me new revelation in these areas.

During a Pastors and Leadership Conference held in Alberta, Canada in 2004, I was prophesied over by three of the apostolic and prophetic keynote speakers that God was sending me into the marketplace and would give me strategies and witty inventions and that millions of dollars were going to flow through my hands. At the time, this seemed impossible and something only the Lord could accomplish. The prophecies bore witness with my spirit, and I knew I was in for quite an adventure. During this time, I was instructed of the Lord to start studying about the Kingdom of God. He showed me if I would focus on building His Kingdom, He would use me far greater than if I focused on building His church.

Coming home one night from a church service, I began to count all of my blessings, including being married to an amazing wife Lisa, having three beautiful and gifted daughters who all love Jesus, knowing the joy of salvation, being baptized with the Holy Spirit, being called into the ministry, experiencing God's faithfulness in our lives, etc. All of a sudden, I blurted out a spontaneous decree from the depths of my soul and at the top of my lungs: "I'm the richest man in Grande Prairie."

Almost immediately, the atmosphere around me began to shift and acceleration began to happen. That guttural decree shifted something in the spirit realm, and I was given a Kingdom key to prosper. It seemed that everything I touched turned to gold and the businesses I prayed for prospered. Businesses started coming to me for investors and for strategies. At first it was thousands of dollars, then tens of thousands, hundreds of thousands, millions, tens of millions and now with all the companies combined, and a new level of faith and authority, we are believing God for hundreds of millions and even billions. I learned that nothing happens in the natural until it is first seen and released in the supernatural.

During this season of marketplace ministry, some people in my precious church were having a hard time accepting the fact that I could still be their pastor while having an effective ministry in the marketplace. A fulltime pastor to them meant being fully devoted to the needs of the church. I felt torn between continuing to minister to the marketplace that God had undeniably called me to and still continuing to shepherd the flock whom I loved and cared for deeply. I recognized my dichotomy of direction and requested a six-month unpaid sabbatical. The church was left in the hands of their former pastor during that time, and I continued to pursue marketplace ministry.

During my sabbatical, I observed that the church on the whole was focused too much on having a glorified body while only admiring the head of the church. I realized in order for the church to be what Christ intended her to be, she must love being in the presence of the Lord and giving him first place or the preeminence in the church. Most churches do not take the time to love the presence of the Lord and to allow Christ to have preeminence and saturate the believers. Some fear if the Spirit starts moving too much there might be wild fire and then what will the people do? Some fear losing control of the service. John the Baptist said, *"He must increase but I must decrease"* (John 3:30).

After the return from my sabbatical, I focused on giving God the preeminence in the church services. Within the first year of taking down the clock and focusing on God's presence, our church doubled in size and there was surplus in the tithes and offerings. People were being drawn because of the presence of God and the freedom in the Spirit. When the time came that our service would normally have been dismissed, I would say:

"Thank you for being here today, and if you must go we understand and we hope to see you here again next week, but for those who want to biggie size your experience with God, stick around while the worship continues because God's got more for you!" During this time, the greatest moves of God took place as we basked in His presence.

God blesses us and gifts us to be a blessing to others. Even the gifts of the Spirit are not focused on our own edification but for the body of Christ's edification. Many of us realize that God has not given us a spirit of poverty, but of faith and of confidence in the promises of God, and so we pray for God to multiply our seed sown which produces great dividends. Since I started praying this way, my "seeds sown" (finances into ministry) have more than doubled what I used to make annually before entering marketplace ministry. The last three years of our pastorate, I did not take a salary from the church but lived completely on our marketplace income. To God be the Glory for His faithfulness and abundant favor! We are not to look to man as our source, nor to the church for that matter.

When we look to man, we put a limit on what God wants to do and can do in our lives. When we look to the congregation or denomination as our source, that becomes our ceiling, so we never increase or accelerate beyond the local church or our own particular stream in the body. When God is our source, the ceiling is limitless!!! The same applies if we are looking to our friends, family, businesses, banks, etc. as our source; we will never go beyond them. Instead of getting a loan, it's great to pay cash. . . while driving my new SUV home and thanking God for this tremendous blessing, (an all-powered, leather seats, seat warmers, sunroof, 4x4), it dawned on me that I didn't praise God nearly enough in the hard times.

Right then, I made a promise to God that if I ever had another hardship I would praise him in it! Well, two minutes later a rock flew up and hit my windshield, "SMACK"!! I almost forgot my promise to the Lord, but I remembered my promise and quickly began to praise God. In the days, weeks, months and years following this promise, I have continued to praise God in the trials and tribulations. This is another major KEY to ACCELERATION in life: to be able to praise God and give thanks in all things. When we can do this, it brings us to a level of victory where we too can say, *"but none of these things move me..."* (Acts 20:24).

11:11

During my early years of ministry, I kept seeing 11:11 frequently on clocks, signs etc. Whenever I would see this, I would be prompted to pray and eventually recognized it as a God wink indicating His blessing and favor. The 11:11 sightings continue to happen along with God's blessing and favor in our family, church and marketplace. Annually, we hosted an Angel Investor appreciation banquet where the companies gave updates to the investors on their progress. We would always open in prayer and give thanks to God for the many answered prayers. All of the CEOs were believers, but I realized there needed to be more emphasis on being Kingdom Companies and running the companies with Kingdom principles.

One of my business associates who happened to be my first investor, Lorne LaRochelle, discovered a website for one of Dr. Bruce Cook's companies. Not long after this, I sent Dr. Cook an email complimenting him on his website and his commitment to seeing the marketplace as a ministry rather than a secular trade. After weeks of exchanging phone calls, prophecies, prayers and emails, we decided to meet each other during my family's summer vacation. We agreed to meet along with my business advisor and mentor, John Anderson, in Gig Harbor just outside of Seattle. Before we knew it, we had 50 Kingdom marketplace people gathered together to seek the Lord. During that meeting, there were many prophecies released, heavenly portals opened, scrolls downloaded, angelic visitations, and glorious worship. I recognized during this meeting that Dr. Cook was not only a prominent business man, but he was also anointed, called and sent by the Lord to be an Apostle and a Prophet. Bruce Cook has since become a dear friend and brother, and we have experienced some amazing divine adventures together.

A month or so later, after returning home, I asked Dr. Cook if he would bring his K.E.Y.S. network leaders to minister to the Grande Prairie marketplace leaders on 11-11-11. He agreed, and we began to prepare for the event. The first thing we did was establish the intercessors to cover the event in prayer. This was vitally important for us to be able to function with freedom as the spiritual warfare was intense. At one point, Dr. Cook called his pastor, an anointed apostle, to pray for us, and we experienced a major breakthrough almost immediately, within 24 hours. We made sure that the people on the team were not novices in spiritual matters.

After months of preparation, the event was upon us. As the people were checking in, the expectation of what God was going to do was intense. In the back of the room, a roundtable of apostles and prophets were getting together to pray and speak over the event and one another. The meeting began with men and woman praying and prophesying in the Spirit at depths I had never witnessed. Throughout the week the messages, teachings and worship were astounding. The depth of the messages were at levels only seasoned ministers could attain. The presence of God was so powerful that nobody wanted to leave. The fellowship among the group was filled with love and affirmation.

This increase in apostolic presence produced three specific things in me: I received an increase in anointing, in revelation, and in authority. Many things were revealed during the services and in dreams during the night, not only for the guests and leaders attending the event, but also for what the Lord was about to do across Canada and the United States. One such revelation from our First Nations representative, Art Auger, was of the eagles from the South joining the eagles from the North. These eagles were identified as the Apostles.

We experienced a supernatural atmosphere shift over our whole city. Prominent businessmen were baptized with the Holy Spirit while others dedicated themselves and their businesses to the Lord. The city's mayor, two prominent businessmen and a First Nations representative were honored by myself as the local host and Dr. Bruce Cook, K.E.Y.S. founder and convener. The level of honoring at the event was overwhelming. Several beautiful swords were presented to honor our special guests and local dignitaries. There were many signs and wonders including a release of spoils over myself, Dr. Cook and many of our guests. Investments and properties which hadn't seen any movement for years began to go public and sell the day following the event. Others testified of their successful hunting endeavors the next week as a result of the K.E.Y.S. event. One man we prayed for even received a $25M cash offer to purchase his business that same week, which he had been praying to be able to sell his business for a profit for 10 years with no prior offers. Everywhere we looked there were "spoils" after the event. This "apostolic invasion" created a "spiritual tsunami" that is still bearing fruit today, including the UNKAP event we co-hosted on 12-12-12 with a dozen apostles from the U.S. and Canada.

APOSTOLIC ACTIVATION FOR ACCELERATION

In my 30 years of ministry, I have learned to ask myself the following questions. These are foundational principles for apostolic ministry.

1. Do I serve in love without entitlement? yes/no

2. Do I love beyond expectations? yes/no

3. Do I give cheerfully, without expecting anything in return? yes/no

4. Do I minister without needing to be ministered to? yes/no

5. Do I rejoice in tribulation and in everything give thanks? yes/no

6. Do I bless those that curse me and pray for those who despitefully use me and persecute me? yes/no

7. Do I forgive those who have wronged me and are indebted to me? yes/no

8. Do I honor all men? yes/no

9. Do I take it patiently when I suffer for doing well? yes/no

10. Do I use self-control and moderation in all things? yes/no

11. Do I want others to succeed even greater than myself? yes/no

12. Do I not just see through people, but see people through? yes/no

13. Do I look for the gold in others and not the dirt? yes/no

14. Do I stay in God's presence and give him preeminence? yes/no

15. Do I speak blessing and not cursing, life and not death? yes/no

NOW DECREE AND DECLARE IT!

Finally, name the 10 areas where you want to experience supernatural acceleration. Here are some examples:

1. Business

2. Church

3. Family

4. Worship

5. Favor

6. Honor

7. Finances

8. Wisdom

9. Knowledge

10. Understanding

Now decree and declare it!

God can use and bless any of his children to do amazing works and He does. We are thankful for the things that God freely gives us including: the prophets, pastors, evangelists and teachers and the equipping they are doing for the body of Christ. Let us make sure that we embrace the gift of the Apostles as well in order to be all that God has designed us to be. In closing, may the Lord accelerate you with Godspeed in all he has for you and yours!

PRAYER OF APOSTOLIC BLESSING AND HONOR
(Read or Speak Out Loud)

"Elohim God, thank you for placing the apostles in your church; please forgive us for not receiving them the way you desired us to. Help us to embrace and honor them as our spiritual fathers and thank you for their knowledge, wisdom and understanding as well as their impartations, prophetic words and discernment that comes from you. We thank you, Pappa God, for sending them to help build us up. We honor them and their pioneering spirit and call, as well as their willingness to take risks.

"Thank you for empowering and releasing them so they can empower and release us to do your will. We do now decree and declare that greater works shall they do than have been done before, for you are doing a new thing in them. We ask that you bless them with a thousand-fold return. As you have asked that you would send forth laborers into the harvest, we ask that you would send forth apostles to every sphere of influence. We also ask for a double portion to the First Nations people whom you sent before us to pave the way and prepare the land. Please forgive us for the many offenses against them and bless them with a two-thousand-fold return.

"Elohim God, thank you also for placing the prophets in your church as well as the pastors, evangelists, and teachers. May their entrance into glory be a glorious one and may they see much fruit for their labors. We decree and declare supernatural abundance of favor over them all, and we bless them in the name of the Lord, our Saviour, Yeshua the Christ, Jesus the King!"

ENDNOTES

1.   http://www.georgebarna.com/2009/10/the-power-of-vision/

ABOUT THE AUTHOR

Charlie Fisher has been a minister for 30 years, a husband for 27 years, and is a father of three beautiful daughters and a grandfather. He is a licensed Bishop and was recently commissioned as an Apostle to the Marketplace. Charlie brings more than 20 years of experience in the business community, including involvement in the following: Owner of Compu-Seller, which provided computer sales, training, servicing and networking. Fisher has served as a key strategy advisor to several boards, advising executives, business owners, and Angel Investors. Fisher has been instrumental in developing and implementing investment strategies as president of a business advisory and angel investment company, www.guidingbusinesstransitions.com, which presently has attracted over 100 "Angels."

His financial strategies have helped to fund several start-up corporations. His greatest honor so far in the marketplace has been to serve (the Lord) as the first international host to K.E.Y.S. Canada under the oversight and direction of founder and apostle Bruce Cook.

CHAPTER SIXTY-EIGHT

APOSTOLIC ENTREPRENEURSHIP & PROPHETIC STRATEGIES

FERNANDO GUILLEN

Last fall we observed and began the Jewish New Year, also known as *Rosh Hashanah*. Inside the studies of the Jewish calendar, this is the year 5773. The '70s decade, represented by the last two digits in the Jewish calendar, is associated with the number seven, which has a direct relation to the Hebrew alphabet letter *ayin,* whose pictogram is an eye. Dr. Robert Heidler and Dr. Chuck Pierce, who have dedicated themselves to the study of biblical times and seasons, have attributed this decade as "The Seers Prophetic Decade." This new prophetic cycle that began with Rosh Hashanah has as a final digit the number three, which corresponds to the Hebrew alphabet letter *guimel,* and is associated to a camel pictogram.

In the remarkable celebration of the Head of the Year 5773 at Global Spheres Center in Corinth, Tex., presided over by Dr. Chuck Pierce, the picture of a camel was in evidence inside a scriptural concept directly associated with and connected to prosperity, considering several Bible scriptures but especially the following:

"Arise, shine; for your light has come! And the glory of the LORD is risen upon you. For behold, the darkness shall cover the earth, and deep darkness the people; but the LORD will arise over you, and His glory will be seen upon you. The Gentiles shall come to your light, and kings to the brightness of your rising. Lift up your eyes all around, and see: They all gather together, they come to you; your sons shall come from afar, and your daughters shall be nursed at your side. Then you shall see and become radiant, and your heart shall swell with joy; because the abundance of the sea shall be turned to you, the wealth of the Gentiles shall come to you. The multitude of camels shall cover your land, the dromedaries of Midian and Ephah; all those from Sheba shall come; they shall bring gold and incense, and they shall proclaim the praises of the LORD" (Isa. 60:1-6).

In view of these prophetic considerations of current time and season related to the letters *ayin* and *guimel* that together form the number 73, we should discern that this is a time when prophetic strategies are fundamental to the liberation of financial resources.

However, every prophetic operation and manifestation has to be aligned to an apostolic dimension in order to materialize.

WEALTH TRANSFER

For many years we have heard prophetic words about "wealth transfer" given by men and women who have a worldwide path, especially Dr. Morris Cerullo, and such words are affirmed in essence in the following Scripture: *"...But the wealth of the sinner is stored up for the righteous"* (Prov. 13:22).

However, even though those prophetic words had been released, we haven't seen their manifestations bringing financial resources to the spreading of the Kingdom. In my understanding, I believe this is due to the fact the prophetic needs to be aligned to the apostolic. But this is the time when we will see the alignment of these two ministry offices in a way increasingly intense and functional.

In this chapter we will take time to analyze in the Scriptures one case of divine wealth transfer that took place in Jacob's life, and the application and principles that case has for each of us today.

"Now Jacob heard the words of Laban's sons, saying, 'Jacob has taken away all that was our father's, and from what was our father's he has acquired all this wealth.'(...) Yet your father has deceived me and changed my wages ten times, but God did not allow him to hurt me. If he said thus: 'The speckled shall be your wages,' then all the flocks bore speckled. And if he said thus: 'The streaked shall be your wages,' then all the flocks bore streaked. So God has taken away the livestock of your father and given them to me" (Gen. 31:1, 7-9).

But, before studying this further, we will look at some transcendental concepts that are going to help us in the development of this subject.

THE POWER OF A SEED

"Then God said, 'Let the earth bring forth grass, the herb that yields seed, and the fruit tree that yields fruit according to its kind, whose seed is in itself, on the earth;' and it was so. And the earth brought forth grass, the herb that yields seed according to its kind, and the tree that yields fruit, whose seed is in itself according to its kind. And God saw that it was good" (Gen. 1:11-12).

In the beginning God determined that everything yields fruit according to its kind of seed. The word seed in Hebrew means *zera*, and denotes the inner potential, offspring, semen. Through this definition we prove then the principle the Eternal establishes for reproduction of all life manifestation, whether animal or vegetable.

MAN'S CREATION PLAN

"Then God said, 'Let Us make man in Our image, according to Our likeness; let them have dominion over the fish of the sea, over the birds of the air, and over the cattle, over all the earth and over every creeping thing that creeps on the earth.' So God created man in His own image; in the image of God He created him; male and female He created them. Then God blessed them, and God said to them, 'Be fruitful and multiply; fill the earth and subdue it; have dominion over the fish of the sea, over the birds of the air, and over every living thing that moves on the earth'" (Gen. 1:26-28).

Man's creation plan would be supernatural; however, the Eternal would rule himself by the established principle for reproduction: everything yields fruit according to its kind of seed. In the case of man, He himself would empty His own seed, so His genetic nature would be inserted into him. For this reason we see that man was made according to God's image and according to His likeness. The word image in Hebrew is *tselem* which denotes illusion, photograph, shadow, or ghost; in fact, it implies a ghost or spirit. But, the word likeness in Hebrew is *demuth* which means similarity or appearance and character, nature.

The fact that the man has received a divine nature through the Eternal supernatural seed, would enable him to a fertility and fructification plan as well as dominion.

SEED ACTIVATION

Although the man has received the supernatural nature through divine seed, we see that the Eternal blesses His plan and declares the Word upon His seed.

The blessing of the Eternal always has a purpose and it is always directed to the activation of seed. The creative power of God's word (*davar*) would activate in the man the divine seed with all of its potential. In order to talk about prophetic plans and strategies in the entrepreneurial realm, we should first emphasize the power which is in the seed. The activation of our seed is necessary in order to us to develop all the entrepreneurial potential and then create entrepreneurship divine strategies.

We can see on the release of the Eternal's blessing upon the man's seed four transcendental words that would activate the seed potential, which are: fructify, multiply, subdue, and dominate. So, let's look at the meaning of these words in the Hebrew context:

- **Fructify** (Heb. *Parah*)

  It means to be fruitful or bear fruit; to branch. It is related to a fertile condition and to the manifestation of making, bearing or producing fruit. It is the capacity of bringing forth life. A seed is a potential tree.

- **Multiply** (Heb. *Rabah*)

  It means to be or become many, to be or become numerous. In essence it is closely related to the capacity of reproducing (of life). It is the external manifestation of internal potential. We reproduce according to a plan, a pattern.

- **Subdue** (Heb. *Kabash*)

  It means to subjugate, force, keep under dominion, imprison, be subordinated, trample. It implies in giving directions, having stewardship of something. It is related to an agreement with the Creator to dominate the environment, and with delegated authority through what is revealed in order to exercise dominion on and over what is multiplied.

- **Dominate** (Heb. *Radah*)

  It means to govern, exercise dominion, position oneself, submit. It has to do with the judging of legislation. It is directed toward establishing governmental legitimacy; the man would be the one commissioned to establish heaven's government on earth, and thus determine the limits of what is legal and illegal.

In Scripture we see that one of the ways the Eternal confirmed the covenant with His people was through the power to acquire wealth.

"And you shall remember the Lord your God, for it is He who gives you power to get wealth, that He may establish His covenant which He swore to your fathers, as it is this day" (Deut. 8:18).

Power in Hebrew is the word *koach* that means abilities, strategies. It is important to have the revelation that the Eternal doesn't give us wealth straightforward, but gives us strategies, abilities so that we endeavor. In the New Testament we see this very clearly through the parable of the talents (Matt. 25:14-30).

We see how the Eternal determined the man's seed potential—a generational, governmental seed. He activated one man and in him the capacity to govern the environment.

ABRAHAM'S CALLING

Scriptures are a type and figure of the New Covenant that was established by Jesus. Abraham, as the faith forefather, is an apostolic type and figure, since one of the true apostle's characteristics is to establish generations or a lineage, because the seed potential which is upon his shoulders. So, we see on the processes which Abraham went through an apostolic plan or model of entrepreneurship.

"Now the LORD had said to Abram: 'Get out of your country, from your family and from your father's house, to a land that I will show you. I will make you a great nation; I will bless you and make your name great; and you shall be a blessing. I will bless those who bless you, and I will curse him who curses you; and in you all the families of the earth shall be blessed.' So Abram departed as the LORD had spoken to him, and Lot went with him. And Abram was seventy-five years old when he departed from Haran. Then Abram took Sarai his wife and Lot his brother's son, and all their possessions that they had gathered, and the people whom they had acquired in Haran, and they departed to go to the land of Canaan. So they came to the land of Canaan" (Gen. 12:1-5).

Twenty-four years later God visited Abraham again. *"When Abram was ninety-nine years old, the Lord appeared to Abram and said to him, 'I am Almighty God; walk before Me and be blameless. And I will make My covenant between Me and you, and will multiply you exceedingly.' Then Abram fell on his face, and God talked with him, saying: 'As for Me, behold, My covenant is with you, and you shall be a father of many nations. No longer shall your name be called Abram, but your name shall be Abraham; for I have made you a father of many nations. I will make you exceedingly fruitful; and I will make nations of you, and kings shall come from you'"* (Gen. 17:1-6).

The apostolic always draws the alignment with eternal purpose. In Abraham's seed is the blessing for the earth's families, and consequently the provision and the financial plans and strategies. It was a royal or governmental generational seed; so, it had an apostolic manifestation. That purpose established in Abraham's seed was going to transcend generationally so that all of the governmental plan was fulfilled.

Jacob inherited that potential of blessing all the families of the earth and his seed is activated when the heavens are opened (Gen. 28:10-22).

He had an encounter at the same place where the Eternal appeared to Abraham. And, because Abraham had built an altar of adoration, the heavens were open on that place. When Jacob gets there he has a supernatural experience and his seed is activated by the *davar* (the Eternal) released upon it. When the heavens open up upon a place, not only supernatural gifts are activated, but also the prosperity seed is activated.

"And behold, the Lord stood above it and said: 'I am the Lord God of Abraham your father and the God of Isaac; the land on which you lie I will give to you and your descendants. Also your descendants shall be as the dust of the earth; you shall spread abroad to the west and the east, to the north and the south; and in you and in your seed all the families of the earth shall be blessed. Behold, I am with you and will keep you wherever you go, and will bring you back to this land; for I will not leave you until I have done what I have spoken to you'" (Gen. 28:13-15).

Jacob had a royal seed which had not been activated, or manifested. The heavens were opened with the purpose of activating that seed; however, he didn't realize what had really happened (v.16).

Jacob was a king, for he had Abraham's seed, but he didn't understand the potential which was inside of him; because of that, he served Laban as a slave for 14 years after his seed had been activated (Gen. 29). Being a king, he worked as a slave. The seed had been activated in Jacob but he didn't have the dimension of it. He was deceived by Laban for not knowing what was inside of him. When we don't understand the potential inside of us, we will always experience losses.

However, what was latent started to manifest. Jacob realized he was the reason for Laban's blessing. While we don't understand the potential within us, we will not be able to prosper. Understanding is the key to the supernatural. There isn't prosperity without venture.

The relationship between Jacob and Laban is an entrepreneurial relationship. Robert Kiyosaki, a bestselling author, in his book *Rich Dad Poor Dad*, dimensions the cash flow in four quadrants, which we will use in this chapter as levels or dimensions of prosperity:

- Employees (wageworker)
- Self-employed
- Entrepreneur
- Investors

Kiyosaki establishes that money is in the center of the two last quadrants, i.e. entrepreneurs and investors, but especially investors.

Jacob started as a wageworker and was deceived by Laban several times. Jacob realized that Laban's prosperity was related to his own prosperity and apostolic seed. From now on we will see how through a prophetic strategy, Jacob went from being a wageworker to an entrepreneur. Prosperity will come with prophetic entrepreneurial strategies and apostolic entrepreneurship.

GIVE BIRTH AND RETURN TO FAMILY TO BE ENRICHED

And it came to pass, when Rachel had borne Joseph, that Jacob said to Laban, *"Send me away, that I may go to my own place and to my country"* (Gen. 30:25).

Every birth in a household seals a new cycle, a new prophetic season. Every child seals a new stage in the family. As soon as Joseph was born, Jacob decided to go back home. Your home needs to be aligned to your eternal purpose. If we don't come back to family, we cannot be enriched.

What will transform you and take you from a wageworker and/or employee mentality and get you wealth will be your decision of doing something for your own family. Turn your heart to your loved ones.

EMPLOYEES AND BOSSES

"Give me my wives and my children for whom I have served you, and let me go; for you know my service which I have done for you" (Gen. 30:26).

In this verse we see how Jacob uses an employee to boss dialogue. He was on an employee or wageworker level. He was working for Laban. Every wageworker provides service. Laban represents the boss or any system that makes you a wageworker. This system which has made us wageworkers knows the prosperity is on the seed potential which is inside of us.

When we have a poverty mentality that conditions us as slaves, we see God as a distant God who is only a boss who gives us orders. But, when God's fatherhood is revealed in our lives, then we understand our Father wants to give us an inheritance; if we are children, then we are also heirs.

YOU ARE THE BLESSING

And Laban said to him, *"Please stay, if I have found favor in your eyes, for I have learned by experience that the Lord has blessed me for your sake"* (Gen. 30:27).

Laban, as a boss, knew that the reason for his blessing was found in the apostolic seed Jacob carried inside him. Bosses know by their own means that "Jacobs" provide blessings and multiplications to them and their companies.

SALARY NOT PARTNERSHIP— LABAN'S ARGUMENT

Then he said, *"Name me your wages, and I will give it"* (Gen. 30:28).

This is the system's argument that wants to keep you as a wageworker. It offers increase in salary but not partnership. Laban wanted Jacob continued at the same level and not increased in level. Bosses propose salaries, and sometimes good salaries, but they don't offer partnership.

Wealth is never on an employees' side, but on bosses' and investors' sides. For an employee, the fact of having a boss can give him/her some stability but it isn't a guarantee of increasing assets.

WORK AND BLESSING

So Jacob said to him, *"You know how I have served you and how your livestock has been with me. For what you had before I came was little, and it has increased to a great amount; the Lord has blessed you since my coming. And now, when shall I also provide for my own house?"* (Gen. 30:29-30).

Jacob is God's blessing for Laban. He enriched Laban due to his diligence. "Jacobs" are those who God use to dignify "Labans." However, under God's plan, Jacob doesn't accept a raise in salary but proposes a partnership.

PARTNERSHIP NOT SALARY— JACOB'S STRATEGY

"So he said, 'What shall I give you?' And Jacob said, 'You shall not give me anything. If you will do this thing for me, I will again feed and keep your flocks'" (Gen. 30:31).

Jacob didn't accept Laban's salary but made a proposal. He had already understood the power of the prosperity and apostolic seed which was inside him. So he didn't want a raise in salary, but proposed going up to a higher level than wageworker, a partnership in the flock-keeping business.

THE IMPORTANCE OF PROPHETIC STRATEGY ON BUSINESS IS ONLY GIVEN BY GOD

"Let me pass through all your flock today, removing from there all the speckled and spotted sheep, and all the brown ones among the lambs, and the spotted and speckled among the goats; and these shall be my wages" (Gen. 30:32).

Prophetic strategy to move forward in prosperity is only given by the Lord. Jacob in his maturity had a prophetic strategy, an entrepreneurial prophetic plan. What is the prophetic strategy God gave him? Even God can be a Laban for us if we see Him only as a boss and Lord. But, it is time to have a partnership with God in our businesses. Seek God's prophetic plan for your business.

HONOR IS THE CONTRACT DISTINCTNESS

"So my righteousness will answer for me in time to come, when the subject of my wages comes before you: every one that is not speckled and spotted among the goats, and brown among the lambs, will be considered stolen, if it is with me" (Gen. 30:33).

If the world moves without principles, the Almighty wants to teach us to walk founded in His principles. Honor is a good principle to bring reliability and clearness to our businesses.

You will never prosper without honesty. It is a principle issue. Jacob demonstrates distinctness of contract and his honor in fulfilling it. Don't negotiate your principles for under them God can cover you.

CLOSING THE DEAL

And Laban said, *"Oh, that it were according to your word!"* (Gen. 30:34).

Laban accepted the proposal. Every one that was speckled, spotted and brown was Jacob's part of the flock. But, as we will see later, Laban was left with the white flock; this is why he accepted the proposal without resistance. He was an exploiter. But he didn't know Jacob had a prophetic strategy.

FOR AN ASTUTE PERSON THERE IS A PROPHET

"So he removed that day the male goats that were speckled and spotted, all the female goats that were speckled and spotted, every one that had some white in it, and all the brown ones among the lambs, and gave them into the hand of his son. Then he put three days' journey between himself and Jacob, and Jacob fed the rest of Laban's flocks" (Gen. 30:35-36).

Laban takes away all natural possibilities to Jacob prospering by removing the male goats that were speckled and spotted and all the female goats that were speckled and spotted and giving them into the hand of his sons three days' journey between them.

While some bosses make all kinds of tricks so you don't prosper, concentrate on your commission and mandate. Don't get sidetracked. Walk in righteousness, not only in morality but also in functional concept. Set your goals. Jacob was concentrated on his prophetic strategy even though his boss would do the impossible in order that this doesn't come to pass.

Laban prepared a snare. He took away all natural possibilities that Jacob could have his streaked, speckled, and spotted flock.

What takes you from one level to another is prophetic strategy. In Jacob's case, this came through a prophetic dream (Gen. 31:1-12).

PROPHETIC STRATEGY

"Now Jacob took for himself rods of green poplar and of the almond and chestnut trees, peeled white strips in them, and exposed the white which was in the rods. And the rods which he had peeled, he set before the flocks in the gutters, in the watering troughs where the flocks came to drink, so that they should conceive when they came to drink. So the flocks conceived before the rods, and the flocks brought forth streaked, speckled, and spotted. Then Jacob separated the lambs, and made the flocks face toward the streaked and all the brown in the flock of Laban; but he put his own flocks by themselves and did not put them with Laban's flock. And it came to pass, whenever the stronger livestock conceived, that Jacob placed the rods before the eyes of the livestock in the gutters, that they might conceive among the rods. But when the flocks were feeble, he did not put them in; so the feebler were Laban's and the stronger Jacob's" (Gen. 30:37-42).

According to the Father's heart, businesses are established under prophetic plans and strategies. This is the power to get wealth. Seek a business prophet, one who can bring a prophetic model for your incomes and your entrepreneurial growth.

What make us rich are the prophetic strategies we may have. With Jacob the flock conceived according to what they saw, that is, the striped rod. One of the definitions for the word vision (in Hebrew *jarjor*) is conception, pregnancy, imagination. This takes us to a spiritual world principle: you conceive what you see in the spiritual world. What you see you get.

Scientifically this is proved by Quantum Physics. There are subatomic particles that are not observed by the naked eye. They are on the universe of probability, and when they are observed, they materialize themselves. They are no longer energy (invisible reality, prophetic world); now they materialize (natural world).

The only thing Jacob did was to use the prophetic strategy God had given him. As with Jacob, God wants to raise us from the prosperity level and take us from the wageworker quadrant to entrepreneur and/or investor. Prophetic strategy raises you from one level to the next.

ANGELS INVOLVED WITH FINANCES

As we have seen earlier, Jacob received prophetic strategy through a prophetic dream. It is important to point out the angelic presence in that dream.

"And it happened, at the time when the flocks conceived, that I lifted my eyes and saw in a dream, and behold, the rams which leaped upon the flocks were streaked, speckled, and gray-spotted. Then the Angel of God spoke to me in a dream, saying, 'Jacob' And I said, 'Here I am.' And He said, 'lift your eyes now and see, all the rams which leap on the flocks are streaked, speckled, and gray-spotted; for I have seen all that Laban is doing to you'" (Gen. 31:10-12).

I truly believe by the measure or metron of apostolic authority, angels are released to fulfill supernatural purpose of financial scope. I have experienced visitations like that in certain moments of my ministry and it has brought breakthrough in the financial area.

Years ago I started being visited by these kind of angels, who appeared to me wearing white clothes and belts and holding a golden scepter; everything they touched turned to gold. Many times I saw them with big bags of golden coins, then after these supernatural visitations I saw gold dust in the physical realm, and sometimes the crystallization of gems.

On other occasions, those angels visited me during the third vigil of the night, and I received many creative ideas which later would become prophetic strategies to generate financial resources.

PROPHETIC TIME OF PROPHETIC STRATEGIES IMPLEMENTATION

This passage also reveals to us that every prophetic strategy of entrepreneurial scope has its prophetic time of implementation in order to reach the superabundance level. Jacob only put the rod in the water trough when the stronger livestock came to the gutters; so, they only conceived strong flocks. There is a right time to apply your prophetic strategy.

BUSINESS SUCCESS

"Thus the man became exceedingly prosperous, and had large flocks, female and male servants, and camels and donkeys" (Gen. 30:43).

With a prophetic strategy aligned to apostolic flow, Jacob became rich. However, he had to activate his governmental capacity, not only his capacity to fructify and multiply. And God activated in him his governmental capacity.

CHANGING NAME

Although Jacob was activated in the prosperity seed, it was necessary for a nature change so he could rule upon the multiplied portion in a way that he wouldn't experience losses. That is why his name was changed.

"And he arose that night and took his two wives, his two female servants, and his eleven sons, and crossed over the ford of Jabbok. He took them, sent them over the brook, and sent over what he had. Then Jacob was left alone; and a Man wrestled with him until the breaking of day. Now when He saw that He did not prevail against him, He touched the socket of his hip; and the socket of Jacob's hip was out of joint as He wrestled with him. And He said, 'Let Me go, for the day breaks.' But he said, 'I will not let You go unless You bless me!' So He said to him, 'What is your name?' He said, 'Jacob.' And He said, 'Your name shall no longer be called Jacob, but Israel; for you have struggled with God and with men, and have prevailed.' Then Jacob asked, saying, 'Tell me Your name, I pray.' And He said, 'Why is it that you ask about My name?' And He blessed him there. So Jacob called the name of the place Peniel: 'For I have seen God face to face, and my life is preserved.' Just as he crossed over Penue the sun rose on him, and he limped on his hip. Therefore to this day the children of Israel do not eat the muscle that shrank, which is on the hip socket, because He touched the socket of Jacob's hip in the muscle that shrank" (Gen. 32:22-32).

The deceiver essence didn't allow Jacob to rule. In his name was his nature. Israel means prince (someone who governs). With the changing of his name, it was activated on him the capacity to rule over what was multiplied.

THERE ISN'T WEALTH WITHOUT COVENANT: THE CONTRACT CLAUSES

Then Jacob made a vow, saying, *"If God will be with me, and keep me in this way that I am going, and give me bread to eat and clothing to put on so that I come back to my father's house in peace, then the Lord shall be my God. And this stone which I have set as a pillar shall be God's house, and of all that You give me I will surely give a tenth to You"* (Gen. 28:20-22).

There wouldn't be Genesis chapter 30 if there wasn't Genesis chapter 28 beforehand. In order to take him to meet his family, his job, and his boss Laban, God first had to take Jacob to a covenant with Himself.

Jacob's tenth established five "clauses" between God and Jacob so that he could have Him as his Lord and God:

- If God will be with me, and keep me in this way
- give me bread to eat
- give me clothing to put on
- come back to my father's house in peace
- the Lord shall be my God

Do not allow the Eternal One to be only your boss, head, or lord. Make Him also your Partner and you will see that the wealth of nations (Isa. 60) will come to you!

ABOUT THE AUTHOR

Fernando Guillen is the Apostle and overseer of Seven Mountains Apostolic Center in Brazil, the Chancellor of Wagner Leadership Institute (WLI) for Latin America, the apostolic leader of W.A.R. (Warriors Apostolic Reformers) Network and a multifaceted trainer, life coach and prophetic mentor who travels up to 50 weeks a year, speaking and empowering people. He is apostolically aligned with Global Spheres and Harvest International Ministry. For more information, visit his websites at www.institutowagner. com or www.apostolofernando.com.

CHAPTER SIXTY-NINE

APOSTOLIC WEALTH

DR. MICHAEL SCANTLEBURY

INTRODUCTION

"And with great power the Apostles gave witness to the resurrection of the Lord Jesus. And great grace was upon them all. Nor was there anyone among them who lacked; for all who were possessors of lands or houses sold them, and brought the proceeds of the things that were sold, And laid them at the Apostles' feet; and they distributed to each as anyone had need. And Joses, who was also named Barnabas by the Apostles (which is translated Son of Encouragement), a Levite of the country of Cyrus, Having land, sold it, and brought the money and laid it at the Apostles' feet" (Acts 4:33-37).

As we move deeper into the restoration of Apostles, the restoration of wealth back to the House of God will become very evident. At the beginning of the Church, in the Book of Acts, we read that money was brought and laid at the feet of the early Apostles, and they distributed it as they saw fit.

APOSTOLIC WEALTH IS
FOR DISTRIBUTION

Please note that the wealth that was laid at the Apostles' feet was for distribution and not for them. The Apostolic has a grace gift to attract wealth to fulfill its God-given mandate.

Wealth has always been a turning point for most churches, either for good or for bad, but with the restoration of the Apostles, God will release greater clarity on how to manage wealth.

As we have elsewhere said, the kings of the Old Testament paralleled the Apostles of the New Testament, so it will be worthwhile to go back to the rules and guidelines that were set down by God, for the establishment of kings.

Long before Israel had a king, God had laid down a set of principles for their function. This can be found in the Book of Deuteronomy:

"When you come to the land which the Lord your God is giving you, and possess it and dwell in it, and say, 'I will set a king over me like all the nations that are around me,' you shall surely set a king over you whom the Lord your God chooses; one from among your brethren you shall set as king over you; you may not set a foreigner over you, who is not your brother. But he shall not multiply horses for himself, nor cause the people to return to Egypt to multiply horses, for the Lord has said to you, 'You shall not return that way again.' 'Neither shall he multiply wives for himself, lest his heart turn away; nor shall he greatly multiply silver and gold for himself. Also it shall be, when he sits on the throne of his kingdom, that he shall write for himself a copy of this law in a book, from the one before the priests, the Levites. And it shall be with him, and he shall read it all the days of his life, that he may learn to fear the Lord his God and be careful to observe all the words of this law and these statutes, that his heart may not

be lifted above his brethren, that he may not turn aside from the commandment to the right hand or to the left, and that he may prolong his days in his kingdom, he and his children in the midst of Israel'" (Deut. 17:14-20).

From this passage several principles can be gleaned, but let's concentrate on what is relevant to this chapter on "apostolic wealth."

Please understand that these principles and guidelines were given long before Israel had a king. One of the things of major concern to the Lord was the issue of wealth.

The Lord gave specific instructions concerning wealth for the king:

1. "He shall not multiply horses for himself" (verse 16); this spoke about military might in the natural. The king's military was not to be in his accumulation of military hardware, but in the Lord.

2. "Nor shall he greatly multiply silver and gold for himself" (verse 17b). This is very clear. The king was not to use his position to multiply wealth for himself. It is similar with the Apostles today. Apostles must not use their anointing and position to build up a financial empire for themselves. However, it is important to note that there is an anointing for wealth upon the Apostolic, but that should never be the primary focus as some will want to make it.

3. "Nor cause the people to return to Egypt to multiply horses" (verse 16b). This is very interesting and carries with it the following understanding - the kings were not to draw their substance from the world or from the pagan systems that existed in their day. In like manner Apostles of today must not rely on the world's

system to acquire wealth or warfare technology to advance the kingdom of God. They must rely on the supernatural hand of provision that the Lord gives.

This was in direct contrast to Saul, because he broke the commandments that were laid down by the Lord regarding the king's office (1 Sam. 8:11-19; 1 Sam. 15:1-9).

Discernment will be a key element in these days as the Lord restores His Apostles back to His Church, as there will be false Apostles who will draw wealth unto themselves and not primarily to further God's Kingdom in the earth.

These principles are very important as we look at the whole issue of wealth as a pillar of the Apostolic.

THE WEALTH TRANSFER

Another powerful scripture that will be fulfilled in this season of apostolic restoration is Prov. 13:22b: *"But the wealth of the sinner is stored up for the righteous."*

Please note that the word of God declares that wealth is stored up for the righteous, and not just the Christian. The righteous spoken of here, are the saints who do not compromise the word of God, who are willing to obey God at His word. However, this wealth is stored up somewhere, and as such, there must be what we call a wealth transfer. In Isa. 45:1-3, the Lord declares:

"Thus says the Lord to His anointed, To Cyrus, whose right hand I have held—To subdue nations before him And loose the armour of kings, To open before him the double doors, So that the gates will not be shut: 'I will go before you And make the crooked places straight; I will break in pieces the gates of bronze And cut the bars of iron. I will give you the treasures of darkness And

hidden riches of secret places, That you may know that I, the Lord, Who call you by your name, Am the God of Israel."

The treasures and riches are hidden and in this hour the Lord is beginning to uncover them to His holy Apostles and Prophets. We are going to see tremendous sums of wealth transferred into the treasuries of the righteous. One of the main avenues of this transfer is through the avenue of business.

This Brings Us To The Issue Of Kingdom Business!

WHAT IS A KINGDOM BUSINESS?

Every so often we need to re-define things in order that they may remain relevant. One thing that is being re-defined with the restoration of Apostles is "Christian Business."

What does it mean to be a Christian businessman or woman? Why should a Christian own a business? What is Kingdom business? A proper understanding of the subject is needed, if we are going to position ourselves to receive the promises God made to us, about wealth transfer and the acquiring of treasure that is hidden in secret places.

In exploring this, one of the very first things that we need to understand, is the fact that Almighty God has made a covenant to bless His people, in order that His Kingdom could advance. Deut. 8:18 states:

"And you shall remember the Lord your God, for it is He who gives you power to get wealth, that He may establish His covenant which He swore to your fathers, as it is this day."

From this passage of Scripture we can learn several things. One is the fact that God confirms the Abrahamic covenant to the seed of Abraham with prosperity. As the children of Abraham through faith, we step into this heritage. There are so many Scriptures that confirm God's promise to prosper His people. So, the first point is that a Kingdom businessperson must have their faith secure in these promises for prosperity.

You must believe that God is with you, and for you, because He wants to make good on His Word. Secondly, it says in that verse, that God gives us the power to get wealth. The first step to receiving power, or ability from God to obtain or acquire wealth, is to have vision for the wealth. The same amount of wealth that existed on the earth from its creation is still on the earth today. It has only changed its form or switched hands over time, but it is still on the earth.

You need to have a vision that includes a strategy to transfer some of that wealth out of the hands of the wicked, and into the hands of the righteous (the Church). As a Kingdom businessman or woman, you can't be satisfied to be in business, just to be in business. You need a large enough vision that would turn God on, to give you the ability to achieve your goals. You need to know where the wealth is located (which market) and come up with a strategy to transfer that wealth.

Isaac knew where to dig for water. I fear that too many Believers enter business without clear direction as to what resource they are trying to tap. They end up doing something in business that they see others doing. They have not studied the market to see where the money is. They limit themselves to their present ability, and settle down in their comfort zones, while God is waiting for them to make a move, so that He can transfer wealth into their hands.

Don't let your present ability limit your vision. You must know where the resources of wealth are in the earth, and devise a plan or strategy to obtain or access some of it. God is going to help you in that. But, if you just want to be in business for some other reason without having a vision to transfer the wealth in the earth from the wrong hands into the right hands, you are not going to trigger God's blessing in any major way.

Jesus said in relation to money, that, *"The sons of this world are more wise in their generation, than the sons of light."* He was observing something that is a tendency with God's people. They tend to rely on God so much, that they don't put forth enough effort in obtaining something. God is with us to give us the wisdom and the ability to get wealth, but we must apply ourselves.

Some Christians in business have unrealistic dreams about God blessing their business, regardless of how non-strategically their businesses are set up to transfer the wealth of the world into their hands. Christians rely too much on God for miracles, and too little on Him who works with us, as we apply ourselves and put forth effort. How convenient! They end up surviving and giving testimony to the God, who always provides what they need. That's great, but it's not the standard for a Kingdom business.

Please understand that wealth is always being transferred from one place to the next, for certain periods of time. As a result, "Kingdom Businesses" need to recognize certain shifts in the market, and move with it. Your power to get wealth is only as good as your vision or your ability to see where the wealth is. Are you in business to obtain wealth? Or are you in it because it's better than working for someone else? Are you in it just to afford a comfortable lifestyle? If you are in the last two categories, you simply cannot expect real wealth for the Kingdom. You can expect whatever your vision allows. So, do you have a Kingdom position for the vision of your business?

Based then on the aforesaid, here are some factors that define a "Kingdom Business."

MENTALITY OF THE KINGDOM

Kingdom businesses must be linked to a larger apostolic paradigm and apostolic purpose or mentality. The ethos, and culture of the business, must reflect apostolic trends such as creativity, discipline, faith, breakthrough, prosperity, success, global mentality and networking.

INVESTING ACCURATELY

It would be a shame for an entrepreneur who is a Believer, with the God-given ability for reaping great financial harvests, to invest inaccurately in the Kingdom of God, particularly when it is this very same God who has blessed him with those finances. This would be a waste, because that entrepreneur would have missed the purpose for which God blessed him with those finances. It would qualify that believer as an unwise steward of the Master's resources.

There are many works in the world today that qualify as "good works," both in the secular world as well as in the church world. You could actually give finances into any of these good works, and be doing well. But, the issue is not about throwing money into the realm of good works. Rather, it is one of investing in those particular projects that are foremost on the mind and heart of God, for the Now!

Everyone who invests in the stock market understands the importance of timing and seasons and trends and demands.

There is a wise time to buy and a wise time to sell, which is usually determined by market trends and product demands. Investing accurately is absolutely related to timing. It is the same with investing in the kingdom of God. As God unfolds His kingdom advancement strategies, we should invest accordingly. In 1 Chron. 12:32 it is stated that the sons of Issachar had understanding of the times, and therefore knew what Israel ought to do. Doing the right or accurate thing depends on understanding the times. Investing into Kingdom works, also depends on discerning the times and seasons of the Lord. If you invest religiously, because it is the right thing to do, then you will still not be investing properly into the kingdom of God.

Many Believers are not aware that God is building something very strategically, and deliberately, according to ancient plans, which means that at present, the Kingdom-building project is in a certain phase, with specific needs and emphases and operations unlike any other time. There is a present kingdom product in demand, by God's timetable. There are present needs that are new and different from those of yesteryear. If you simply give to be doing something good, without understanding the Kingdom demands, the Kingdom market trends, the Kingdom timing and seasons, you will invest inaccurately. If you give to churches that are not building according to the timing and seasons of the Lord, but are involved in traditional religious activities, you will invest inaccurately.

Accuracy in the area of Kingdom activity is totally dependent on a proper discerning of the times. The times reveal to us where God is currently active in advancing His

Kingdom. Jesus said he would only do what he was seeing the Father do, not what he saw the Father do at some former period. Many financial investments end up in works that God is no longer emphasizing. God has moved on, and man must constantly discern His migration and move with Him, in order to be spiritually accurate. You have to become a "prophetic Believer" to know where God is currently building. You need to develop an ability to hear God and to receive revelation truth.

A great example could be found in the context of the Early Church. When the Apostles were teaching new revelation in the midst of an old and well-established religious center, people had to choose between the two, and commit to the right one, in order to be accurate. If Believers at that time continued to sow their finances in the old Jewish Temple, and not in the new apostolic church, they would have been investing wrongly. They could not know the difference apart from a prophetic ear, or an ability to understand truth non-traditionally.

Giving into traditional religious good works is not investing accurately in God's Kingdom. It might still accomplish some earthly good, and it might still earn you some points in the records of Heaven, but it will not advance the invasion of God's Kingdom on the planet in the present season. It will not be supporting His eternal purpose for the present. God's Kingdom advancement on the earth can only be funded by a people who can discern the timing of God.

Kingdom accuracy is not equal to every good, religious, well-established work. There are a lot of religious works that have built worldly kingdoms, instead of a House for God to dwell in. Not everything we see with our physical eyes that looks like church is in fact church according to God's design. The need for discernment in these last days, to know the true Church and the current speaking and workings of God, is great. Ecclesiastes Chapter Three is a worthy passage to meditate on, to appreciate the value and importance of understanding the times, in relation to doing things. Verse 17 (b) says; *".... there is a time there for every purpose and for every work."* Accuracy in Kingdom investment is in knowing what God is doing at the present time.

BABYLON WILL BE JUDGED

Babylon is a demonic system in the earth set up by the devil. This system controls most of the kings of the earth, commerce and trade and is very anti-Christ.

"Then one of the seven angels who had the seven bowls came and talked with me, saying to me, "Come, I will show you the judgment of the great harlot who sits on many waters, "with whom the kings of the earth committed fornication, and the inhabitants of the earth were made drunk with the wine of her fornication." So he carried me away in the Spirit into the wilderness. And I saw a woman sitting on a scarlet beast which was full of names of blasphemy, having seven heads and ten horns. The woman was arrayed in purple and scarlet, and adorned with gold and precious stones and pearls, having in her hand a golden cup full of abominations and the filthiness of her fornication. And on her forehead a name was written: MYSTERY, BABYLON THE GREAT, THE MOTHER OF HARLOTS AND OF THE ABOMINATIONS OF THE EARTH. I saw the woman drunk with the blood of the saints and with blood of the martyrs of Jesus. And when I saw her, I marvelled with great amazement" (Rev. 17: 1-6, NKJV).

At this current time Babylon still controls the wealth of the earth and has been mandated by the devil to destroy the apostolic and prophetic. They know that once these two ministry gifts are fully restored to the Church, their kingdom is coming down. As a matter of fact, the Lord has already given us the script – Babylon is going to fall and a decree will be issued in the Heavens, and the Apostles and Prophets are to rejoice at her demise:

"They threw dust on their heads and cried out, weeping and wailing, and saying, 'Alas, alas, that great city, in which all who had ships on the sea became rich by her wealth! For in one hour she is made desolate.' "Rejoice over her, O heaven, and you holy apostles and prophets, for God has avenged you on her!" (Rev. 18:19-20, NKJV).

This is why there is a clarion call going out in the Spirit, through the Apostles and Prophets to all of God's people who are still trapped in Babylon, to come out of her. There are many, because of lack of understanding, who are trapped in Babylon. However, in this hour God is releasing the wisdom and revelation through His holy Apostles to draw them out of Babylon.

"And I heard another voice from heaven saying, "Come out of her, my people, lest you share in her sins, and lest you receive of her plagues. "For her sins have reached to heaven, and God has remembered her iniquities" (Rev. 18:4-5, NKJV).

I submit to you, that as soon as those who belong to the Lord come out of Babylon, it will signal the end of that polluted system. They will be used of the Lord, to effect a large portion of the wealth transfer.

It will be similar to what happened to the Egyptians when the Israelites left. Only this time, the effects will be far more devastating.

In the Book of Genesis there is an account of an incredible incident that took place when the Israelites were about to depart from Egypt. Scripture records this as follows:

"And the Lord said to Moses, 'I will bring one more plague on Pharaoh and on Egypt. Afterward he will let you go from here. When he lets you go, he will surely drive you out of here altogether. Speak now in the hearing of the people, and let every man ask from his neighbor and every woman from her neighbor, articles of silver and articles of gold'" (Ex. 11:1-2, NKJV).

"And the Egyptians urged the people, that they might send them out of the land in haste. For they said, "We shall all be dead." So the people took their dough before it was leavened, having their kneading bowls bound up in their clothes on their shoulders. Now the children of Israel had done according to the word of Moses, and they had asked from the Egyptians articles of silver, articles of gold, and clothing. And the Lord had given the people favour in the sight of the Egyptians, so that they granted them what they requested. Thus they plundered the Egyptians" (Ex. 12:31-36, NKJV).

That was incredible. Imagine the Egyptians actually giving the Israelites their wealth? Talk about the wealth of the sinner being laid up for the righteous. The favor of the Lord accomplished it.

The Lord is releasing this same favor as He calls His people out of Babylon. If you are called to be a Kingdom businessman or woman today, this is the time to dismantle any or all of Babylon's structure and spirit that may exist in your business.

However, in the midst of the wealth transfer that is taking place, and will continue to take place as the Apostles are fully accepted into the Church, there is a caution.

Let us resist any temptation to do as the Israelites did and build a golden calf with this wealth. As it happened, the Israelites made wealth their god (Ex. 32).

As with every move of God, there are going to be excesses and falsity and certain ones will make money their god, thereby setting him or herself up to become like fallen Babylon, a dwelling place for demons:

"And he cried mightily with a loud voice, saying, "Babylon the great is fallen, is fallen, and has become a dwelling place of demons, a prison for every foul spirit, and a cage for every unclean and hated bird" (Rev. 18:2, NKJV)!

CONCLUSION

I want to conclude this chapter with the following powerful admonition from Timothy:

"If anyone teaches otherwise and does not consent to wholesome words, even the word of our Lord Jesus Christ, and to the doctrine which accords with godliness, he is proud, knowing nothing, but is obsessed with disputes and arguments over words, from which come envy, strife, reviling, evil suspicions, useless wranglings of men of corrupt minds and destitute of the truth, who suppose that godliness is a means of gain. From such withdraw yourself. Now godliness with contentment is great gain. For we brought nothing into this world, and it is certain we can carry nothing out. And having food and clothing, with these we shall be content. But those who desire to be rich fall into temptation and a snare, and into many foolish and harmful lusts which drown men in destruction. For the love of money is a root of all kinds of evil, for

which some have strayed from the faith in their greediness, and pierced themselves through with many sorrows" (1 Tim. 6:3-10, NKJV).

Editor's Note: This chapter was originally included in *Five Pillars of the Apostolic*, which was published by Word Alive Press Inc. in 2000, and has been used by permission of the author.)

ABOUT THE AUTHOR

Apostle Michael Scantlebury is originally from the twin-island republic of Trinidad & Tobago, and is now a Canadian citizen; he resides in Vancouver, B.C., Canada with his wife Sandra, and their two daughters and son.

He received Jesus Christ as Savior and Lord in November 1979, and was called into the ministry several months later. He then received three years of intensive training at his home church, Barataria Church of God (an affiliate of the Assemblies of God), after which he functioned as the Associate Pastor of Ekklesia Teaching Centre. In 1992, Dr. Scantlebury then went on to another local church where he functioned as part of the leadership in several capacities, such as Pastoral Minister with direct responsibility for the men, young converts, cell groups, planting of other churches, among other things. He functioned in that capacity until the Lord called him to Canada in 1997, where he now functions as the Founder and Senior Elder of Dominion-Life International Ministries, a young, multi-ethnic, multi-racial, vibrant and growing Body of Believers he founded in 2002. He is also the Founding Apostle of an Apostolic

Network (KIN) Kingdom-Impact International Network, and has a Doctor of Divinity degree.

Apostle Scantlebury has made several radio and television appearances and travelled and ministered in the Caribbean, South America, North America, Asia, Africa, Australia and Europe, conducting Ministry Training Seminars and preaching in churches and conferences. He is also the author of over a dozen books, which include a trilogy on the Apostolic — *Five Pillars of The Apostolic, Apostolic Purity,* and *Apostolic Reformation,* and also *Kingdom Advancing Prayer Volumes I–III, I Will Build My Church—Jesus Christ.* His latest books are *The Fortress Church* and *Leaven Revealed,* which have been highly recommended! Even his recent autobiography is titled, *Born to Be an Apostle.*

His wife Prophetess Sandra has become his travelling partner and they minister out of a strong apostolic/prophetic anointing, and have a tremendous desire to see the Church come to full maturity and unity for greater function in the earth.

A man who has given himself to the preaching and teaching of the gospel of the Kingdom, to the integrity and authority of God's Word, all based upon a Spirit-filled life, are the words that best describe Apostle Michael Scantlebury. To learn more or to contact him, visit his web sites at www.dominion-life.org or www.kinternationalnetwork.org.

CHAPTER SEVENTY

KINGDOM STEWARDSHIP

CHRISTOPHER JAMES

Kingdom Stewardship does not come easily. It takes a life dedicated to keeping our eyes on the Perfect Steward, Jesus. Scripture says if we keep our eyes on Him, the Author and Perfecter of our lives and faith, we will be changed from glory to glory. Jesus emptied Himself and came as an humble child to ultimately offer His life as a sacrifice for our sins. We need to follow His example and do likewise. This is not an easy process; it requires death to self. For the serious follower of Jesus, it is a life pursuit, which yields great benefits in this life and the life to come.

Rightly so, since those that are serious in their walk with Jesus are focusing on their relationship with God while expanding and perfecting Jesus' Kingdom here on earth. More simply said, Kingdom and Relationship are vital. They are core to our becoming good stewards, and real followers of Christ.

Biblical Stewardship speaks of our responsibility to serve God and even spread the Good News of Jesus Christ. The 1828 version of Webster's Dictionary defines this as, "In Scripture and theology a minister of Christ, whose duty is to dispense the provisions of the Gospel, to preach its doctrines and administer its ordinances." And the truth is that as a disciple of Christ, we are all called to minister to God and others using the gifts and talents we have.

Stewardship covers every aspect of society, not just Religion. Many of us have heard of what is called "The Seven Mountains." They are Government, Education, Media, Economy, Family, Celebration, and Religion. They cover all of aspects life. Os Hillman and Johnny Enlow have written extensively on the subject. In his book, *The Seven Mountain Prophecy*, Johnny Enlow writes of the vision he had of seeing the Seven Mountains and seeing little lights climbing each mountain. These lights were people assigned to their respective mountain. When these believers had a problem that seemed unsolvable, they would cry out to God for the answer. The Lord in a laser-like beam would shine down on His disciple with the needed answer and provision. Most all of us are called to one of these mountains or areas of influence.

We, as stewards in our respective areas of influence, are called to retake all of what the Devil has stolen or repossessed. This may seem impossible, but presently God is supernaturally enabling His Bride (remnant) to accomplish this. We need to remember the story on how does a mouse eat an elephant? That is one bite at a time. With His empowerment, we are to partner with Jesus to establish His Kingdom and expand it until the whole world is His with everything being under His feet. WOW, this is exciting! We are called to be co-heirs and joint-heirs with Christ. In the spirit of Elijah we are to prepare the way of Christ's Return.

We are all products of our environment and the experiences we have in this world. Many of the authors writing this book are from the United States of America.

We are products of its culture and perceive things through very different eyes than most of the world. Since the latter part of the '40s, the U.S. has greatly expanded our markets around the world. This was accomplished by the creation of the Federal Reserve early in the 20th century, which led us from the gold standard into the debt-based fiat money system, which we are in now.

World War II caused us to go into debt and essentially we used debt to expand our industries and world-wide trade and help rebuild other nations through the Marshall Plan. Debt has not only affected almost every facet of our lives, but it has become so ingrained in our culture that we are addicted to it. Most of us readily buy things that we want. We buy it on credit, which increases our debt. This practice has led to gluttony to attempt to satisfy our desires. As a nation, we are addicted to a gluttony for things. This certainly includes food. Obesity is rampant. This is the nature of flesh. Our affluence through the flesh is leading us to effluence in our bodies, our souls, and spirits.

OUR SPIRITUAL CONDITION

This leads me to Scripture, which speaks of our spiritual condition. We have sown to the flesh and we are reaping what our flesh has lusted for. Job 20:20 in the NASB says, *"Because he does not have the peace within, he cannot retain anything that his heart desires."* In the flesh we will never have enough. John D. Rockefeller, the wealthiest man in the world a century ago, was once asked, "How much is enough?" He reportedly answered, "It is just a little more."

To be good stewards, we need to discipline ourselves. We are not to indulge the flesh. Solomon pursued life and even its indulgences with a vengeance, coming to conclusion that the world and its pursuits were vanity of vanities and can never satisfy. God put eternity into our hearts (Ecc. 3:11) and the only thing that satisfies is our relationship with God.

SOME QUALITIES OF A GOOD STEWARD

Besides discipline, several qualities of a good Kingdom Steward are Relationship with Father God, Jesus, and Holy Spirit; Faithfulness/Consistency, Responsibility, Integrity, Hunger for the Word, a Dedicated Servant, and Always Seeking the Truth/While Exposing the Evil.

Relationship with Father, Jesus, and Holy Spirit/Attentiveness to the King—To be a good steward we must know our master well, very well. We must sit as His feet. Most are familiar with the story of Mary and Martha in Luke 10. The key verse here is 39, where Mary is identified as *"Mary, who sat at Jesus' feet and heard His word."* The key is our relationship with the Lord and hearing/knowing His Word. I came to the Lord as an adult in June 1979, confessing and making Jesus the Lord of my life. This happened through a church that was practicing "Walk Through the Bible" (in a year). That very day I started reading through the Bible every year.

This was more than fortunate for me, because I had little Christian training as a child, adolescent, and young man. Up to my adult conversion I had more than been pursuing the world and all of its destructive, supposed benefits. Later that year I went on a trip to Eleuthera, Grand Bahamas. While kicking back and reading the Word, a gardener who worked close by said, "You do well in reading the Word. It will be a guide to your life… (and much more)." I was encouraged and more than blessed at the time. In looking back at this short, but powerful interchange, I think it is possible the older man could have been an angel.

For us to become all that we can be in becoming good stewards and real followers of Christ, we must know Jesus, our King, and soon coming Husbandman very well. We must pursue our personal relationship with Him. Studying the Word individually and corporately in Bible study groups, will help build the foundation solidly on the Rock. Within a month of coming to the Lord in June 1979, I joined five weekly Bible studies.

About three years ago, I was recommended by a good friend that our ministry, Living Waters Ranch (LWR), sponsor a conference called "Communing with God" with Dr. Mark Virkler. The conference took our attendees to new levels of relationship with God. I recommend Mark's book *Dialoguing With God* for pursuing God more deeply. Two Biblical characters that wonderfully characterize an exceptional relationship with God are Enoch and Abraham. Abraham was called the friend of God. May we all aspire to greater depths of relationship with God as these two did.

WE ARE THE BRIDE

Another Bible character that we should consider emulating is Esther. Many of us know the story of Esther, which is written in the book of Esther. Almost 10 years ago my wife, Debbie and I attended a conference at City Bible Church in Portland, Ore. Among the excellent contributors was Tommy Tenney. Tommy had written a book by the name of *One Night with the King*, which was later made into a movie. It was based on the life of Esther. At that time many people were identifying with the Scripture, *"For such a time as this,"* which helped this movement catch fire. My understanding of this was the Lord was planting a hunger in us for our identifying as a bride for our coming Husbandman, Jesus.

In looking further back to 1998, we sponsored a conference called "Preparing the Bride." To me these spiritual signs were helping the Bride look forward to the Wedding Feast. One of the key messages in Esther was her desire to please the King. The other candidates for becoming queen sought worldly trinkets and the like. Only Esther had the heart to singularly desire to please the King. This is almost a perfect picture for those desiring to qualify as becoming the Bride of Christ. We are to deny ourselves (quenching our fleshly desires) so that we please the King. This all speaks of longing for a greater and deeper Relationship with our King Jesus. For each of us to become better stewards, we must pursue our relationship with Jesus.

FAITHFULNESS/OBEDIENCE

One of my favorite Names for Jesus is "Faithful and True," which comes from Rev. 19:11. Jesus was faithful perfectly to the Father's will and He spoke only those words that He heard the Father speaking. Jesus was the Perfect Steward and He is our Model. To become an excellent steward, we must be obedient to what He tells us to do. Once we have learned to identify His voice, testing it for consistency with His Word and feeling inner peace, we will have confidence to carry out His instructions.

From the Parable of the Sower in Luke 8:15, a steward is to be like the good soil, *"But the ones (seeds) that fell on the good ground are those who, having heard the Word with a noble and good heart, keep it and bear fruit with patience (endurance)."*

God is faithful to perform His word; He is always ready to perform His word. To become an excellent steward, we must be fully faithful to Jesus and always ready to carry out the will of the Father.

Dedicated Servant: Jesus, our perfect example, is a Dedicated Servant. He came to earth as a child, emptying or laying aside much of His glory to do so. Phil. 2:5-8 says, *"Let this mind be in you which was also in Christ Jesus, who, being in the form of God, did not consider it robbery to be equal with God, but made Himself of no reputation, taking the form of a bond-servant, and coming in the likeness of men. And being found in appearance as a man, He humbled Himself, and became obedient to the point of death, even the death on the cross."* Furthermore, Mark 10:45 says, *"For even the Son of Man did not come to be served, but to serve and give His life as a ransom for many."* As stewards, we are to follow His example, denying ourselves and carrying out the will of the Father.

Our Assignments: Rev. 12:11 says, *"And they (the church) overcame him (Satan) by the blood of the Lamb and by the word of their (the church's) testimony, and they did not love their lives to the death."* Jesus' blood and our testimony have great power. Our assignment in becoming good stewards is to share our testimony with its great power to destroy Satan's Kingdom and thereby advance the Kingdom of Jesus Christ. Therefore, let us be willing to share our testimony of God's faithfulness in our lives.

LEARNING TO DEPEND ON THE LORD

My Testimony and Assignment: In 1983 I made a small investment in a Christian mining venture in the Central Mountains of Idaho, just west of Challis and some 90 miles north of Sun Valley. About a month later, a 7.3 magnitude earthquake destroyed much of the tunneling, causing the company to shut down. The General Partner (GP) would not quit and sent out pleas for help. When I received one certain tape from the GP sharing his call not to quit, I responded and arranged to visit him and the mine. While inspecting the property and the quake damage, I sensed that I was to help the GP and later move to Challis. We set up a new partnership with my financial backing. Due to my existing commitments with my professional trustee business, I had to wait until I found a buyer for my business. It took me three years until I could find the right buyer and move to Challis.

During that time I visited Challis 10 times. One possible wrench in those plans was my former wife had serious health problems and there was the question whether she wanted to make the move or not. If it was the Lord's will, she would have to want to make the move. We made the move in June 1987 from the west coast of Florida to a 12-acre ranchette a few miles north of Challis. We hadn't sold our house before we moved. There were no nibbles for our Florida property for three months.

After a good amount of prayer, I committed to tithing against the margin debt I had incurred to buy the ranchette in Idaho. In short order, the Florida property sold. Praise God, He had taught me some five years earlier to tithe in the most difficult of circumstances. According to Mal. 3:10-12, He proved true that He would open the floodgates of heaven when I tithed. However, I don't advise people to follow my example with the method I used unless God says to. Through careful prayer and proper Scriptural testing, I came up with the method I used. But, everyone should hear God and study Scripture for themselves.

Over the years, much prayer had gone up for my wife's health with long periods of fasting thrown in. My walk with the Lord had continued to grow, especially through the daily devotional times in the morning with the Lord and while reading the Word every morning.

In the mining business, we brought in a partner who had real skills in Oil and Gas exploration. Unfortunately, he had greater skills in taking advantage of the GP and me. Within two years of joining us, he forced us into bankruptcy. In addition, he tried to destroy the GP, claiming that he did not follow SEC rules for disclosure. It was a very difficult time for the GP and for me, too. Both of our wives sued for divorce. And the new partner tried to draw me into the bankruptcy as a GP since I had other assets. In prayer, the Lord said not to worry. The Christian attorney for the partnership and the GP strongly advised me to get an attorney to defend myself. I followed the Lord's advice and didn't. Obedience is better than sacrifice. In retrospect, if I had not followed the Lord's advice, my new attorney would likely have drawn me into a big court fight.

Through these difficult times, I learned to depend more and more on the Lord. My faith was growing. One of my serious shortcomings at that time was "fear of man." Because of inside insecurities, I tried to please man. From time to time, I still have to give that one to the Lord. In my adolescent years I became a braggart. While as a securities salesman in my early 30's, I would exaggerate when there was never a need to. When I read Prov. 8:13, the Lord convicted me of my "perverted tongue." I asked Him to forgive me and to stop me before I lied, exaggerating the truth. The Lord in His faithfulness stopped me and set me free. Thank you Lord for Your mercy.

Another big problem that ended up surfacing in my early 40's was my spoiled little boy attitude. If I didn't get my way, I would rant and rave. I used to say, "I've had to eat a lot of crow." Through seeing how God has worked in my life, I can see that He does work "all things" for good for those that love Him. Even now I jest that I have learned to enjoy eating raven. Humility comes oftentimes by our being humiliated. A good steward should meet all of the qualifications in 1st Timothy and Titus. I can honestly say that I have good reason to be humble.

Debbie and I recently celebrated our 20th Anniversary. With the Lord's encouragement and guidance, we have built Living Waters Ranch on Garden Creek in Challis. We have turned an old sheep ranch into a beautiful Eden in the desert that serves the Body of Christ. We've sponsored many conferences over the years that have helped the Body mature. The last four conferences we have sponsored were based on preparing for harder times. It has been a real honor to serve the Risen King and His Bride.

Your assignment from the Lord is to become a good steward. We must all give an account of what He has entrusted to us. Write down the godly desires that the Lord has put into your hands and heart. Ask Him what has He placed into your hands and heart. Ask Him to stir up the gifts that are in you.

Pray: "Lord, open our eyes of understanding to see you and the assignment You are giving us. May we bless You and help prepare the way of Your return."

THE CONDITION OF OUR NATION WHERE TIME IS GETTING SHORT AND JUDGMENT IS AT THE DOOR

Several months back, a fine young man with whom I am well-acquainted made a comment on how a certain action would negatively affect his credit score. I was amazed that this young man was so concerned for his ability to take on more debt. Our culture is so wedded to debt. We don't realize that the borrower is a slave to the lender. We as a country and most individually are in bondage to our appetite for more that doesn't satisfy.

The U.S. economy is very complex. We are so dependent on one another to our own harm. What happened in the latter part of 2001 and 2008 and the years following should warn us that when the velocity of money slows down, it can and will cause severe problems. Couple that with our current and growing debt, the likelihood of increasing interest charges, and the possibility of other geophysical strokes of judgment, and it is only a matter of time until a financial collapse or global economic correction occurs. Our former way of life is in serious jeopardy and may soon end. The writing is on the wall.

At the time of this writing, late September 2012, I am amazed that this hasn't happened much sooner. Many have prayed for delay and the Lord in His mercy has answered, delaying the inevitable. I've spoken about the current condition of the U.S. economy because it directly speaks of our country's lack of conservative stewardship. If we had disciplined ourselves and shunted our appetite for stuff, this could have been delayed longer. But, the real problem with our country is SIN. We need the Lord to convict our hearts and bring enough judgment to our country that will drive us to repentance.

Get Busy: In Psalm 90, attributed to a prayer of Moses, verse 17 commissions those called to be His stewards: *"And let the beauty of the Lord our God be upon us, and establish the work of our hands for us; yes, establish the work of our hands."* Get busy in becoming the steward and joint heir of His Kingdom that God has called you to be. Get busy. Ps. 89:20, 24 speaks of David: *"I have found My servant (steward) David; with My holy oil I have anointed him, My faithfulness and My mercy shall be with him, and in My Name his horn shall be exalted."* Become the servant/steward that David became.

Open up your hands with palms facing upward toward the Lord. Receive His anointing. Receive His blessing. Receive Him. Receive. Now go forth and pour out His love and blessing to others.

In the Name of Jesus and with the Blood of Jesus, I bless you to bless others by becoming the steward that you are called to be. Thank you LORD.

ABOUT THE AUTHOR

Christopher James has been married for 20 years to his wife, friend, and life partner, Debbie. Together they manage Living Waters Ranch, a spacious, modern and full-service conference and retreat center near the Salmon River in beautiful Central Idaho in Challis. Christopher is a "retired" financial services executive, pilot, and avid golfer. He and Debbie operate several businesses, serve on various Boards, oversee an international ministry network, and enjoy their many friends and family members and life together. To learn more or contact them, visit their website at www. livingwatersranch.org.

CHAPTER SEVENTY-ONE

FOUR KEYS TO CREATING & STEPPING INTO ACCELERATION

WENDE JONES

I first began exploring this idea several years ago as I began to experience divine acceleration in my life. What is it and how do we step into it? I wanted to understand what provoked it, how to sustain it and what to do with it in order to glorify God during it! I didn't realize at the time what a loaded question it was or how important it was to the body of Christ to understand it and move into it. More recently, I have been commissioned as a workplace apostle and ordained in ministry. God has challenged me to trust him in business decisions at a greater level and to move forward in faith and obedience without knowing all the answers ahead of time. As I have done that, God has blessed my business with supernatural increase through His riches in Christ Jesus.

Let's start by defining it in the natural sense; what is acceleration? Acceleration is defined as "an increase in the magnitude of the velocity of a moving body, i.e., an increase in speed." This is a positive acceleration; yes, a decrease in speed is a negative acceleration. I had not even thought of it from this perspective until I began writing this chapter and

God brought a whole new perspective on it for me to share. Another concept of acceleration that is important to discuss is the fact the acceleration also happens when an object stays at the same speed but changes direction. I believe this is critical for the body of Christ to understand in these times. I believe God is shifting our direction to completely align us with His purposes and our assignment so sometimes when it seems we aren't accelerating, we really are because we are shifting direction. For the purposes of this chapter, when I speak of acceleration I am speaking of positive acceleration, which I believe is how most think of it; if I am speaking of negative or a decrease in acceleration, I will address it specifically.

I remember a few years ago, as I began experiencing this divine acceleration, that sometimes it seemed I was moving so quickly and could feel it but at other times it seemed as if I had actually slowed down, or was in negative acceleration. I felt in these times that I wasn't doing something right, that I had done something to upset God, because otherwise, why wasn't He accelerating me now like He had before? I could feel myself going through "withdrawal" symptoms when I was in these times of negative acceleration. I found myself feeling lonely and sad and maybe even forsaken during these times. Why couldn't I feel the intentionality, favor and momentum of God like I had before?

I began to realize that these were the shifts, the changes in direction He was working me through which at times required negative acceleration. God wants to make sure we are always prepared and equipped for our assignment, for the next thing He is doing and bringing to pass through us. This requires negative acceleration at times to ensure we are staying pressed into Him, seeking Him and always putting Him first. I believe negative acceleration is used by God to keep us humble and submitting to Him at all times. It is very easy to get caught up in acceleration and often find ourselves out of step with God and doing things in our own strength instead of His. As we move through times of positive acceleration, He slows us down so we can comprehend the magnitude of the shift and allow Him to prepare us for the next level of acceleration.

FOUR KEYS

What causes acceleration? I believe there are four keys to creating and stepping into acceleration:

- **Intimacy with God**

- **Identity in Christ**

- **Alignment in our Assignment**

- **Unity in the Body**

INTIMACY WITH GOD

Everything starts from our intimacy with God which only comes by spending time with Him. How do you get to know someone? You spend time with them! What happens when you spend lots of time with someone? You recognize their voice on the phone or in the hallway; you know their heart and what moves them; you get to know their family and friends; you know how they think and you know what they do. As we spend time with God, we can discern His voice (from all the other ones in our head); we can understand what brings Him joy and sorrow; He directs us to His family and friends (critical relationships in the body, unity); He tells you what He is thinking and what He would do in any situation (through the Holy Spirit).

Our intimacy with the Father is the number one critical component in our lives! Jer. 29:13 says, *"You will seek me and find me when you seek me with all your heart."* What does seek with all your heart really mean? Does this mean just spending time with Him in church on Sunday and maybe bible study on Wednesday? Let's look at the definition of the word seek to answer this question. The word "seek" means to go in search of or quest of, to pursue or to follow. God is calling us to pursue Him with all our hearts. Pursue means to follow with earnestness, go in search of, hunt down, occupy oneself with, accept as authority and adopt opinions of, to watch and to attend to closely as a calling or profession. Have we made God our calling and profession? Have we hunted him down lately?

Pursue also means to keep eyes fixed upon while in motion, keep mind upon while in progress, to keep up with. Do we keep our eyes fixed upon Him while we are in motion? Are we keeping up with God? These two meanings begin to address acceleration and the need for it. First God expects us to keep moving and progressing while keeping our eyes fixed upon Him. Often we get moving and forget the second part; we forget to keep our eyes fixed on Him. Before we know it we are out of step, out of His timing and out of our assignment. Secondly, pursue means to keep up with. God needs us to accelerate to keep up with Him.

Dr. Gordon Bradshaw and I were recently talking about this concept and he said acceleration catches us up to God. This is a very profound statement that triggered additional revelation on acceleration and the importance of it. Why do we need to catch up? How did we get behind? We took our eyes off of Him while we were moving or we stopped moving; either way, we end up out of time, out of step with God and He needs to accelerate us to catch up to where He is! Isn't that great? God has a plan for us to catch up to Him when we get behind to make sure we can realign with Him to step into our assignment and complete it. God really does provide us with everything we need to do what He has called us to.

Lastly, the word *pursuit* means to move behind in the same path or direction, hence to go with. This is the capstone, the arrival of our pursuit as we move in behind God in the same path. What happens when you move in behind something that is already moving? For example, in racing, a car will move in behind the lead car and tuck into his jet stream; this is called drafting. It works the same with bicycles, airplanes, trucks and geese. What happens when you are drafting? You accelerate to greater speeds with less effort because you have moved in behind the lead car and moved out of the wind resistance. The lead car is taking all the resistance; therefore, you can move faster while conserving energy and fuel.

This is such an incredible vision the Lord gave me to see that He is in the lead, and He is taking the resistance on our behalf so we can tuck into his jet stream; we can draft and accelerate with ease! Now we are in complete alignment with God and we are in the "now" of who God is and what He is doing. He goes right, we go right; He goes left, we go left in unison, flowing in His movements, breathing in what He is breathing out, moving to the rhythm of His kingdom! Acceleration catches us up to the "now" of God. This is critical because this is the only place we can operate in our full power and authority that we have in Christ, is in the "now." This is where you come face to face with God, the "I Am"! This is where the heavens are opened and we can apprehend that which we need to do, that which we are called to.

The word "all" means the whole of, the greatest possible, every and nothing but. When we seek Him we are to seek him with the greatest possible heart, the whole of our heart. Folks, we have to be all in, holding nothing back, surrendering and committing everything to our pursuit of Him. The first key to acceleration is to increase our intimacy with God by getting to know Him, by hunting Him down and making Him our cause. And then to move in behind Him in the same path to catch His tail wind, His jet stream, so He can accelerate us to catch up to Him.

Matt. 6:33 says, *"Seek ye first the kingdom of God and his righteousness and all these things will be added to you."* Have we hunted down God's kingdom to understand it, to walk in it and to be a part of it?

IDENTITY IN CHRIST

This leads us into the second key to acceleration which is our identity in Christ. Do we really know who we are? Do we understand our citizenship in His kingdom and that it is now here on earth? Until we begin to really believe who we are in Christ, we will not be able to carry out our assignment. If we haven't hunted down God and sought His kingdom above all else, we can't begin to comprehend the magnitude of His kingdom nor our citizenship rights, privileges and responsibility in it! Do we understand the power and authority that is truly ours as sons and daughters of God? As royal citizens in His kingdom?

Understanding who we are is so important to understanding what we have been called to do for His kingdom, what our calling is, our assignment, our purpose! Often as Christians we ask each other, "How long have you been saved?", which translates to "How long have you known God?" God challenged me a year ago to begin asking people, "How long has God known you?" He said to me, "Wende, tell my children how long I have known them so they will know how much I love them." This was an incredible revelation and every time I speak on this subject, God gets so excited and He can hardly wait for me to tell them how long He has known them. God gave me a teaching for the body last year called "Chosen, Created and Called" to help us truly understand who we are and how long He has known us so we can step into the fullness of our identity in Christ.

Eph. 1:4 says, *"For he chose us in him before the creation of the world to be holy and blameless in his sight."* So, when did God choose us? Before the creation of the world!

Gen. 1:27 says, *"So God created man in his own image, in the image of God he created him; male and female he created them."* God created man after he created the world and saw that it was good. So, if God created us after the world, that means He had actually chosen us before we were created, according to Eph. 1:4. God chose us before the creation of the world and before he created us!

Rom. 8:28 says, *"And those he predestined he also called; those he called he also justified; those he justified, he also glorified."* Eph. 1:11 says, *"In him we were also chosen, having been predestined according to the plan of him who works out everything in conformity with the purpose of his will."* When did He predestine us? Before He chose us, so before the world was created, He chose us! He chose YOU!

The question was, "How long has God known us?" God has known us since before the world was formed! God has been intentional with us not our whole lives but rather His whole life! Since the earth was null and void, God knew us. Since before the creation of the world, God thought about me and He thought about YOU. How intentional have we been with God? Our efforts pale in comparison to His efforts but praise God, He gave us a Savior so that we could be redeemed, reconciled back to Him and could spend our entire lives seeking Him, pursuing Him, hunting Him down and being intentional with Him!

It's never too late to become intentional in our relationship with Him. If you are at a crossroads in your life, become more intentional with God, spend more time with Him and get to know Him as He knows you! If you are struggling, trying to figure out why the visions or prophecies God gave you have not come to pass, spend more time with Him; hunt Him down and ask Him. If you are not moving in the full joy, peace and righteousness of the Holy Spirit, spend more time with God and seek Him for the keys of the kingdom!

Jer. 33:3 says, *"Call to me and I will answer you and teach you great and unsearchable things you do not know."* Call to God; He is waiting for you. He chose you, He created you, He called you and He predestined you. His thoughts of you outnumber the grains of sand and you are fearfully and wonderfully made. He created you in His image and he knit you together in your mother's womb (Ps. 139).

Eph. 1:18-21 speaks to our power and authority that is ours as His sons and daughters. *"I pray also that the eyes of your heart may be enlightened in order that you may know the hope to which he has called you, the riches of his glorious inheritance in the saints, and his incomparably great power for us who believe. That power is like the working of his might strength, which he exerted in Christ when he raised him from the dead and seated him at his right hand in the heavenly realms, far above all rule and authority, power and dominion, and every title that can be given, not only in the present age but also in the one to come."*

Do we believe this; do we walk in this power and authority? Imagine what our world would look like if the entire body of Christ walked in this power and authority! Cities and nations would be transformed, goat nations would become sheep nations and the kingdoms of this world would become the kingdom of our Lord and Christ!

We have the power that raised Christ from the dead in us! Are we walking in this power? Are we moving in the authority of Christ? Are we commanding the storms to be calm? Are we raising the dead? Are we healing the sick? These are all things Christ did when he walked the earth because he was one with the Father. He left us his Holy Spirit so we could do greater things than he. Let's see this in scripture. John 14:12-21 says:

"I tell you the truth, anyone who has faith in me will do what I have been doing. He will do even greater things than these, because I am going to the Father. And I will do whatever you ask in my name, so that the Son may bring glory to the Father. You may ask me for anything in my name, and I will do it. If you love me, you will obey what I command. And I will ask the Father, and he will give you another Counselor to be with you forever--the Spirit of truth. The world cannot accept him, because it neither sees him nor knows him. But you know him, for he lives with you and will be in you. I will not leave you as orphans; I will come to you. Before long, the world will not see me anymore, but you will see me. Because I live, you also will live. On that day you will realize that I am in my Father, and you are in me, and I am in you. Whoever has my commands and obeys them, he is the one who loves me. He who loves me will be loved by my Father, and I too will love him and show myself to him."

We have to begin to believe who we are so we can believe what God has called us to do and walk in that authority here on earth today.

ALIGNMENT IN YOUR ASSIGNMENT

Acceleration comes from alignment with God in your assignment. As we begin to discover our true identity in Christ, then we can begin to discover our calling and election. 2 Pet. 1:10 says, *"Therefore my brethren be all the more eager to make your calling and election sure and you shall not fall."* This is the third key to acceleration: alignment in our assignment. Do we know what God has called us to do here on earth, and why we have the skills and giftings He gave us, and what to use them for? The youth today are lost and killing each other because they don't feel like they have a purpose. We have taken God out of the schools, which has stripped our youth of the hope of Christ. We first must begin to walk in our assignment so we can help others step into theirs. Our hope comes from knowing we are His and He has a mighty calling on our lives and has predestined us for His purposes.

To save a lost and dying world, to destroy Babylon and to take back that which was lost (souls, resources, land, time, relationships, etc.)—that is our mandate, our corporate assignment. How we carry this out is based on our gifts and talents God has given us. We are all unique and so is our calling, also. How I carry out this mandate will be different then how you carry it out but we must work together to achieve the purposes of God. I need you so I can complete my calling and you need me so you can complete yours. The body of Christ must unite and come together to complete each other so that together we can defeat Babylon and see His kingdom come.

I realized several years ago the only way I could figure out my purpose, my assignment was to spend more time with my creator, the one who predestined me for my assignment, the one that purposed me before the creation of the world, God my Father. He had the answers I was looking for and I needed to improve my relationship with my Father, the one who created me and knit me together in my mother's womb. I also needed to spend time with God's people, His apostles, His prophets, His teachers, His Pastors and His evangelists. I needed to hear what they were hearing from the Lord. I needed to understand the times and hearing what God was saying to others helped me to gain understanding of what God is doing.

UNITY IN THE BODY

So, the last key to acceleration is unity in the body of Christ. The body of Christ must come together as one to complete their individual and corporate assignments. We need prophets and apostles in our board rooms. We need teachers, evangelists and pastors on our staff to reach out to our employees, to love them and lead them to the fullness of who they are in Christ. We need businesses uniting in communities to make a difference, to create new jobs and to work with churches and city government to solve community problems. The body of Christ is called to work together to transforms man's ways, man's systems and government (Babylonian systems) into God's government and God's ways. Remember the definition of acceleration is the "velocity of a moving body."

It is this final step, this unifying the body of Christ, that creates momentum across the land to speed up the advancement of His kingdom. The body of Christ must come together and unite for this final acceleration to happen; we must complete each other so we may complete the work of God. The body of Christ needs to be like interlocking jigsaw puzzle pieces. Interlocking pieces are snapped into place, locked in with the piece next to them and when you hold up the puzzle, the pieces don't fall apart, they remain interlocked. The body of Christ needs to be locking arms, interlocking one member to the other, one assignment with the other, and when it is threatened or attacked, it remains locked. When it is held up to the light, it remains in one piece and does not scatter or fall away.

This is advancing the kingdom of God; this is the final step to acceleration, to catching up to God, to operating in the "now" with God and taking down Babylon and rising up as a nation with the government of God on our shoulders! This will carry God's righteousness throughout the land across the earth, and God will be honored and glorified and His kingdom order will be established!

Isa. 9:6-7 says, *"For to us a child is born, to us a son is given, and the government will be on his shoulders. And he will be called Wonderful Counselor, Mighty God, Everlasting Father, Prince of Peace. Of the increase of his government and peace there will be no end. He will reign on David's throne and over his kingdom, establishing and upholding it with justice and righteousness from that time on and forever. The zeal of the LORD Almighty will accomplish this."*

May God bless you as you accelerate in His service for His purpose and glory.

ABOUT THE AUTHOR

Wende Jones is a native Oregonian and has spent most of her life in the Pacific Northwest. She resides in the Beaverton area with her husband and her two daughters when they are not away at college, with her third daughter and grandchildren close by.

Wende is founder and CEO of Agile Business Services, a software development company that focuses on building applications for the web and mobile devices for her clients that are spread out from Oregon to Washington, D.C. She has her credentials as a certified management consultant (CMC) and is a founding member of the Northwest Christian Chamber and serves as Chairman of the Board. She is a published author of *The God Port: Accessing God in Real Time.*

Wende also serves as an advisor for KEYS Network, is a member of the GEMS Network and is on the board of directors for Nehemiah Project International Ministries because of her desire to see other Christian business owners excel and build sustainable and profitable kingdom businesses. Wende is an accomplished speaker and business consultant and enjoys educating CEOs and other top executives on technology and innovation. She speaks in Christian marketplace groups, conferences and venues to encourage, edify and train employees, leaders and business owners for their marketplace mission field. Whether CEO of a business or pastor of a church, we are all called to minister to those God puts before us.

Wende truly believes that if we are all moving in our calling and election, we are in full-time ministry in the sphere of influence we have been called to! To learn more or contact Wende, visit her websites at www.wendejones.com or www.agilebusinessservices.com.

CHAPTER SEVENTY-TWO

ASK FOR & FOLLOW THE ANCIENT PATHS

LARRY TYLER

Early mornings with God have become a habit since I was 11 years old. "God will always, regardless of the time, show up and want to talk," I can hear my mother's voice say. She stressed repeatedly to me as a youth the need to start each day with God—no matter where I am. These early morning times with God are a time to pray, read and study the Bible, meditate and communicate with Him. I've come to know real communication is primarily listening!

For the past year I've learned to listen to God more through prayer journaling, by asking specific questions and then writing down what I think He's saying to me. I believe God has things to say to me about my future, my destiny and the desires He has placed in my heart to help accomplish His purposes and help bring forth, establish, build, expand and multiply His Kingdom on earth. I ask questions and imagine Jesus sitting in front of me answering them.

One morning as I wrote my first question in my journal, "Father, what is on your heart this morning and what do you want to say to me?" I clearly heard Him say, *"Ask for and follow the ancient paths."* I was not sure what he meant by this response. However, my mind went immediately to hiking in the mountains of North Carolina, which my wife and I do weekly. We often take old paths that are faint to the eye, grown over and mostly hidden by weeds and brush from lack of regular use, but paths nonetheless.

Sometimes we follow old logging roads that are almost reclaimed by nature out of curiosity and with a desire to capture that next great picture, since my wife is a photographer. Besides getting great exercise, venturing on these old paths has always rewarded us with a sense of adventure, great sights and photo opportunities. My mind went next to my vocational career. I seemed to always be looking for and taking the hidden paths, seeking a better way, looking for the simple and practical path to provide a solution. However, as I have learned in my career, the curious individuals, the ones offering solutions that went against the status quo, were usually on a path by themselves, alone, wondering if they were made differently than others.

God directed me to Jer. 6:16 which says, *"Thus says the Lord, stand by the ways and see and **ask for the ancient paths, where the good way is, and walk in it, and you shall find rest for your souls...**"* (NASB, author's emphasis). I learned through some research that the ancient path was God's Word – the only absolute and trustworthy standard for life. The "good way" meant pleasant, prosperous, excellent, cheerful, and agreeable.

For the past four years I have been asking God (Jer. 33:3 – *"Call to me, and I will answer you, and I will tell you great and mighty things, which you do not know."*) which path to take to have maximum fruit and impact for the Kingdom. I spent 40 years in the finance field as a financial manager and have a passion for helping and serving business owners so their businesses will prosper. This passion has intensified even more during the current economic recession. My prayer was,

"Show me Lord how I can help business owners, especially those with Kingdom businesses, to prosper during these challenging times." Many businesses have been and are still going through difficult times. My question to God was, "Why the tough times, Lord?" His answer to me was Deut. 29:6: *"I took you through the wilderness for forty years and through all that time the clothes on your backs didn't wear out, the sandals on your feet didn't wear out, and you lived well without bread and wine and beer, **proving to you that I am in fact God, your God"*** (MSG, author's emphasis).

GOD IS THE PROVIDER

God wants business owners to acknowledge and know that He is the PROVIDER and not ourselves, our businesses or our intelligence. God created man in His own image and placed inside of man the DNA to follow God's "good ways." With the fall of man, and the departure from God's "good ways," many people today have very little peace, rest or prosperity. Such a state is not walking in the *ancient paths.*

Over the past several months, since He spoke to me that morning about asking for the *ancient paths,* God began showing me some of His *ancient paths.* These are the paths he showed our spiritual forefathers – paths the patriarchs traveled – Abraham, Isaac and Jacob. I felt, as I was taking or rediscovering these *ancient paths,* that I was back again on one of my hiking adventures, picking my way through thick brush and weeds following an old forgotten path.

Recently some trusted individuals suggested that I investigate what it means to be apostolic or to be an apostle, according to Eph. 4:11. I knew of the terms but wasn't clear on what they mean or how an apostle functions in the church, society and workplace. Through research, prayer and talking to others, I found that an apostle is one that is sent forth or ahead, like an ambassador sent to a foreign country, to represent the king and to inform the king's subjects of the king's plans, ideas and the ways of his government. In other words, an apostle is a path or way shower, telling, showing and taking action on behalf of the King to advance His Kingdom – like a GPS system gives us directions to a specific destination. Also, an apostle has the heart of a father, loving unconditionally and serving with all that is in them - being a bridge between where individuals currently are in their walk with the Lord or in their business and where God designed them to BE.

During my research, I recognized for the first time that throughout my career, I had been apostolic in my approach to serving and being a father to others and helping lead the way to better paths, especially when it came to business. I thought of the many times I had felt isolated and different from most of my peers and co-workers, because of my desire to forge a path, one I felt strongly to be the truth, but with few followers, and mostly skeptics. I realized an apostle is much like another term used today in business—an innovator.

Innovators make up approximately 2.5% of the population and pursue new ideas and paths; they challenge others to see and think of how the world could be. They rely heavily on their intuition and trust their gut and suffer some level of inconvenience to espouse an idea or path of action that feels right or to show and lead the way.

As a path or way shower, I had felt obligated during my career to obey the words in Isa. 30:8-9: *"Now go write down this word of mine concerning Egypt, so that it will stand the end of time...For if you don't write it, they will claim I never warned them, "Oh, no." they'll say, "You never told us that!"* Now that I am self-employed, serving on the board of directors of two large financial companies that are Kingdom-focused, and as CFO of several small companies owned by a Kingdom entrepreneur, I have the same burden to both warn and teach people concerning God's ways and more time to help others. So, let's explore some of God's *ancient paths* now.

God says in Hosea 4:6, *"For a lack of knowledge My people perish."* Following are some of the **ancient paths** I believe God desires we take to be successful and blessed in our businesses.

WHAT IS IN YOUR HAND?

Like Moses in Exodus 4, God is asking us, *"What do you have in your hand?"* Moses answers, "A shepherd's rod." God says to Moses, "Throw it down on the ground." Later God tells Moses, "Grab it by the tail." What I believe God is saying to us is that all we are designed to be and have belongs to God. Give up the right(s) to who we think we are, our experience, expertise, what we know, what our job title is, what we are in the natural, what we own or possess personally and commit it ALL to God. Look, see, observe all we are and have etc. from God's perspective (pick up the rod by the tail) and be ready and available to be used by God in ways we wouldn't expect. What IF? - We did this in our businesses? *This is the ancient path of looking for and pursuing God's perspective.*

In Ex. 4:24 God says something very surprising to the man who is to lead God's people out of slavery and captivity and into the Promised Land. Moses had not circumcised his son (obeyed God's commands). God was going to kill him! God had prepared Moses for 80 years to meet with Pharaoh and was marching him forward to one of the biggest events of all history. This, for me, is hard to swallow. Moses was God's hand-picked leader for this major event. God was ready, willing and able to kill Moses for his lack of obedience and delay the release of His people from Egypt! God is SERIOUS about our obedience to His ways and commandments. God talks repeatedly in Deuteronomy about the blessings we will receive by obeying all His laws (Deut. 28:1). I've never read in the Bible that following God's ways was like a cafeteria—where we get to pick and choose which laws we want to obey and live by! *This is the ancient path of total and full obedience.*

God made man and woman with incredible desires and motivational needs such as: significance, love and acceptance, authority, honor and respect, peace of mind, security, provision, contentment, to be understood and to understand correctly. We all at times are very much like the woman that Jesus talks to at the well in John 4. She had spent most of her life looking and searching for love and acceptance in all the wrong places. Instead of coming daily to Jesus' well of living water to seek Him first and have our needs met and quenched as only He can, we by-pass Jesus' well and seek to have our needs met in our own way.

We forget, especially in developed nations, the importance of clean water for drinking and cooking. In biblical times, cities formed around water supplies and succeeded and thrived or failed based on the existence of water. Today, many times we fail to acknowledge and live based on the "living water" that is provided for us freely by God. We dig our own wells to find and meet those needs that only God can truly satisfy. What happens when those wells we dig go dry or the water becomes sour? *This is the ancient path of seeking and coming to God's well first to satisfy our needs.*

Money is a big thing to God. Not in the sense that it is or should be a god in our lives but money does play a significant role in each of our lives in regard to how we direct or invest it or as most people would say— spend it. Life is about choices and those choices are based many times on how we direct or invest our money, time, energy, words and resources. If we base our choices on God's purposes for our lives rather than our own, we will no doubt bring about or see a good return for making those wise choices – as based on God's promises like Matt. 6:33. What do we have available to us to use in our businesses daily and moment by moment to practically help us in this area of directing our money toward God's purposes?

Many are familiar with Tommy Newberry's bestselling book, *The 4:8 Principle*, which used as its thesis the verse – Phil. 4:8—as a standard or guideline for thinking the way few people think versus the way most people think.

WHAT IF?

What If?—(our minds work best when responding to a question)—We used Phil. 4:8 as the standard for how we direct money in our businesses? We would base our money direction choices on those things that are: true, pure, noble, just, lovely, virtuous, of good report or praiseworthy. What If?—We went on a fiscal or monetary diet and used Phil. 4:8 as the basis for the diet? Do you think the businesses that went on the diet would have any excess cash? If you were one who went on the diet which resulted in excess cash, what would you do with the excess? Would you then be able to help satisfy that desire that God placed for fulfilling your part of the Great Commission with the excess cash that was shed as a result of your diet? *This is the ancient path of seeking God's best way (the 4:8 principle) for directing your money.*

As I was meditating one morning I could hear the rain hitting the roof and driveway. I saw myself in the rain but it wasn't raining water—it was raining provision— God's provision for me. The provision was far more than money; it was a great and healthy marriage, and a strong, healthy body I could use to exercise, hike, hear and see God's beautiful creation. It was love, knowledge, wisdom, understanding, clear thinking, a hunger for live and nourishing food, a peaceful and beautiful home, good friends and relationships, cars that never needed repairs, daily bread, vivid imagination, child-likeness even at 62 years of age, talents and many other things I really never considered as provisions from God.

God clearly then spoke these words to me, "What are you doing with the provision I've provided for you?" I responded, "Over and above meeting our needs, I tithe; I give the best I can to others over and above my tithe; I give away ideas and things I've learned and experienced in my life; I love others to the best of my ability. I help others that need help when I see or become aware of needs and I invest some of the money to provide for emergencies and future retirement."

God then asked, "How do my purposes get accomplished in My Kingdom on earth?" I answered, "You work through people like myself and use relationships and the provision that you rain on people to accomplish your purposes and bring about your Kingdom on earth." I recalled then so many business owners I had consulted with, especially the past four-and-and-half years of this recession, and during the years I was a commercial loan officer. Many had great ideas, inventions and businesses that went under, or the ideas and dreams were still on the shelf due to a lack of funding and other types of provision or help. God then said to me, "It is the FLOW of my provision, which you now acknowledge is more than just money, by and through individuals and businesses that My will and purposes are and will be fulfilled on earth. Many times it is with the full cooperation of those individuals but it isn't always. In other words, My son, it's from the FLOW of My provision through people's lives and shared or passed on to others that My will is generally accomplished. The key is FLOW."

NO PLAN B

I realized how important several aspects of God's Kingdom are and how His Kingdom operates: God's plan A for bringing forth His Kingdom on earth is through people and relationships; there is no plan B, we are it; God is truly our provider (Phil. 4:19) and provision is much, much more than money; FLOW of all the many types of provision provided by God is essential and necessary to accomplish His will and purposes.

God asked me, "What did you do with the excess provision I provided you?" I answered, smugly, remembering the parable of the talents and knowing I had invested some of my excess provision, "I invested it Lord for emergencies and for retirement." God then said, "Well done, son, but where and how was the excess invested? How did those you entrusted with those funds invest them? Would I be pleased with where and how the money was used? Were any of the funds used to build churches, spread the Good

News of My son's life, death and resurrection? Were any of the funds used to make disciples of all the nations or feed the poor, disadvantaged and homeless? Were any of the funds used to take care of orphans and widows or the least of these? Were any of the funds used to teach and educate business owners on My Kingdom economic principles and how to successfully manage businesses such that there will be excesses that can help others in need – what I call *Compassionate Capitalism?"* Were any of the funds loaned to or invested in other Kingdom businesses like yours to help bring forth witty ideas and inventions and help grow and prosper dreams other entrepreneurs and business owners had—what I call *Entrepreneurial Lending*?

As those monies were His, I had to ask myself the question, "Is this investment and how and where these funds are invested by this investment company or by myself something that God would be pleased with?" I was beginning to understand that God's provision to me and others was meant to be a blessing and help to supply other's needs as well as my own. God then directed me to what I call "radical kingdom business" – 1 Tim. 6:18: *"...do good, to be rich in good works, to be generous and ready to share"* (NASB). A similar and parallel scripture passage is 2 Cor. 9:6-11. *This is God's ancient path of FLOW of His provision to us and through us to accomplish His purposes on earth through Compassionate Capitalism and Entrepreneurial Lending and Investing.*

For the previous four years, many businesses throughout the world have experienced difficult times financially. In my talks with business owners, I can see and feel their frustration, anxiety and stress with not exactly knowing what to do. I asked God, "Father, what can I tell these business owners that will help or what can I do? Please guide me to help provide root solutions."

In Acts 4 the apostles were experiencing *"pushback"* (defined as—force back with or by power, opposition, attack from an enemy, move back by force or influence, negative or unfavorable response, persecution) from society and Jewish leaders. They would return from public meetings to the company of friends, family, like-hearted and like-minded associates for networking, support, encouragement and prayer. In Acts 4 God gives us a "pattern" of how we as Kingdom business owners and business men and women should handle threats, problems, issues and opportunities or "pushback" in our businesses.

A similar example is found in Daniel 2 where Daniel and his three friends were experiencing "pushback" even to the point of death. A common element in both of these situations is the coming together of a few individuals – those whom were relationally involved either by prosperity or pain to lay out their issues.

FIVE THINGS TO CREATE BREAKTHROUGH

The apostles in Acts 4 did five things to create breakthrough that are a pattern for what I believe can and should be done today:

- Come together "as one" in a safe community of believers to debrief from time in the marketplace and lay out their biggest threats and opportunities to their businesses with the context being a focus on seeking first the Kingdom of God (Matt. 6:33).

- Access heaven via prayer

- Receive anointing from heaven to act

- Receive fresh authority

- Receive new instruction to administrate their breakthroughs

One vehicle for a safe community of believers is a Master's (God's) Mind group. The goal of such a group is to come together to collaborate and explore ideas about how the Gospel of the Kingdom of God can be expressed within businesses. The group is a platform to invite the Holy Spirit to partner and lead business owners to the best and brightest ideas and strategies not only to save businesses but to help them thrive.

God's solution and perspective to business and financial problems is found in 2 Chron. 7:14: *"and if my people who are called by My name humble themselves and pray, and seek My face and turn from their wicked ways, then I will hear from heaven, will forgive their sin, and will heal their land."*

The key ingredient and tool to bring about solutions and strategies in Kingdom businesses is prayer, seeking the face and mind of Christ. 1 Cor. 2:16 says, *"...but we have the mind of Christ."*

The picture or vision God gave me of what is possible with Kingdom businesses when a Master's Mind's mindset was applied to a business along with the application of Kingdom economic principles in the business was that of Ex. 8:19. Kingdom businesses would bear witness and testimony to God's greatness in their businesses such that others and those not of the household of God, point their finger at something that happens before their eyes that is so unmistakably *"of God"* that they call out, testify and say: *"this is the finger (Spirit and power) of God."*

When Adam sinned, I believe man lost the upper bandwidth that God created us with. In John 16:13 Jesus says, *"When He, the Spirit of truth has come, He will guide you into all truth... and He will show you things to come."* Jesus is saying, 'I want to show you your future. We can know God's will and His plan for our life, although right now, we don't have the upper bandwidth to see or observe it. But when the Spirit of truth comes, He will give us the upper bandwidth to see things to come.' Knowing our assignment and having and knowing the vision from God—we can thus—through the Holy Spirit—who is both inside us and outside of this natural realm—be provided information from our future possibilities for us to see, observe, and call those things that are not as though they are.

Bottom line—the Holy Spirit has the answers, strategies, words, etc., whatever we need and desire to complete the business vision God has placed within us. *This is the ancient path of collaborating with family, friends, like-minded and like-hearted believers and the Holy Spirit in prayer to seek and receive God's perspectives and root solutions to and strategies for business and financial issues.*

Heb. 12:1-3 says, *"Do you see what this means—all these pioneers who blazed the way, all these veterans cheering us on?" It means we'd better get on with it. Strip down, start running— and never quit! No extra spiritual fat, no parasitic sins. Keep your eyes on Jesus, who both began and finished this race we're in. Study how he did it. Because he never lost sight of where he was headed—that exhilarating finish in and with God—he could put up with anything along the way: Cross, shame, whatever. And now he's there, in the place of honor, right alongside God. When you find yourselves flagging in your faith, go over that story again, item by item, that long litany of hostility he plowed through. That will shoot adrenaline into your souls!"* (MSG).

Many businesses have been holding on since 2008 and are like tumbleweeds being blown to and fro by the winds of constant change in the economic landscape. Are you running helter skelter seeking worldly solutions that hopefully will work for your business?

As I read through the Gospels and visualize or imagine what Jesus did and had to go through and endure during His ministry, I feel the landscape was much tougher in His time than it is today. In fact, Jesus accomplished the vision set before Him by God such that He was rewarded by being placed in "the place of honor," the scriptures say. Jesus' path wasn't easy but He succeeded, as the scripture in Hebrews above says, because "He never lost sight of where He was headed." He went through His daily routine with the picture of the end in mind. Jesus never lost sight of the vision God placed on His heart, despite tough times, difficult people that were constantly after Him and the betrayal of His closest friends.

BE VISION-LED

One of Jesus' secrets to success while on earth, which can also be yours as well, is that He was vision-led. Vision is a picture of the end result. It is about seeing where you want your business to end up. Vision is an inner knowing of exactly what your business is doing and why. You can see, feel, taste, hear and almost physically touch where you want to end up. Vision is the power that drives purposeful activity and decisions in your business. Vision brings clarity which in turn brings cash into the business. The vision is the bridge to the company's future. Vision provides the context for everything you do in your business.

Redemption of mankind via the cross, resurrection and ascension to God's right hand was what drove Jesus' thoughts and activities during His ministry on earth. What drives your business activities and decisions?

Start with and stick with pursuing the vision (also called purpose, intent or your "Why"). Prov. 29:18 says, *"Where there is no vision, the people are unrestrained..."* (NASB). In other words, without a clear picture of the business future or God's revelation to you of your business purpose and to use that vision as the guiding light for activities and decisions, we and our businesses will be out of control, undisciplined and will fall under judgment.

Hab. 2:2 implores business owners to write the vision down, make it plain and available to all so that the employees will be enthusiastic, energized and motivated and will succeed. 1 Chron. 4:10 says we are blessed mightily when we pursue God's purposes. Neh. 2:17-18 records a beautiful example and model for us of how sharing the vision given by God and placed in our hearts with employees, and trusting the Holy Spirit to impress the employees with similar thoughts, creates enthusiasm and inspiration for working toward and fulfilling the vision.

Does your business matter? Your business matters to the extent you create an emotional (relational) connection with your customers and employees. People don't buy (dollars are certificates of appreciation from customers) what you do—they buy WHY (your vision, intent or purpose) you do it! *This is the ancient path to clarity and success in your business—pursue your vision as effectively as Jesus pursued His.*

God desires to bring about His Kingdom on earth through and by His people and their businesses. Through the prophet Jeremiah, God is directing business owners, like using a current day GPS system, toward success and fulfillment in their businesses. Like punching the address you desire into the GPS system to guide you to a destination, God is saying to all of us, ASK for the *ancient paths* (directions) and I'll show you the shortest and best way to the destination. The path I lead and guide you on will bring REST to your soul. God made us for Himself and our souls are restless until they find REST in Him. Who today in their business wouldn't want a much better pathway to success which also produces or operates from REST? I asked and God responded by showing me some of His ancient paths:

- *The ancient path of looking for and pursuing God's perspective.*

- *The ancient path of total and full obedience.*

- *The ancient path of seeking and coming to God's well first to satisfy our needs.*

- *The ancient path of seeking God's best way (the 4:8 principle) for directing your money.*

- *God's ancient path of FLOW of His provision to us and through us to accomplish His purposes on earth through Compassionate Capitalism and Entrepreneurial Lending and Investing.*

- *The ancient path of collaborating with family, friends, like-minded and like-hearted believers and the Holy Spirit in prayer to seek and receive God's perspectives and root solutions to business and financial issues.*

- *The ancient path to clarity and success in your business—pursue your vision as effectively as Jesus pursued His.*

ABOUT THE AUTHOR

Larry Tyler has over 35 years of experience partnering with business owners, entrepreneurs and their businesses in a wide range of industries, helping them to bridge the gap between where they currently are and where they want to be.

He is founder and CEO of Up Your Business LLC, a business consulting and advisory enterprise, whose mission is to inspire business owners and entrepreneurs to reach their potential, to dream bigger and to develop their strengths and talents. Larry helps business owners to develop ways to improve revenue, profit and personal fulfillment in their business as well as improve their ability to obtain the capital they need from lenders and investors to successfully sustain and grow their businesses. Larry's experience allows him to assist others to navigate the challenging and often daunting process of pursuing their entrepreneurial dreams.

Larry is a requested speaker in entrepreneurial classes in area colleges which are taking advantage of his experience in working with business owners. He is the author of *Romancing the Loan—14 Principles for Opening Your Lender's Vault* and *Cash Flow Basics for Business Owners—Strengthening the Foundation of Your Business.*

Larry has both an MBA and BS in business administration. He continually learns, applies and shares sound business principles and Kingdom economic principles acquired from his professional experience, his customers and a steady diet of reading leadership, business, motivational and biblical books. His satisfaction comes from being instrumental in another's journey to success.

Larry can often be seen during his spare time with his wife Vickie, a writer and photographer, hiking the many mountains or traveling along the many rivers in western North Carolina taking pictures for cards, calendars and posters they produce or for their articles, books or speeches. To learn more or contact him, visit his website at www.upyourbusiness.biz.

APOSTOLIC CULTURE

CHAPTER SEVENTY-THREE

APOSTOLIC WISDOM TO REDEEM THE CULTURE

DR. TED BAEHR

The entertainment industry in Hollywood is an influential world force.

When I am in my office, I am only about 45 miles north of the heart of the entertainment industry in Hollywood, California. The drive takes an hour...or two or three, if there's traffic.

Increasingly, I am called to speak around the world in faraway places such as Poland, Ukraine, India, Japan, or the border of Laos. When I step on the plane, I find Hollywood movies and television programs. When I go into the jungle of the highlands of Thailand, Hollywood is still very close nearby—there are satellite dishes run by generators connected by exposed wires, which bring Hollywood entertainment into the flimsy grass huts of the people. The children in these villages try to dress like the Hollywood stars they idolize and try to mimic their lives—right down to the smoking, drinking and sexual promiscuity.

Hollywood is not just a geographic place anymore, but a huge entertainment industry that reaches the world, for good or ill. Aided increasingly by foreign investments, it is the United States of America's voice to people everywhere, especially the youth. As Jesus told the leading spokespeople of His day, *"It's not what goes into the mouth that defiles a man, but what comes out of the mouth, this defiles a man"* (Matt. 15:11, CSB). All too often, what comes out of the mouth of our entertainment-oriented culture are movies such as *Hostel, Kill Bill, Sex and the City,* and *Saw IV.*

Countless scientific studies of different kinds, including longitudinal studies of the effects of the media, have clearly shown the powerful influence that the entertainment media has on people's cognitive development and behavior, especially children, teenagers and young people, who represent the biggest audience for entertainment programming from the mass media, including Hollywood. In fact, according to media consumption statistics from the Motion Picture Association of America (MPAA), by the time he or she is 17-years-old, the average child will have spent up to 63,835 hours watching movies, videos and TV programs, playing video games, or listening to music.

In comparison, by the time he or she is 17-years-old, the average child will have spent only 11,000 hours in school, 2,000 hours with their parents, or 900 hours in church if they regularly go to services. Thus, in one year, the average child might spend about 3,755 hours watching movies and television, listening to music or consuming other media, but only about 52 hours in church (if they attend once a week).

In 2000, the Surgeon General of the United States agreed with four top medical groups, the American Medical Association, the American Academy of Pediatrics, the American Psychological Association, and the American Academy of Child and Adolescent Psychiatry, as well as countless psychological and neurological experts, that violence in the mass media is contributing to increased violent behavior among children and teenagers.[1] Not only that, but many scientific studies from other sources, such as education professor Diane Levin, author of *Remote Control Childhood? Combating the Hazards of Media Culture,* and psychologists like Dr. Victor Cline, Dr. Stanley Rachman, Dr. Judith Reisman, and Dr. W. Marshall, have found that viewing sexual images in the media has led to increased sexual activity among children and teenagers and increased deviant behavior, including rape.[2] Furthermore, a 2001 Dartmouth Medical School study of New England middle-school students, reported by the National Cancer Institute, found that viewing drug use in movies and TV programs leads to increased drug use among children.[3]

A long-term study released in 2002 proved, once again, the negative effects of today's popular visual media on children, teenagers and young adults. Published in the journal *Science,* the study found that teenagers and young adults who watch more than one hour of television, including videos daily, are more likely to commit violent crimes and other forms of aggressive behavior. The study, led by Dr. Jeffrey G. Johnson of Columbia University and the New York State Psychiatric Institute, followed children in 707 families in two counties in northern New York state for 17 years. Adolescents and young adults who watched television for more than seven hours per week had an increased likelihood of between 16 and 200 percent of committing an aggressive act, including criminal behavior, in later years.

The study found a link between violence and viewing any television, not just violent programming. This study is important not only because of its long-term nature but also because it proved a link between television viewing and violent criminal behavior apart from environmental characteristics such as low family income, living in an unsafe neighborhood and parental neglect.[4]

"The evidence has gotten to the point where it's overwhelming," Dr. Johnson says.

A study by the Rand Corp. in 2001 and 2002 of American children aged 12 to 17, reported by the Associated Press, found that those children who watch a lot of television with sexual content are about twice as likely to start having unmarried intercourse during the subsequent years as those with little such exposure. "Exposure to TV that included only talk about sex was associated with the same risks as exposure to TV depicting sexual behavior," the Rand. Corp. said.[5] A more recent study led by Dr. Jane Brown of the University of North Carolina of children aged 12 to 17 had similar findings that exposure to media sex leads to increased sexual promiscuity among teenagers. "The media are also important sources of sexual norms for youth," this study reported.[6]

All of these studies about the negative effects of the media are incredibly disturbing. This is especially true in light of studies by the Parents Television Council in 2006 and by the Henry J. Kaiser Family Foundation in 2005 showing that the amount of violence and sexual content on television has doubled since 1998 and a 2005 study by the think tank Third Way that the number of pornographic pages on the Internet has risen more than 3,000 percent since 1998![7]

When I drive to Hollywood to preview a movie at a screening, I visit studio executives to help them understand this influence they are having on the children and grandchildren of the United States and the world. The good news is that many of them are listening. The type of entertainment being produced is gradually moving away from salacious, ultra-violent, R-rated movies to family films with faith—movies such as *Amazing Grace, Prince Caspian,*

The Nativity Story, and *The Lion, the Witch and the Wardrobe.* Even Rocky Balboa has found faith in Jesus Christ. Now, every studio is pursuing the Christian faith-based audience.

Even so, there remains a large residue of movies with rotten values in the bloodstream of the culture, and the entertainment industry is still producing a significant number of rotten movies and television programs are still being produced. So, while many factors contribute to establishing society's mores, Hollywood no doubt has a secure foothold as the epicenter of what is popular and what is not. Clearly, what happens in Hollywood does not stay in Hollywood. What Lindsay Lohan wears, Justin Timberlake sings and George Clooney says will ripple its way not only to the heartland of America but well beyond. Indeed, the culture clash thrives from Kansas to Kiev.

READY TO COLLIDE

Sometimes, the influence of the mass media of entertainment on faraway places helps us to reflect on our own problems and vulnerabilities as well as our influence on the culture of the world. For two years in a row recently, I spoke in Kiev, a city in Ukraine that's emerging from totalitarian suppression. The pastor of the church where I preached told me that his father had been tortured for his outspoken faith in Jesus Christ in the very hotel where I was staying. Now this pastor has a megachurch of over 1,000 and a growing group of almost 200 churches. The mayor of Kiev is his Spirit-filled Christian friend. The president, whose wife is from America, is a thoughtful Christian. Business is booming.

Yet on the other hand, Ukraine has the highest rate of AIDS/HIV, prostitutes and women sold into white slavery in

Europe, and at night the streets are filled with empty alcohol bottles. In 1994, there were only 183 registered cases of HIV, but by 2004 that number had grown to more than 68,000.[8] "Ukraine...has replaced Thailand and the Philippines as the epicenter of the global business in trafficking women," an article from *The New York Times* noted.[9] While sin was no stranger when communism reigned in Ukraine, one cannot help but notice how consumerism has adversely affected the nation's youth.

So, it is the best of times and the worst of times for the people of Kiev. They asked me to teach them media wisdom to navigate the treacherous rapids of the changing culture—a culture that seems to be at war with itself. The communist oppressor of the East has left in disgrace and the materialistic pornography of Hollywood has blatantly and seductively taken its place. Two great rivers of conflicting cultural values have converged into a raging torrent of cultural confusion. A churning flood threatens to sweep aside a bright future for the precious next generation.

How do people navigate the cultural rapids? In Japan, a homeschool conference has grown phenomenally in the past few years as families consider taking their children out of schools where materialism is so rapacious that young girls are selling themselves to buy iPods. These Japanese flocked to listen to my talks on cultural wisdom in search of guidance.

What is happening, why is it happening, and how do the messages of the mass media of entertainment influence us, our children, each society and the world as a whole? Is there any hope? Can we navigate a safe passage to reach the still waters and green pastures of Christ's kingdom?

THE DECLINE OF NATIONS

Observant pundits on all sides of the political spectrum have correctly noted a steady decline in the last century in the quality of culture. There has been a weakening of faith, an abandonment of values and an eroding of civility in our culture. The work of shaping our culture requires God's wisdom to use the right tools so that He will be glorified.

In their CD *The Decline of Nations*, Dr. Ken Boa, a highly respected theologian and philosophy scholar, and Bible teacher Bill Ibsen point out three symptoms of decline: (1) social decay—the crisis of lawlessness, the loss of economic discipline, and finally, growing bureaucracy; (2) cultural decay—the decline of education, the weakening of cultural foundations, the increasing loss of respect for tradition, and the increase in materialism; and (3) moral decay—the rise in immorality, the decay of religious belief, and the devaluation of human life.[10]

Dr. Ken Boa and Bill Ibsen state that "symptoms of decline synergistically rot a nation from the inside out, making it vulnerable to attack from a variety of enemies." Then they ask the critical question: What objective measures of social and cultural health can be used to determine how America is doing? To answer this question, they cite a report published in 1993 by William J. Bennett, the former U.S. Secretary of Education, who notes that between the 1960s and the 1990s there was:

- A 966 percent increase in the rate of cohabitation

- A 523 percent increase in out-of-wedlock births

- A 370 percent increase in violent crime

- A 270 percent increase in children on welfare

- A 215 percent increase in single-parent families

- A 210 percent increase in teenage suicide

- A 200 percent increase in the crime rate

- A 130 percent increase in the divorce rate

- A 75 point decrease in the average SAT score

"Improvements were made in the violent crime rate, welfare and teenage suicide in the 1990s," Boa and Ibsen state. "However, the breakdown of the family remains of particular concern. Indicators point to nurturing relationships as a key factor to maintaining a stable society, while mass media entertainment often fills the voids left by family breakdown."[11]

SUCH A TIME AS THIS

All too often, the prosperity of God flows into fruitless endeavors as succeeding generations begin to disregard the root of their wealth. America's ancestors planted the seed of God's blessing and left a rich inheritance in this land. But God has no grandchildren. He has only first-generation descendants who yield to His Spirit, live in His grace, and enter His kingdom. If those children become selfish, indolent, or corrupt, they eventually stew in their own sin. As God warned the Israelites:

"Be careful that you don't forget the LORD your God by failing to keep His command—the ordinances and statutes—I am giving

you today. When you eat and are full, and build beautiful houses to live in, and your herds and flocks grow large, and your silver and gold multiply, and everything else you have increases, [be careful] that your heart doesn't become proud and you forget the LORD your God who brought you out of the land of Egypt, out of the place of slavery" (Deut. 8:7-18, CSB).

It is true that God's kingdom will never end and that it is advancing into the far reaches of the world. But, many cultures that once embraced the values of Christianity, have turned away from the Word of God as the cornerstone of their civilization. When this happens—when people forget to love God and follow after the false gods of selfish desire—they fall from His blessing. Those familiar with the Word of God know that at the end of human history there is great news. In the meantime, we will face trials and tribulations as Christian civilization ebbs and flows to all areas of the globe.

Yet, in the midst of such cultural collapse, it is important to remember that God has called His people to go on His adventure into the entire world. He has called them to preach the good news that will redirect the tidal wave of conflicting cultures. His people constitute His Body, the Church, which has braved paganism and persecution to build hospitals, schools, orphanages, and loving homes that have civilized societies. The Church is here for such a time as this.

In Kiev, the church where I preached conducts street ministries to reach the unsaved, youth ministries to rescue the rebellious, and schools to lead the children out of darkness. Other ministries at the church reach orphans and vagrants and bring the good news to performing artists. This is the grand old story of Christian faith. In the midst of cacophony, the people of God proclaim good news and restore lost souls. Where the gospel takes root, faith and peace replace animosity. Where God's grace is lifted up, war-torn lands become green pastures where children and families can flourish.

To quote from a paper titled "Ethics in Communications" from the Pontifical Council for Social Communications, "Viewed in the light of faith, the history of human communication can be seen as a long journey from Babel, site and symbol of communication's collapse (cf. Gen. 11:4-8), to Pentecost and the gift of tongues (cf. Acts 2:5-11)—communication restored by the power of the Spirit sent by the Son. Sent forth into the world to announce the good news (cf. Matt 28:19-20; Mark 16:15), the Church has the mission of proclaiming the Gospel until the end of time. Today, she knows, that requires using media."[12]

ENOUGH ALREADY!

For a few days, my e-mail box was deluged by reviews from so-called evangelical Christian sources touting a New Age occult movie called *Conversations with God*. This movie was produced and directed by a man named Stephen Simon, who is a relentless proponent of New Age movies through his organization called the Spiritual Cinema Circle. What is strange is that this movie (to which Movieguide® gave only one star and a minus four) has received much praise from the reviewers of other evangelical movie sites. These reviews raise the question: Has the Evangelical Church gone the way of God's frozen chosen mainline denominations?

When I was in a mainline seminary in New York in the mid 1970s, the ecumenical Thursday night service was led by Hilda the White Witch, who was introduced by the bishop of New York. The Indian faker Sri Chinmoy, who claimed to be able to levitate, gave the Easter service, and the Lucifer Trust established their headquarters at the Cathedral of St. John the Divine.

Most of the frozen chosen were oblivious to this occult takeover of the mainline churches. Those with a modicum of faith came to realize 25 years later (and too late) that these denominations were dead. They began to start splinter groups, which are now reviving the biblical faith.

The sea of e-mails I receive touting Luciferian movies such as *Conversations with God* is a heartbreaking déjà vu indicating that the Evangelical Church is turning into the Church of "do what you want" of Aleister Crowley. Like Telemachus, all we can say is, "Stop! And, wake up to the Good News and to the deliverance that only comes through Jesus Christ and His holy Word written."

WHAT CAN WE DO?

One of the primary building blocks of the culture, the mass media, is a tool of communication, entertainment, and art. Although anyone may misuse a tool, most people involved in the mass media as creators, regulators, and consumers are conscientious individuals who want to do the right thing, as they understand it. However, those who make up these groups often forget that their mass media choices have ethical weight and are subject to moral evaluation. Therefore, to make the right entertainment choices, they need to develop discernment and understanding, especially in light of all the studies indicating the extremely negative effects of the mass media of entertainment, especially on children and teenagers.

Even many of the most astute Christians, however, have become desensitized to cultural degradation. Many do not understand the consequences of different worldviews. They also are ignorant of the persuasive power of the mass media of entertainment, which creates the culture in which we live and move. Consequently, they do not know how to develop the discernment, knowledge, understanding, and wisdom to be more than conquerors within the cultural turbulence created by all the forms of mass media. The good news is that there are effective ways for us and our families to learn how to be culture-wise and media-wise.

FIVE PILLARS OF MEDIA WISDOM

As the director of the TV Center at City University of New York, I helped develop some of the first media literacy courses in the late 1970s. Since then, years of research have produced a very clear understanding of the best way to teach media literacy. Specifically, there are five pillars of media wisdom that will help build the culture-wise family.

Pillar 1

Understand the influence of the media on your children. In the wake of the Columbine High School massacre, CBS president Leslie Moonves put it quite bluntly: "Anyone who thinks the media has nothing to do with this is an idiot."[13] The major medical associations have concluded that there is absolutely no doubt that those who are heavy viewers of violence demonstrate increased acceptance of aggressive attitudes and aggressive behavior. Of course, media is only one part of the problem—a problem that could be summed up with the sage biblical injunction, *"Do not be misled: 'Bad company corrupts good character'"* (1 Cor. 15:33). As the results of thousands of studies on youth violence prove, watching media violence causes violence among children. Bad company corrupts good character— whether that bad company is gangs, peer pressure, or violent television programs.

Pillar 2

Ascertain your children's susceptibility at each stage of cognitive development. Not only do children see the media differently at each stage of development, but also different children are susceptible to different stimuli. As the research of the National Institute of Mental Health revealed many years ago, some children want to copy media violence, some are susceptible to other media influences, some become afraid, and many become desensitized. Just as an alcoholic would be inordinately tempted by a beer commercial, so certain types of media may tempt or influence your child at his or her specific stage of development.

Pillar 3

Teach your children how the media communicates its message. Just as children spend the first 14 years of their lives learning grammar with respect to the written word, they also need to be taught the grammar of 21st century mass media so that they can think critically about the messages being programmed for them.

Pillar 4

Help your children know the fundamentals of Christian faith. Children need to be taught the fundamentals of Christian faith so that they can apply their beliefs and moral values to the culture and to the mass media of entertainment. Of course, parents typically have an easier time than teachers with this pillar because they can freely discuss their personal beliefs. Yet even so, it is interesting to note that cultural and media literacy and values education are two of the fastest-growing areas in the academic community—a trend most likely due to the fact that educators are beginning to realize that something is amiss.

Pillar 5

Help your children learn how to ask the right questions. When children know the right questions to ask, they can arrive at the right answers to the problems presented by the mass media of entertainment. For instance, if the hero in the movie your child is watching wins by murdering and mutilating his victims, will your children be able to question this hero's behavior, no matter how likable that character may be?

EDUCATING THE HEART

Theodore Roosevelt said that if we educate a person's mind but not his heart, we create an educated barbarian. Cultural and media wisdom involves educating the hearts of children and teenagers so that they will make the right decisions throughout their lives.

The truth of the secure hope available only in Jesus Christ is great news that needs to be shouted from the housetops. The people of God have a wonderful opportunity to manifest His grace. However, we first need to ascertain the state of cultural affairs. The work of shaping our culture requires God's wisdom to use the right tools so that He will be glorified.

One day more than 70 years ago, two literary giants in England stood talking about language, stories and religion.

In the middle of the conversation, the taller gentleman blurted to his slightly balding companion, "Here's my point: Just as a word is an invention about an object or an idea, so a story can be an invention about Truth."

"I've loved stories since I was a boy," the other man admitted. "Especially stories about heroism and sacrifice, death and resurrection.... But, when it comes to Christianity . . . well, that's another matter. I simply don't understand how the life and death of Someone Else (whoever he was) 2000 years ago can help me here and now."

The first man earnestly replied, "But don't you see, Jack? The Christian story is the greatest story of them all. Because it's the Real Story. The historical event that fulfills the tales and shows us what they mean."

About a week later, Jack—also known as C. S. Lewis, the author of the classic books MERE CHRISTIANITY and THE CHRONICLES OF NARNIA (among many other works) -- announced his conversion to Christianity to a friend. Lewis attributed much of his decision to his conversation with J. R. R. Tolkien.

Of course, Tolkien is the author of one of the greatest books of the 20th century, THE LORD OF THE RINGS, which has been transformed into a magnificent movie trilogy by director Peter Jackson. Although Tolkien, a Roman Catholic, didn't always see eye to eye with Lewis, who was more inclined toward Protestantism, they both understood the truth of the Ultimate Story.

STORYTELLING AND MYTHMAKING

As Tolkien and Lewis said so long ago, stories matter deeply. They connect us to our personal history and to the history of all time and culture. Human beings are meaning seekers and meaning makers. We strive to connect ourselves to our experiences and the experiences of others. We are addicted to those "aha!" moments in our lives when we see meaning, purpose, and significance.

Stories help us do this. They bring us laughter, tears, and joy. They stimulate our minds and stir our imaginations. Stories help us escape our daily lives for a while and visit different times, places, and people. They can arouse our compassion and empathy, spur us toward truth and love, or sometimes even incite us toward hatred or violence.

Different kinds of stories satisfy different needs. For example, a comedy evokes a different response from us than a tragedy. A hard news story on page one affects us differently than a human interest story in the magazine section or a celebrity profile next to the movie or television listings. While different kinds of stories satisfy different needs, many stories share common themes, settings, character types, situations, and other recurrent archetypal patterns. They may even possess a timeless universal quality.

Many stories focus on one individual, a heroic figure who overcomes many trials and tribulations to defeat evil or to attain a valuable goal. We identify with such heroes because we recognize that we are each on our own journey or quest. How a hero's journey informs and illuminates our own journey is significant. We look for answers in stories.

However, every story has a worldview, a way of viewing reality, truth, the universe, the human condition, and the supernatural world. Looking carefully at a story, we can examine the motifs, meanings, values, and principles that it suggests. For example, a story can have a redemptive Christian worldview that shows people their need for salvation through a personal faith in the Gospel of Jesus Christ, or it can have a secular humanist worldview that explicitly or implicitly attacks Christianity. By examining a story's worldview, we can determine the cultural ideals and the moral, philosophical, social, psychological, spiritual, and aesthetic messages that the story conveys, as well as determine the emotions the story evokes.

Movies and television programs are the storytelling media of our age!

LEARNING FROM HISTORY

Part of the reason for the breakdown of morality in movies and television today and in the culture at large, and the resulting society breakdown, is that people of faith retreated from being salt and light in the culture.

From 1933 to 1966, Christians were one of the predominant forces in Hollywood. During that period, the Roman Catholic Legion of Decency and the Protestant Film Commission (which started several years after the Legion of Decency) read every script to ensure that movies represented the largest possible audience by adhering to high standards of decency. As a result, *Mr. Smith* [went] *to Washington, It* [was] *A Wonderful Life,* and *The Bells of St. Mary's* rang out across the land!

It took 10 years and God's grace acting through three dedicated Christian men to position God's people to be such a powerful moral influence on Hollywood. As the videotape *Hollywood Uncensored* all too clearly demonstrates, prior to the involvement of these Christian men in 1933, American movies were morally bankrupt—full of nudity, perversity and violence. From 1922 to 1933, church-going men and women tried everything, including censorship boards, to influence Hollywood to make wholesome entertainment. Nothing succeeded until Christians volunteered to work alongside the Hollywood studios to help them reach the largest possible audience.

When the Protestant Film Office closed its advocacy offices in Hollywood in 1966 (in spite of many pleas to stay by the top Hollywood filmmakers), not only did it open the floodgates to violence (*The Wild Bunch*), sex and Satanism (*Rosemary's Baby*), and perverse anti-religious bigotry (*Midnight Cowboy*), it also caused a severe drop in movie attendance from 44 million tickets sold per week to about 20 million.

PREPARING TO REDEEM THE MASS MEDIA OF ENTERTAINMENT

In 1946, at the height of the Golden Age of Hollywood inspired by the Protestant Film Office and the Catholic Legion of Decency, I was born to Theodore Baehr (whose stage name was Robert "Tex" Allen) and Evelyn Peirce, both successful stage, screen, and television actors. Growing up in New York, I followed in my parents' footsteps, performing in commercials, movies, television, and stage.

It wasn't until 1975 that my life turned. While I was financing independent movies for Canon Films, a friend suggested that I read the Bible, which changed my perspective both professionally and personally.

Filled with the Holy Spirit through my newfound faith in Jesus Christ, I decided to attend seminary at the Institute of Theology and received a Doctor of Humanities (HHD) degree from Belhaven College. To pay for my seminary, I accepted a position as the Director of the Television Center at the City University of New York and started the Good News Communications ministry in 1978.

In 1983, the great movie producer Ken Wales (*The Pink Panther* and *Christy*) introduced me to George Heimrich and George's work at the now-defunct Protestant Film Office. Inspired by George Heimrich and George's beloved wife Lucille, I began contacting prominent members of the entertainment industry, and in 1985, formed the Christian Film & Television Commission™ ministry and MOVIEGUIDE®: A Family Guide to Movies and Entertainment. Heimrich donated his Protestant Film Office files to the ministry, where they now reside. The ministry uses the same vision for positive change in those files to redeem the values of the mass media of entertainment according to biblical principles by influencing key entertainment executives to adopt higher standards and by informing and equipping the public, especially parents with children and families.

As a result of conversations with Sir John Templeton beginning in 1988, the Christian Film & Television Commission™ ministry initiated the Annual MOVIEGUIDE® Faith & Values Awards Gala and Report to the Entertainment Industry in 1992 in Los Angeles. The Gala, which now also features the prestigious John Templeton Foundation $50,000 Epiphany Prizes for Inspiring Movies

& TV, the Templeton Foundation $25,000 Kairos Prize for Spiritually Uplifting Screenplays by New Screenwriters, the MOVIEGUIDE® awards for the top 10 family movies and the top 10 mature audience movies of the preceding year, and the Grace Award for Inspiring Performances in Movies & TV, seeks to acknowledge those movies, TV programs and actors truly deserving of praise, and those persons responsible for bringing them to the screen.

To add glamour to the event, actors and actresses are invited to emcee and be presenters of the awards. Music and entertainment are also added to make it a memorable event. We also hand out Bibles and other redemptive materials to carry out our mission to reach Hollywood for Christ.

Within the context of an elegant affair, I present MOVIEGUIDE®'s "Report to the Entertainment Industry." Through careful analysis of box office figures and MOVIEGUIDE® criteria on all the major movies released (nearly 300 a year) by the six studios controlling the industry, I give valuable and unique information to the highest-level Hollywood leaders through a high-impact presentation. Thus, the purpose of the Gala and the Report is:

- To encourage filmmakers to continue to make movies with moral and spiritually uplifting values;

- To share the concerns of the majority of the American public in regards to the negative influences of today's movies; and,

- To present an in-depth study of the annual movie box office and not only dispel myths that extreme sex, violence and nudity sells, but also to show that family movies and movies with morally uplifting, Christian values and positive Christian content make the most money by far.

Many studio executives and entertainers are getting the message. More good movies are being made each year. Hollywood is being redeemed.

Furthermore, the Report to the Entertainment Industry provides the analytical tools to make great, successful movies and entertainment, so it is the basis for the HOW TO SUCCEED IN HOLLYWOOD (WITHOUT LOSING YOUR SOUL) courses.

GOOD NEWS—REDEEMING THE ENTERTAINMENT INDUSTRY

In the 30 years since meeting George Heimrich, we have implemented many efforts to regain the influence in Hollywood that Christians once had. To God's glory, many studio executives and entertainers are getting the message. More good movies are being made each year. Hollywood is being redeemed. Every major studio now has a Christian, faith-based film division, and several studios are doing major movies with strong Christian content. In fact, the number of movies being produced with strong, explicit Christian content or values has increased by 2,900 percent since 1985!

This doesn't mean, of course, that the studios are not doing bad movies anymore, but it does mean there are fewer and fewer bad movies, and an increasing number of good ones. It's our prayer that the movie industry will make more and more commendable movies and remove all offensive elements from them.

Why am I saying these things? I say them for this simple reason: Hollywood can be redeemed and its negative influence on our culture reversed! It is critical that people of faith and values become the best communicators through the mass media of entertainment. The New Testament uses five Greek words that we translate as preaching in English. The most common word is "kerysso," which Jesus uses 63 percent of the time. It means to go into the marketplace to proclaim or herald the good news of the Gospel, and this includes in movies and television.

Hollywood already holds the world as a captive audience. As God uses people like you and me to redeem this international culture-shaper, His kingdom will influence the nations more and more for His glory, reaching many with the good news of Jesus Christ, and leading them to believe in His name. You can help redeem the mass media of entertainment. You can tell the stories God has laid on your heart. And you can pray for and support other godly storytellers.

ENDNOTES

1. See "Joint Statement on the Impact of Entertainment Violence on Children," Congressional Public Health Summit, July 26, 2000.
2. See pages 87-110 of *The Media-Wise Family* by Dr. Ted Baehr, Chariot Victor Publishing, 1998.
3. Press release dated 03/23/01 by the National Cancer Institute.
4. Jeffrey G. Johnson, Patricia Cohen, Elizabeth M. Smailes, Stephanie Kasen, and Judith S. Brook, "Television Viewing and Aggressive Behavior During Adolescence and Adulthood," *Science*, Vol. 295, No. 5567, 29 Mar. 2002, pp. 2468-2471.
5. Associated Press and *Seattle Times*, 09/08/04.
6. Reuters, 04/03/06.
7. Parents Television Council, 2006; *Los Angeles Times*, 11/10/05; and, Associated Press, 07/27/05.

8. "Report on the Global AIDS Epidemic 2004," UNAIDS, 2004, no. 52.

9. Michael Specter, "Traffickers' New Cargo: Naïve Slavic Women," *The New York Times*, January 11, 1998.

10. Dr. Ken Boa and Bill Ibsen, *The Decline of Nations*. Atlanta, GA: Reflections Ministries, 2005.

11. Ibid.

12. Pontifical Council for Social Communications, Vatican City, June 4, 2000, World Communications Day (cf. Vatican Council II, Inter Mirifica, 3; Pope Paul VI, Evangelii Nuntiandi, 45; Pope John Paul II, Redemptoris Missio, 37; Pontifical Council for Social Communications, Communio et Progressio, 126-134, Aetatis Novae, 11.

13. Leslie Moonves interview, Associated Press, May 19, 1999.

REFERENCES

- Ted Baehr & Pat Boone, *The Culture-Wise Family*. Ventura, CA: Regal Books, 2012.

- Ted Baehr, *How to Succeed in Hollywood (Without Losing Your Soul)*. Washington, DC: WorldNetDaily/WND Books, 2011.

- Ted Baehr, *So You Want To Be in Pictures?* Nashville, TN: Broadman & Holman, 2005.

- Ted Baehr, *The Media-Wise Family*. Colorado Springs, CO: Chariot Victor Publishing, 1998.

- Neal Gabler, *An Empire Of Their Own*. New York: Crown, 1988.

- Lajos Egri, *The Art of Dramatic Writing: Its Basis in the Creative Interpretation of Human Motives*. New York: Simon and Schuster, 1960.

- David Lowenthal, *No Liberty for License: The Forgotten Logic of the First Amendment*. Dallas: Spence Publishing Company, 1997.

- H. Richard Niebuhr, *Christ And Culture*. London: Faber and Faber, Ltd, 1952.

- Tom Snyder, *Myth Conceptions: Joseph Campbell and the New Age*. Ada, MI: Baker Books, 1995.

- Jack Vizzard, *See No Evil*. New York: Simon & Schuster, 1970.

ABOUT THE AUTHOR

Dr. Ted Baehr is founder and president of Movieguide®: A Family Guide to Movies, Entertainment and Culture (www.movieguide.org) and the Christian Film & Television Commission®, a Christian advocacy group in Hollywood. He is the co-author of *The Culture-Wise Family* with legendary entertainer Pat Boone. He is also Chairman of the Advisory Board of the Christian Institute for the Study of Media, at the Center for the Arts, Religion and Education (CARE), at the Graduate Theological Union (GTU) at the University of California at Berkeley.

He has spent the majority of his life in the film and entertainment business. After studying abroad at the University of Munich, Germany; Cambridge University, England; and Bordeaux and Toulouse Universities in France, Dr. Baehr graduated with high distinction in Comparative Literature and as a Rufus Choate Scholar from Dartmouth College. He then received his Juris Doctor degree from New York University School of Law, where he served as editor. He attended seminary at the Institute of Theology and received an honorary Doctor of Humanities (HHD) degree from Belhaven College.

For more information on protecting your children from the influence of the mass media of entertainment by teaching them how to be media-wise, read Dr. Ted Baehr & Pat Boone's new book: *The Culture-Wise Family*. This book is available at most bookstores, on Amazon.com and at www.movieguide.org, or by calling 1-800-899-6684. To learn more, visit his website at www.movieguide.org, or contact Dr. Baehr at MOVIEGUIDE®, 1151 Avenida Acaso, Camarillo, CA 93012, or by phone 805-383-2000.

CHAPTER SEVENTY-FOUR

THE OMNIPOTENT GOD (& THE IMPOTENT CHURCH?)

DR. ERIK A. KUDLIS

It appears there has been adopted an updated and modernized version of the most recited prayer in human history, the "Our Father..." (Lord's Prayer), newly revised by much of the Church in an effort to be "relevant" and "inoffensive." Here is a copy of it, as updated from the original in Matt. 6:9-13 (author's revision/parody):

> "Figurehead God, which art in heaven,
>
> We acknowledge Thy name,
>
> Thy kingdom come,
>
> Thy will be done,
>
> On earth as it is in heaven,
>
> Except for the following:
>
> In our schools,
>
> In our governance,
>
> In our voting,

In our view of sanctity of life,

In our economics,

In our system of jurisprudence,

In our sanctity and definition of marriage,

In our morality,

In our courts and in our laws,

In any other areas we may choose ...

Give us this day, our daily bread, but if you don't the government will, so don't concern yourself with this minor detail anymore,

And forgive us our debts, because our creditors might not,

As we forgive our debtors, especially if they are in the big banking system, and are especially needy and deserving of rescue and bonuses in these times.

And do not lead us into temptation, because we have found our way there ourselves,

But deliver us from the evil one if he exists,

For Thine is the kingdom and power, and the glory somewhere, for we have our own kingdom, power, and glory here. Aperson and aperson."

In the original Our Father prayer Jesus modeled for His disciples, *"Thy will be done on earth, as it is in heaven"* meant something very specific. It was the assignment and call to bring heaven's culture to earth, not earth's culture to heaven. To bring heaven's culture to earth, meant to influence and impact, in a meaningful way, the culture of earth with heaven's culture.

Jesus made an incredible statement in Matt. 28:18-20, which is otherwise known as "The Great Commission."

"All authority has been given to me in heaven and on earth. Go therefore and make disciples of all the nations, baptizing them in the name of the Father, and of the Son, and of the Holy Spirit, teaching them to observe all things that I have commanded you; and lo, I am with you always, even to the end of the age."

Because all authority has been given to Him, Christians are instructed to be "enforcers or implementers" of His authority, i.e. making (by moral force, by training, educating, and modeling) disciples of all nations. This means having an impact so as to train, as a disciple is one who is taught. Jesus, Himself, tells us who His disciples are in John 10:31,32: *"If you abide in My word (My culture, my principles and precepts for living), you are my disciples indeed."*

This is bringing heaven's culture into the earth in a real and meaningful way, a way that invades and influences all aspects of society, the "seven mountains" so to speak, as elaborated on by visionaries like Bill Bright, Loren Cunningham, Francis Schaeffer, Lance Wallnau, and others; these "Seven Mountains" include government, education, media, arts and entertainment, religion, family, and business. Obviously, the more discipled individuals there are in any of these mountains, the more the power and influence of heaven will manifest in any particular sphere.

Most interesting, however, is the phrasing of the Great Commission, which indicates the making disciples "of" all nations, not "in" all nations. Nations are meant to be discipled, i.e., taught, instructed, and made to conform to the Master Teacher, in this case, the Lord Himself. These nations are brought into submission to Christ's authority, taught and trained to be Christian nations in principle, demonstrating Christian behaviors. We should perhaps clarify, that the United States was founded by Christians, for the purpose of promoting life, liberty, and the pursuit of happiness, i.e., the right to property. It has a Christian heritage and foundation, but should have no "state" religion; rather, it should be discipled by operating under the principles and the liberties given by the Creator.

What is the byproduct or end result of this discipling of the nations? It is teaching them to observe all which God has commanded. It is in their observation and heeding of these commandments, precepts, principles, that discipleship is demonstrated. It is the increase and release of the authority Christ has been given in heaven, manifested on earth in the nation or nations, with the resulting blessings of increased liberty and prosperity.

If "thou shalt not steal" and "thou shalt not kill" were truly the law of the land, and the people of the nation were discipled to walk in it, we would not need large police forces, huge prisons, huge insurance policies, etc. Godliness is profitable for any person, any city, any state, any country, any culture. Monies saved if these necessary services were minimal, could be invested and put into productive use, goods, and services, so standards of living could increase, and the human condition improved.

For Christians, God's culture, Heaven's culture, SHOULD supercede and take precedence over all earthly, man-made cultures.

Paul writes in Gal 3:27-28, *"For as many as of you as were baptized into Christ have put on Christ. There is neither Jew nor*

Greek, there is neither slave nor free, there is neither male nor female; for you are all one in Christ Jesus."

For those Christians who have NOT put on Christ, and have NOT been discipled by, or have NOT submitted to the authority of His Word, His precepts, and His principles, then cultural and other factors/differences that affect perception and govern actions, will still exist: male/female, Jew/Greek (nationality), black/white (racial differences), rich/poor, etc. Inevitably and sadly, these qualities show up in the voting booth.

In the kingdom and culture of heaven, all of these – race, sex, nationality, social status, and economic status – should be relatively inconsequential, having little impact on behavior or belief, as all individuals are equal in God's family, one and the same before God, submitted to, and operating in, His culture, in His assignment for their life. Only Christianity offers true deliverance from racism, sexism, and other social prejudices. Only Christianity can offer this, because it changes the innately sinful nature of man, and does not simply "band-aid" or legislate over man's nature to cover the wound.

WHAT IS MEANT BY "THE CHURCH?"

God only has one church, though men's thinking may differentiate by denomination or other separating factor, thereby saying in effect, *"I am of Paul, I am of Cephas (Peter),"* as we are specifically instructed not to do. These differences are only in the mind of man, not of God, and are described as carnal, meaning earthly, sensual, and devilish.

Christ does not have multiple churches, just one. He only has one bride, and is not a polygamist. In heaven, it's true there will be multitudes of every tribe, tongue, color, kindred. The church will be like a bride, not a cornucopia of concubines. None of the differences that can seem so important to us are necessarily of significance in the culture of heaven, and none of these of themselves will include or exclude anyone from experiencing the culture and eternity of heaven.

Rev. 5:9b-10 among other verses (7:9-17), summarizes the ultimate fulfillment of the Great Commission. *"You were slain, and have redeemed us to God by Your blood, out of every tribe and tongue and people and nation, and have made us kings and priests to our God; and we shall reign on the earth."* This is the Great Commission in its intent, ultimately fulfilled, as demonstrated by the Church reigning over the nations on the earth.

Many individuals in the United States at this time are suffering the consequences of fiscal and governmental irresponsibility. People cannot find jobs. Unemployment is at all-time highs, despite the "massaged" numbers to make the dire situation appear less serious than it actually is. The federal government is at war with many state governments. States and cities are declaring bankruptcy and devolving into lawlessness, something never even remotely thought possible just a few years ago.

Some say we are in a double dip recession; others say we are in a bubble yet to pop, with this period only being the prelude of worse to come, even though short bursts of bright times in the economy can temporarily give the impression that all is well and getting better.

Many blame Wall Street and the big banks which are too big to fail. Many blame politicians. Others blame judges or the U.S. Congress. Many point to government policies that facilitated the playing out of our current circumstances, and I happen to believe government policies were and are, by and large, directly related to the woes currently being experienced by the American populace.

While all of these may have been complicit players in the causality of today's woes, and may share some blame, the truth is none of them are ultimately to blame.

If it is true that many of the present woes are a result from previous and present U.S. governmental policy, it is of utmost importance to remember that the politicians involved were elected, and administrators/judges/agency heads, appointed by those elected. They were elected by voters. The majority of voters in America claim to be, or identify themselves, as Christians. Apparently they did not obey the Great Commission, have never heard of the Great Commission, or do not know, or care to know, how to enact the Great Commission, and are not disciples themselves.

If, on the other hand, all voters who identified themselves as Christians, had the intent to disciple this nation, many of the political elite responsible for causing or contributing to the nation's demise, would never have been elected.

No pro abortionist would have had a chance. No one who favored the redefining of marriage to be anything other than one man and one woman, the scriptural standard, would have dared to run for office. No one who favored increasing government debt would have been elected. No one who played the "race card," preying upon old wounds, and unforgiveness, would have had a chance for election, as their motives and methods would stand in sharp contrast to the true culture of heaven, the principles of the Kingdom of God which foster reconciliation, healing, forgiveness, peace, righteousness, joy.

THE IMPOTENT CHURCH

The root causality of our woes in fact, lies at the feet of what I would call the "impotent" church, a church that has failed to impregnate our culture and society with the seed of heaven.

*"You are the salt of the earth; but **if the salt loses its savor,** how then shall it be seasoned: It is then **good for nothing, but to be thrown out and trampled underfoot by men"** (Matt. 5:13, author's emphasis).*

Salt that has lost its savor, has lost its characteristic constituent. Thrown out means removed from use, disposed of, discarded, as being of no further practical use, value, or benefit. Trampled means walked over, walked upon, or treated as insignificant, subdued and under forced submission, as in "the devil is under our feet." Unfortunately, it seems he is over our heads more than under our feet in current political reality.

Catholic parochial (elementary) schools, for example, have been closing on a national basis, withering under mandates for teaching curricula, the increasing costs for private education, competition from charter schools, and the effects of difficult financial times. In a recent year alone, nearly 180 Catholic Schools closed, losing 34,000 pupils. In Los Angeles, enrollment has dropped by 2,000 per year for nearly 10 straight years.

The same parents that pay taxes for others' children to attend public schools are forced to find increasing funds for the chance at a private Catholic or Christian education for their children. The oft-proposed school voucher system would have allowed not just Catholic parents to send their children to a private learning environment, but would at the same time have allowed parents from poor neighborhoods at least the option of being able to send their children to a school of their choice, without having their children locked into underperforming schools that might be in their own neighborhood.

Educational unions, the NEA, the Cabinet-level Department of Education, and liberal politicians, have been successful at maintaining the educational monopoly currently in place, as a free market competitive system is nothing they can control...and therefore do not want. Ironically, and tragically, the very same families who would often most benefit from vouchers, routinely and statistically by a wide margin, vote for the very same candidates and parties that crush the opportunity their children might have had.

And, while the Catholic schools may have been good at teaching their students, they obviously failed in teaching parents to exert political influence. If Catholic families alone became politically active, vouchers could have been political reality today. Freedom to choose would have liberated the educational system, and the shackles of the educational monopoly been broken.

Beyond this one example, however, and more to the point of this chapter, is the question: "How is it that a miniscule percentage of the population can drive the entire national agenda on an issue, while the silent Christian majority, hides in its church buildings, blessing itself, talking prosperity, the forgiveness of sins, God's goodness and righteousness, yet remaining impotent or ineffective in establishing any of the authority Christ spoke of in a real and meaningful way?" Name just one of the Seven Mountains that today demonstrates the discipleship and dominion called for in the Great Commission!

To my way of thinking, the events cited herein are simply illustrations of the saltless church, "good for nothing except to be trampled under the foot of men," that Christ spoke about. The increasingly impotent church in the U.S. has lost its savor.

The church appears to be in full retreat, having been thrown out of the school system, and with efforts underway to remove Christian influences from every facet of American life, under the manufactured theory of separation of church and state. Humanism, i.e., man's wisdom replacing God's, has like a plague been infecting every vestige of American life. The secular humanists love it, but the church and the masses are baffled, like sheep without a shepherd, for the most part silently enduring the consequences... the high cost of low living, with worse yet to come.

This is not to say the church has totally failed in all things. But, like the regional churches in the book of Revelation, the Holy Spirit is saying, *"Nevertheless I have this against you..."*

Adam and Eve were the first people in the Bible to lose their dominion. As we look at the situation, we might ask, "Whose fault was it they failed in their assignment to have dominion in the garden? Was it the devil's fault for tempting them?"

It was true that the devil temped and bewitched them with lies, and half-truths, but it was their responsibility to govern within God's commands.

If someone is given a garden to manage, and it becomes overgrown with weeds, one cannot blame the weeds. We blame those who should be the managers of the garden. It is the manager's or caretaker's failure and irresponsibility or incompetence that made room for, allowed, and permitted the growth and eventual dominance of the weeds.

How in the United States can the Church exercise its dominion? While it might not be the same in other countries, or in other parts of the world, here we are able to exercise our dominion in the voting booth. By openly supporting and voting into office "good gardeners" that can create the garden we want to have, and God wants to have, we can set and redirect our garden, or our country's future.

Adam and Eve yielded dominion to the devil, and the church in the United States has done the same. Adam and Eve were driven out of the garden, and the Church has been driven out of schools, law and the courts, arts and entertainment, and government policy. Efforts are openly and blatantly underway to remove Christianity from all aspects of American life, only humoring the church as a figurehead of sorts to save some face. Our culture now is embracing the scriptural form of godliness, but denying the authority and power thereof over real life events.

Never before has there been a greater need for repentance in the corporate church for its lack of stewardship over the precious heritage given by our founding fathers; hence, the urgency of this book, and others like it, which are now calling for a partnering with the apostolic. The apostolic and prophetic are being raised up to correct and instruct the church, leading it from repentance to restoration, much like a prodigal son wallowing in a pig pen of what life never needed to be, to a restoration of influence and dominion in the Seven Mountains of Culture.

AUTHORITY IS KEY

While others may disagree, I believe the foremost, and perhaps easiest mountain in which to regain influence, is the sphere of government. I believe it is foremost, because in most cases it impacts, influences, and has dominion over all of the others. One will never repair the sphere of education, without first dealing with the government.

The church corporate must awaken to the power it has, and choose to use it. Jesus said to Peter, *"...And I say to you that you are Peter, and on this rock I will build my church, and the gates of Hades shall not prevail against it. And I will give you the keys of the kingdom of heaven, and whatever you bind on earth will be bound in heaven, and whatever you loose on earth will be loosed in heaven"* (Matt. 16:7-19).

Here Jesus describes the passing on of His authority as revealed to Peter, that He Jesus is the Christ, the Son of the living God, endowed with God's very own authority, as again declared in the Great Commission, that power which will be passed on to disciples present and future for the building of Christ's church.

Keys denote authority. Keys lock or open doors. Keys either permit passage by opening, or deny passage by locking. As the church, we, given the opportunity we have here in the United States, have possession of Christ's authority, to either permit or deny what transpires in our society. Binding or loosing, in essence, has to do with permitting or forbidding.

This authority, when properly administered, renders hell's best efforts to resist both helpless and ineffective. However, having authority and using it are two different things. One can have authority and fail to use it. Sometimes the enemy is "permitted" to do something, by our failing to "forbid" it. This is a sin of omission rather than a sin of commission.

In the very first prophecy given to the young child and future prophetic leader of the ancient Israel nation, Samuel, the Lord declared he would strip away the authority and destiny of Eli and his legacy, as his sons made themselves vile, and he (Eli) did not restrain them (1 Sam. 3). His failure to restrain his sons corrupted and weakened not only the "church" (ecclesia) as God's people at that time, but the nation (ethnos) itself. He failed to use the authority God had given him for his sons and the nation, with the gravest of consequences.

In much the same way, Adam, as previously discussed, failed to walk in his dominion and authority in the Garden of Eden, and was driven out into a grievous existence. And as mentioned before, blatant, open, and vicious efforts have been loosed in the United States to drive out and remove the influence and dominion of the church from its rightful place of possession and occupation.

What has the church loosed or permitted, by its inaction, or its failure to walk in its authority, and its failure to restrain evil? Rampant spirits of homosexuality, pornography, violence, crime, the breakdown of the family, lawlessness, covetousness, corruption, and a seemingly endless host of other evils have emerged, to the point where not only the church, but society as a whole has become overwhelmed by the flood of iniquity that has been released and the consequences loosed into our nation. No one seems to know what to do to solve these social problems. Restoring righteous living seems like an impossibility. Restoring academic excellence to our schools seems like an impossibility. Restoring fiscal sanity to our government and financial integrity to our stock markets seems like an increasing impossibility.

Demonic powers can use flesh and blood for their own evil purposes, make no mistake, as Jesus told the Pharisees they were of their father the devil.

In John 13:18-30, John writes how the devil himself entered Judas Iscariot at the time and for the purpose of the betrayal of Jesus.

But how is it that demonic powers can use flesh and blood? While it is beyond the scope of this brief chapter to fully investigate and enumerate in what ways that might manifest, seeing as how entire books, and many books at that, have been written on this subject, for our purposes, it's best to keep things simple.

It is absolutely critical to understand, that whatever principles an individual, a culture, or a society believe in and adhere to, or live by, those same principles release and allow a principality to manifest and operate in the earth. Principalities are loosed to operate where principles that govern allow it to.

For example, where individuals believe abortion should be allowed, that murderous spirit is given the go ahead, or "loosed" to operate. Where individuals do not believe that taking innocent life should be allowed, that murderous spirit is then bound, restrained, not allowed to operate freely. What the president believes, and his leadership appointees to Health and Human services believe, will determine what is loosed in the land.

Not all individuals are equally of "value" in allowing demonic principalities to operate. One strategically placed individual at the top of a mountain or sphere of influence can alone do untold damage by releasing murderous demonic spirits. Herod, in his vain attempt to murder the Christ child before He could come of age, sent his troops into Ramah, slaughtering every male child under two years of age. You can only imagine the sheer brutality and horror of the event, but the gruesome and horrifying details lie buried beneath the simplicity of a few Bible verses. You can bet there was weeping and wailing in Ramah, as the impact of one strategically placed individual's decision, destroyed both children and families in an entire region.

Homosexual activists and those who would choose to redefine marriage, for example, are well aware that key individuals, properly placed, can determine the policy for the entire nation. Understanding this, they have been successful in changing the entire national policy, in the military, in the courts, in political leadership. How is it that a fringe minority, something less than one percent of the entire population, can drive social policy for the entire nation, when the 50% Christian majority seems powerless, lacking the potency to resist it? How can this be possible?

The major force for this change in national policy over the last 20 years, has not been the homosexual community alone. Rather, it has been the elected politicians, who in turn have appointed revisionist judges. The greatest tragedy has not been merely the implementation of these new "politically correct" beliefs, but the sadder truth that these politicians would not have been elected, unless supported by some of the Christian majority. The "less than 1%" has been successful in implementing its will, while the 50% church has failed and is in full defensive position, losing ground every day.

When a U.S. President appoints Cabinet-level leadership hostile to the principles of God, and czars accountable to no one, to rule over domestic territories, you can easily understand that the principles these leaders subscribe to release corresponding principalities that are then free to operate.

Leadership, on the other hand, that operates by the principles of God's Word, releases God's Spirit to operate, and establishes the authority of Christ in the land. At the same time, it binds the operation of demonic spirits that war against God's people. This is discipling a nation, teaching it to adhere to all the precepts and principles God has given us to live by and prosper.

Right now, it is easy to see, that demonic spirits are freely and actively establishing territorial dominion, and "binding" the church from operating in its beliefs and authority. The world—and our nation—are upside down, and the woes that come upon those that call evil good, and call good evil, are coming upon us all.

When small-time politicians are no longer afraid to stand up, and openly and unconstitutionally use the authority of their office to condemn and persecute anyone who dares express a personal scriptural belief, one realizes a dangerous time is at hand. It most frighteningly reveals their mindset, that the church and its beliefs are culturally irrelevant, weak, and not to be feared. Even more frightening is the possibility they are right!

Change must happen IN the church first, and THEN, it will manifest outside the church, with the church becoming an agent of change in society as Jesus designed and intended. It must and will start with repentance, and a turning from its wicked ways, wherein many of the self-identified Christians continually vote into office Herods, Ahabs, and Jezebels, and then wonder why there are serious problems, otherwise known as consequences of sin.

The Bible tells us how our land (country) can be healed in this familiar verse, 2 Chron. 7:14, *"If My people, who are called by my name shall humble themselves, and pray, and seek My face, and turn from THEIR wicked ways, then I will hear from heaven, forgive THEIR sin, and heal their land."*

CALLING OUT ELIJAH

Prophetic and apostolic agents of change will not be greeted warmly. They will be viewed by society, and often by the "religious" as troublemakers.

When Elijah came to confront Ahab, and the prophets of Baal, during the severe famine in Samaria (1 Kings 18), Ahab upon seeing Elijah said, *"Is it you, you troubler of Israel?"* To which Elijah answered correctly and accurately, *"I have not troubled Israel, but you have, and your father's house, because you have abandoned the commandments of the Lord and followed the Baals."* Then outnumbered 450 to 1, Elijah defeated and had killed the politically-entrenched prophets of Baal, which led to death threats from Jezebel.

We are living in our time of the Samarian famine, and God at the very same time is calling out His Elijahs against all odds, and against all threats.

If you've been alive for any length of time, and in the church for any length of time, you've no doubt heard numerous prophesies about the glorious end-time revival and harvest...our churches will be filled, our wallets will be filled, and it will be heaven on earth.

In my opinion, heaven on earth will not occur until Jesus comes, but the other things will come the same way they came throughout the entire Old Testament, especially the Book of Judges, when suffering became so bad, people had no choice but to come to God in repentance.

The story in Luke 15 of the prodigal son who could no longer tolerate the suffering of lack, eating shriveled corn husks in the pen with the pigs, is a New Testament example. Then, recognizing the lifestyle and heritage he had lost, he came to his senses and returned to his father's house in humility and repentance. Similarly, when the church repents of its lack of stewardship over the United States of America, and comes back to the founding father's house in repentance, these, among other things, will begin the great inflow and great outpouring that has been prophesied. Our churches need to be prepared. It's only a few years away. It is time to prepare.

With the inevitable apocalypse that will cover the earth, will come incredible opportunities for the gospel, and for wealth transfer. The perplexing times will call forth visionaries, those with answers and problem-solving skills given by the Holy Spirit....Daniels....Davids....Josephs, those who have answers when no one else does. They will not emerge necessarily from the political elite, but be relative unknowns whose only credential may be that they can hear from God. What an incredible credential....

They will be business people, perhaps small-time sheepherders in the backlands of small business, who, like David, only see opportunity when the Goliaths emerge. They will participate in the great wealth transfer, and help others to enter in as well. It will be a potential time for retaking the mountains of our culture.

It will be a time of mind-numbing tumult in the earth..... life as we have known it will be a thing of the past....it will be a time unlike any other, and we are entering it NOW.

"Is there not a cause?" David said to his brothers shortly before killing Goliath. So will be the call to repentance from the apostolic to all the church, saying, "Is there not a cause?" There has never been a greater cause or greater need for the church, and for the United States of America, as we move into the end-time harvest of souls. He that hath ears to hear, let him hear....

ABOUT THE AUTHOR

Dr. Erik A. Kudlis is president of Erik's Design Build Associates, Inc., an award-winning design and construction corporation in Connecticut. With more than 25 years of experience in men's ministry, Dr. Kudlis was commissioned as a minister to men in 2001 by Dr. Edwin Louis Cole and the Christian Men's Network. Considered a "Watchman on the Wall," Dr. Kudlis has been involved in or conducted hundreds of ministerial events nationally and internationally in nine countries. Author of *Creating A Better Life: Three Keys to Possessing Your Destiny*, the preceding content was excerpted and formatted for *Aligning With The Apostolic* from his soon to be released book, *The Omnipotent God: And His Impotent Church?* He can be reached via email at erikak@comcast.net.

CHAPTER SEVENTY-FIVE

BECOMING A VOICE IN THE STORM

MARK W. PFEIFER

AN APOSTOLIC WARNING GOES UNHEEDED

The wind had a name. The ancient maritime voyagers called it Euroclydon. It presented one of the greatest terrors of ocean travel during the time of the Romans. It was the enemy of any and all vessels sailing across the waves of the Mediterranean Sea. Like a mythical dragon casting its shadow over all who sailed its waters, the name of Euroclydon was cautiously uttered on the lips of nervous sailors when the chilly winds of autumn began to blow across the sea. Even experienced seamen dared not set sail after the month of October.

But it was a beautiful autumn morning that day on the shores of Fair Havens!

The rising sun greeted the owner of an Alexandrian ship standing on deck with his captain and a Roman centurion named Julius. As they discussed the feasibility of continuing their journey at sea they were joined by a fourth man, but he had little credibility. He was neither a military man nor an experienced sailor. He was a prisoner in their custody.

Accused of sedition against the government, he was on his way to the court of appeals in Rome to plead his case before the emperor. His name was Paul.

Paul put forth a warning to the centurion about the perils of traveling this late in the year, during the season of Euroclydon's fury, but the advice of the ship's captain prevailed over Paul's counsel. After all, they were enjoying the sunshine and soft ocean breezes of a beautiful Mediterranean morning. What could possibly go wrong? The order to set sail was given and Paul was quietly moved to the holding facility below. As well-wishers shouted a bon voyage, the ship charted a course for Rome.

Before long, Euroclydon came calling. The first hint of his presence came in the form of dark clouds circling ominously overhead. Then, his advanced winds hit the boat from sail to stern like menacing gremlins announcing the arrival of their king. Soon, Euroclydon himself came upon the scene and fell upon the small vessel with all his fury. The craft was seized by the monstrous waves like unfortunate prey caught in the paws of a playful cat. The sail was retracted, the life boat secured, cables were wrapped around the hull of the boat and the crew hunkered down, hopelessly praying that Euroclydon would spare them from a long and painful death.

At this moment God dispatched an angel right in the middle of Euroclydon's fury. He had a message to deliver to a Change Agent on that boat who was fulfilling his Kingdom assignment. Unhindered by the raging seas, the angel appeared to Paul in the dark belly of the creaking and groaning ship with a strategy from heaven. In short order, Paul ascended from his incarcerating lair with the first words of hope spoken on the vessel since Euroclydon's arrival. After a humble and well-deserved, "I-told-you-so,"

Paul became the voice of God to the centurion, the captain and the crew in the midst of the storm. He restored their lost hope by assuring them everyone onboard would be spared from death...if they obeyed his every word!

THE EMERGING VOICE

An amazing thing happened that night on the fragile North African vessel: The prisoner became the leader. Recognizing the mark of leadership and wisdom on the apostle, the centurion commanded everyone to listen to Paul's words and follow his instructions. Paul subdued and took dominion of the vessel, not through coercion and control, but by leveraging his wisdom and concern for their well-being to show the entire crew a superior plan to preserve life. He was so concerned for the people onboard that he fixed breakfast the following morning for the entire crew—all 276 of them!

This is how God wants to raise up marketplace leaders all over the earth. In every city and nation under heaven, He is preparing an army of presently unknown people to take the helm of sinking ships. Like Paul, their primary means of influence will come in presenting people with a superior model of life. Their irrefutable wisdom will solve life's most complex problems. Their genuine concern for humanity will earn respect and trust. How do the children of God garner influence in the world? They earn it during times of crisis!

Perhaps not everyone will listen when soft, southern breezes blow across life's harbor. Human nature is typically blind to possible danger when good times abound. However, when Euroclydon comes calling, God's hidden servants will snap into action and take advantage of the opportunity. In the midst of crisis, He will present a company of people to the world who will provide amazing hope and wisdom in anxious times. This is why many future leaders are largely unknown at this time. God is saving them for just the right season when their grace and wisdom will be needed in order to preserve life.

Not everyone on that boat was worthy of being saved, mind you. This was not a class of school kids going on a fieldtrip. They were, by and large, an unbelieving and ungodly group of people who did not acknowledge God. They were just like the people who live all around you and me. They were idolaters, adulterers, God-mockers and atheists. However, God loved them enough to give them Paul, who displayed such love and grace in the storm that everyone wanted to follow his orders. People took notice when Paul went to work preserving lives on that battered boat.

The same was true with Joseph in Egypt and Daniel in Babylon. They rose to prominence during times of national crisis because they knew how to use the wisdom of God to solve problems, provide solutions and answer tough questions. Even though they were surrounded by unbelievers and idolaters, God acted on their behalf and preserved life for entire nations. When God sets Change Agents in the midst of the world to "subdue" and "take dominion" of it, the heavenly strategy is to do so without the use of brute force and control. God wants to bless us so we can be a blessing to others. Influence is gained by leveraging the wisdom and compassion of God to help others and reveal His glory to a lost and fallen world.

KINGDOM LEADERS IN HIDING

I've labored the point of this story because I want you to experience that terrible Mediterranean storm. I want you to feel the fear and hopelessness on board that vessel. I want you to see the despair on the faces of the crew. Does it seem familiar?

Do you see the same thing around you today?

Do you see yourself in the midst of it?

Envision yourself like Paul, emerging from the bottom of the boat with a calm and reassuring word from God to a battered and exhausted world. Why do I want you to see this? Because this is what you and I will be doing as Kingdom leaders in days to come.

You may see your life as insignificant right now. You may feel like Paul did when he was locked away in the darkness of the ship's brig. But hold on! In times of great crisis, God will raise up people just like you whom He has equipped and trained to preserve life. Like Paul, perhaps much of your training has come in times of previous peril throughout your life. Remember, this was not Paul's first time at sea. It wasn't even the first time he had been in trouble. According to 2 Cor. 11:25, he had already been shipwrecked three times before!

God releases His servants from the most unlikely places. They are plucked from the Nile River, freed from Pharaoh's prison, pulled from the bottom of a boat, delivered from a fiery furnace and led out of the wilderness. His timing is impeccable. When people are in crisis, having given up all hope in their own abilities to survive, look for the Kingdom Leaders to arise! You may be one of those whom God is preparing behind the scenes at this very moment. Can you sense it? Do you feel like you've been hidden away in the belly of a ship, unseen and unheard, being readied for a specific task? Be patient! God is saving you for just the right time!

Little did the centurion and ship owner know they would follow the orders and owe their lives to the man they had shackled and thrown in the bottom of the boat. While they might have seen themselves as superior to the seasoned apostle in the beginning, they soon found out how much they needed him. Their future was in his hands. When the man of God took his place as the duly appointed representative of God to a needy and hungry group of people, everyone was blessed!

FIVE VOICES IN THE MIDST OF THE STORM

Like Paul, we need to take our place as God's representatives on the earth in order to extend His Kingdom rule. Make no mistake, Euroclydon is coming and God is preparing people just like you to represent Him and speak with His voice in the midst of the storm. There are five voices people need to hear in the midst of crisis. They are just as powerful today as they were when Paul uttered them 2000 years ago:

1. God's Kingdom leaders provide a voice of WISDOM: There is a supernatural wisdom that comes from God. The Bible says in Jas. 1:5, *"If any of you lacks wisdom, let him ask of God, who gives to all liberally and without reproach, and it will be given to him."* If you ask for wisdom, God will give it to you with no strings attached. Not only that, He will also give it to you

liberally! The world needs this kind of wisdom in the day of crisis.

Wisdom comes from a combination of education and experience. Education comes to you in the form of classrooms, books, mentoring, CD's, conferences, etc. Every person reading this chapter who has determined to become a kingdom leader should constantly seek and take advantage of educational opportunities. We should forever be a student. *"A wise man will hear and increase learning,"* Solomon said in Prov. 1:5.

The other component of wisdom – experience – comes from applying what you have learned to everyday life. You don't normally plan for these events; they just happen. When you face a crisis or tough decision, you can apply the education you have received in practical ways. This is how you learn to be a Change Agent. Like Paul, every experience becomes training for the next challenge. Having sailed the open seas and been shipwrecked three times, Paul had the confidences he needed in a crisis. In your experiences today, God is preparing you for greater challenges tomorrow! Don't despise this season of your life. Emulate Paul and learn all you can so you can continue to move forward in your training.

2. God's Kingdom leaders provide a voice of HOPE: Hope is necessary for motivation. Without hope for the future, there is no power for the present. When Paul emerged from the bottom of the boat, he spoke a word of hope and salvation to the entire crew. Even as they reaped the consequences for their

foolish decisions, Paul displayed hope in the midst of despair.

If you sense the desire to be a kingdom advancer in your world, hope will be one of your most powerful tools. The apostle Peter said, *"But sanctify the Lord God in your hearts, and always be ready to give a defense to everyone who asks you a reason for the hope that is in you, with meekness and fear"* (1 Pet. 3:15).

For years I was taught that the emphasis of this verse was "defense." Accordingly, I was armed with a litany of doctrinal arguments I could use against any opposing voices. What we missed was the reason why people should be attracted to us in the first place. Look at the verse again. It says that we should be ready to give a reason for our hope, not our doctrine.

Say, when was the last time someone came up to you and said, "Why are you so hopeful all the time?" Or, "Why are you so positive about everything?" Or, "Why do you always believe the best about people?" Or, "Why do you always believe good things will happen?" Or, "Why do you believe that things will always work out for the best?"

Many times?

A few times?

Sometimes?

Never?

It is the evidence of hope in a believer's life that Peter assumed people would ask about. In order to be a kingdom man or woman, you need to adopt an attitude of hope when it comes to people and situations. Hope is an acronym for Having Optimism Past Everything. It is faith applied to the future. We have an undying faith that God will have His way in all things. We believe this fact because the Bible says, *"...all things work together for good to those who love God, to those who are the called according to His purpose"* (Rom. 8:28). This is the voice that gets people's attention.

3. God's Kingdom leaders provide a voice of REVELATION: God is the Originator of all great plans and strategies. We need to know how to find God's marching orders and battle plans in the hour of need. This type of revelation carries an authority people recognize. This is what people noticed about Jesus. Matthew records their reaction to His revelation when he wrote, *"And so it was, when Jesus had ended these sayings, that the people were astonished at His teaching, for He taught them as one having authority, and not as the scribes"* (Matt. 7:28-29).

   Revelation knowledge can rest upon a businessperson, salesperson, housewife, student, executive or factory worker to change their world just as much as it does on a preacher. God is interested in using His people to bring wisdom and hope to all spheres of life. Revelation from heaven makes people sit up and take notice of you. Even unbelievers will many times respond to the authority of God when it is spoken through His children.

4. God's Kingdom leaders provide a voice of DIRECTION: The world is a confusing place. People lose their way and turn to all sorts of things to make sense

of life. They ask, "Why are my parents divorcing? Why does my dad reject me? Why am I drawn into abusive relationships? Why am I depressed? Why am I so angry? Am I really gay? Why do people hate me? Why do I want to kill myself?" Instead of being uncomfortable around such honesty and avoiding these questions, the church needs to embrace these people and offer a voice of direction for them. In order to be a Change Agent, you must not be afraid of getting your hands dirty with humanity. We must offer practical solutions to real-life problems with wisdom and love.

5. God's Kingdom leaders provide a voice of COMPASSION: The world needs to see the compassion of Christ in His church. In so many cases, the world has seen the church only as a place where holy people gather to look pretty and talk about how sinful everybody else is in the community. They see us as inwardly focused, concerned only with making money and preserving our public image. It doesn't matter that we in the church may not see ourselves that way. This is how the world often views us. This is something we need to change.

Compassion will be the best form of evangelism in days to come. Acts of compassionate outreach affect communities more than event-driven extravaganzas where religious superstars grace glittery stages in the spotlight. Trying to compete with Hollywood and Las Vegas entertainment is insanity. Most local churches can't come close to these productions; they simply don't have the necessary funds to create a level playing field. The good news is we don't have to. Compassion is free! Paul showed compassion in the midst of the storm when he displayed genuine love and concern for the crew. This is our pattern. This is our hope.

CONCLUSION

Armed with wisdom, hope, revelation, direction and compassion, God's kingdom people are being positioned by God right now to make a difference on the earth. Their influence will be gained by serving mankind rather than by coercion and control. If enough of these people come forth, over time, we can make a difference. Don't ever doubt that these five voices bring change. Indeed, they are the only things that truly bring change to the earth.

Let's join them!

ABOUT THE AUTHOR

Mark Pfeifer is founder and Senior Pastor of Open Door Christian Fellowship in Chillicothe, Ohio, a church he planted in 1991. He is also the Lead Apostle of the Soma Family of Ministries, an Apostolic Network headquartered in Chillicothe. He founded and presently oversees several schools including the Southern Ohio School of Ministry with multiple locations and the Soma Business Institute, an entrepreneurial training ground for aspiring business owners. He and his wife, Nicki, have three children, one grandchild and reside in Chillicothe, Ohio. To learn more or contact Mark, visit his websites at www.markandnicki.com, www.somafamily.com and www.opendoorohio.com.

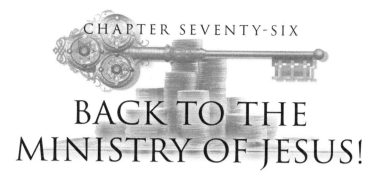

CHAPTER SEVENTY-SIX

BACK TO THE MINISTRY OF JESUS!

HENRY FALANY

The only thing that can turn this world around is a move of God. For that to happen, our part is basically two-fold. We must pray in the Spirit of 2 Chron. 7:14, and we must return to the apostolic ministry of Jesus Christ.

LIKE A BULLDOG ON A BONE!

In the spirit of Paul's heart in Phil. 3, we must re-focus on *the "knowledge of Jesus Christ our Lord, count everything else as dung, purpose to know Him and the power of His resurrection and the fellowship of His suffering; we must follow after this one thing—JESUS!—forgetting the past and everything else as we reach forth, pressing for the mark of the prize of the high calling of God in Christ Jesus!"* (author's paraphrase).

The message that the Lord has given me for the churches and all ministries as we minister around the world is this: we must get back to the basic ministry of Jesus.

It amazes me how most ministries, even "Spirit-filled" churches, are ministering much differently than Jesus did. They want Jesus' results, but they don't minister Jesus' way.

Jesus' mission statement is Luke 4:18-19:

"The Spirit of the Lord is upon me, because he hath anointed me to preach the gospel to the poor; he hath sent me to heal the brokenhearted, to preach deliverance to the captives, and recovering of sight to the blind, to set at liberty them that are bruised, To preach the acceptable year of the Lord."

In Acts 10:38, Peter gave a summary of the ministry of Jesus when he said, *"God anointed Jesus of Nazareth with the Holy Ghost and with power: who went about doing good, and healing all that were oppressed of the devil; for God was with him."*

Do you remember that Jesus said in John 14:6, *"I am the way"*? He also said in John 14:12, *"Verily, verily, I say unto you, He that believeth on me, the works that I do shall he do also; and greater works than these shall he do; because I go unto my Father."*

We must remember that Jesus isn't just the way for us to get to Heaven. His way of life and ministry is also the way we get others to Heaven. He said in John 8:12, *"I am the light of the world."* He also said in Matt. 5:14, *"Ye are the light of the world."* Then in verse 16, He said, *"Let your light so shine before men, that they may see your good works, and glorify your Father which is in heaven."*

Paul tells us in Eph. 2:20 that the church is built on the foundation of the apostles and prophets with Jesus as the chief corner stone. And Paul also tells us in 2 Cor. 12:12 that the signs of an apostle are signs, wonders, and mighty deeds.

I am convinced that we, the church, need to take a fresh look at the ministry of Jesus. I call it, "a fresh revelation of an old truth." If we are to experience the revival of the ages with souls being swept into the Kingdom, I declare to you it will only happen His way. The world must begin seeing the miracles, which is Heaven manifesting in their lives.

Now don't take me wrong when I say this, but I believe we need to do a little in-house repair before we get so excited about our outreaches. When Jesus prayed His heartfelt prayer in John chapter 17 he said, *"I'm not praying for the world, but for the ministers"* (author's paraphrase). They represent the churches and ministries that are the harvesters. That is why we must get the light (Jesus) on in the church, which is the body of Christ.

The focus of Jesus' ministry as laid out in Matt. 4:23 was preaching, teaching, and healing. His command to us in Matt. 10 was to preach and heal. In Luke 10, He commanded the seventy to heal and then preach.

JESUS DIDN'T PRAY FOR THE SICK—HE HEALED THEM!

If I could encourage the body of Christ in anything, it would be to re-read the four Gospels and the book of Acts with a fresh and open mind. It will change your life and ministry. One thing you will discover is that Jesus never prayed for the sick. Not once! Nor can you find the Apostles praying for the sick in the book of Acts, which happens to be the book that we, the body of Christ, are still writing.

Jesus didn't pray for the sick; He healed them. Jesus also said that He did nothing unless he saw the Father doing it (my paraphrase of John 5:19-20 and verse 30, and 8:28-29). In other words, He maintained a relationship with the Father that allowed Him to hear clearly from Heaven on every issue. Jesus moved in the gifts in a very simple but profound way. That's why one time He spits in a blind man's eyes, another time He makes mud from spit and rubs it in the fella's eyes and tells him to go wash in the pool, and another time He just says, *"Receive your sight."* There were three different methods that got the same results: blind eyes were opened. But, notice that there was a constant in all three cases. That constant was that Jesus witnessed in His Spirit what the Father showed Him in each case, and He did that.

Our ministry should never be about "method" but about developing a relationship with Him through the Word and prayer that takes us to a new level of hearing from the Holy Spirit and moving in all nine of the gifts of the Spirit.

Jesus was the Spirit of prophecy, but let's take a fresh look at how the Spirit of prophecy did it. Too many "Spirit-filled" churches are focused on the prophetic, or having a word for people, as the fulfillment of "moving in the gifts." Now, again, don't get me wrong; I believe in the prophetic and move in it myself. My wife, Grace, is a seer and sometimes has words and visions for everyone in the meeting. It is a wonderful manifestation of the Holy Spirit. We also bring the prophets into our church to speak and prophesy fresh words over our church and the people. A prophetic word can be very powerful, as it can unlock things and set people free. But, it is not central to the ministry of Jesus Christ.

What I am getting at is that too many churches are satisfied with that dynamic of the prophetic ministry. They will have church beginning with praise and worship, preach a sermon, then line the people up, or call them out, and have words for them. That's great and wonderful, but it will not attract the unsaved world to your church. What it does attract is Christians who want a "word" to make them feel good. I feel that sometimes it even borders on the Christian version of going to a palm reader or psychic to read your future.

In Matt. 11:4, when Jesus confirmed to John the Baptist's disciples that He was the Christ, He told them, *"Go and shew John again those things which ye do hear and see: The blind receive their sight, and the lame walk, the lepers are cleansed, and the deaf hear, the dead are raised up, and the poor have the gospel preached to them."*

I believe that I am real safe in telling you that Jesus has shown us right here what we need to do to get the light on and burning bright in the Church. The world is sick and hurting and they need to start hearing the ministries report what Jesus told John's disciples.

T.L. Osborn called healing, "The Lord's dinner bell." Smith Wigglesworth called it, "The maidservant of salvation." In Mark 7:27, Jesus called it, *"The children's bread."*

In Mark 1:29-34, when Jesus healed Peter's mother in-law, it says that by nightfall all the sick in the whole city were gathered at the door. In Acts 9:32-35, when Peter healed Aeneas, it says that the whole country saw what God did and everybody in the region turned to the Lord.

In Acts 8:5-13, when Philip went down to Samaria, it says he preached Christ, cast out devils, and healed many. The results were that *"there was great joy in the city"* and everybody turned from witchcraft to Jesus.

If that is the way Jesus and His disciples did it, why would we think we should do it any differently?

ABOUT THE AUTHOR

Henry Falany was a pioneer in the white water rafting industry, starting a business in his late teens that grew to employing more than 20 people by the time he was twenty. Eventually, this grew into an international business that included camping trips to the Caribbean and horse breeding. Henry's business ventures became the training ground for the Holy Spirit, who was constantly at work in both him and his wife, Grace.

Henry and Grace sold their business in 1989 to follow God in a new direction—pastoring a revival church and pioneering new realms of the Spirit. Now, after more than two decades in ministry, including 23 years of founding and pastoring a local church, it is clear that God has used the millions of miles of experiences that He led them through to birth a very non-traditional, apostolic ministry for these last days. Henry's book on the spiritual history and contributions of California to the church and kingdom of God, titled *God, Gold and Glory!*, documents the spiritual heritage of the Golden State and has inspired many in the body of Christ.

Henry and Grace travel and minister as modern-day revivalists with an apostolic and prophetic anointing and experience many healings and miracles in their meetings. Pastor Henry's preaching is often salted with a lot of country humor and interesting illustrations, often based on stories and life experiences in the great western outdoors, and southern swamp and bayou upbringing. You can find more information about Henry, Grace, and the ministry God has given them at www.mariposarevivalcenter.org.

CHAPTER SEVENTY-SEVEN

HEALING ROOMS MINISTRIES: AN APOSTOLIC BIRTHING OF A WORLD-WIDE VISION

CAL PIERCE

THE VISION

It was July 22, 1999 that we re-dug the wells of healing and opened up healing rooms in Spokane, Wash. The healing wells of John G. Lake were waiting to be re-dug since 1935 when he passed away. I knew for this work to be available to the whole body of Christ, the focus must come off of a man, John G. Lake, and onto the Holy Spirit. Even though John G. Lake brought an amazing work to us, we must build upon that work. To have increase, we must go higher. There is a tendency to focus on what a man has done rather than what the Holy Spirit is doing.

By focusing on the Holy Spirit, the work of Healing Rooms can go into every nation and every city in every nation. Where the Holy Spirit is, His anointing is available to every believer. God said if your vision is as big as the world, it wouldn't have to be any bigger.

EVERY CITY IN EVERY NATION

After we opened the first healing room in Spokane, we began to have visitors who came from around the world. They saw what was happening in Spokane and expressed a desire to have the same work in their city. We knew that we must have a work that could be duplicated in every nation. We developed, by the leading of the Holy Spirit, a model of operation for every healing room. It is this model that helps us to maintain the integrity of every healing room. Every healing room, no matter what nation, must be a safe place for the sick to go.

The power to heal the sick is the same, no matter where a healing room is located. The key that we bring is that healing comes by the power of God. When we pray three team members to a room, one puts 1,000 to flight, two put 10,000 to flight and three put 100,000 to flight. There is power in the unity of God's people. A healing room will accomplish three key things in every city: 1), equip the saints for the work of the ministry; 2), bring unity in a city as all the body of Christ can come together and minister in a healing room; and 3), bring healing and restoration to God's people. One requirement to start a healing room in a city is if there are any sick people there. We haven't yet seen a city that didn't meet that requirement.

THE STRATEGY

We had an operational model that could be duplicated; now we needed a strategy to take it to the world. For me, this was unfamiliar territory. I came into this ministry with a business background. I received a degree at college in business administration. I was in the real estate development business when renewal came to our church, Bethel Church in Redding, Calif. Since I wasn't formally trained in Biblical principles, all I could do was ask the Holy Spirit, who is my teacher, what to do. By His direction, we formed the International Association of Healing Rooms (IAHR).

This would be the framework for a worldwide work. We asked the leadership team of our local church to bless and commission us and send us out, and they did. Through IAHR, we began to identify national directors, in the U.S., regional directors who oversee state directors in their sphere of influence. Each national director works with our IAHR offices in Spokane to transcribe our training materials into their language. They also co-ordinate training and conferencing in their nation to grow the work throughout their country. We are constantly looking to improve this strategy. We cannot continue to reach a changing world with old wineskins. We are currently looking to identify divisional directors who will oversee groups of nations with national directors.

REFORMING CULTURE

We quickly realized that to get the body of Christ healed, we had to change cultural thinking. To do this would require a renewing of the mind according to Rom. 12:2. For too long, the church has justified their condition, rather than their position. We had to explain why we were sick, rather than why we were healed. The revelation that healing was in the atonement had to come to believers so that they would embrace God's will to heal them.

THE SPIRIT OF RELIGION

The spirit of religion had to be overcome by releasing truth. The spirit of religion had established a culture in the church that caused a believer to go by what they see, rather than by what the Spirit of God wants to reveal. Jesus cautioned us, not to walk by sight, but by the Word of God. When we walk by sight, we see sickness in the body of Christ, and then bring the word down to our experience, rather than have our experience changed by raising it up to the level of the Word.

FROM GREEK TO HEBREW MINDSETS

The spirit of religion works through a Greek mindset that causes a believer to walk by sight. This spirit will cut off faith and not fulfill the will of God. Faith is not activated by what we see; it comes by what we hear. Without faith, the Bible says, it's impossible to please God. We can't please God because without Faith His will isn't being fulfilled. So we found ourselves having to reform cultural thinking about healing by renewing the minds of believers to think with Hebrew mindsets.

Basically, a Greek mind goes by what it sees and a Hebrew mind goes by what it hears the Spirit saying. The Greek thinking has caused us to believe the devil has the power to make us sick, but God who has more power can't make us well. When a believer realizes the Holy Spirit is in them for the fulfillment of the will of God, then they can partner with Him, as His vessel, and move in power to destroy the enemy's work.

NATURAL REALITY
TO KINGDOM REALITY

Only with the Hebrew mind, will revelation come to a believer. Only by the Holy Spirit, can we understand the fullness of truth. Cultural transformation comes when we set our minds on the things above, not on the things that are on earth, (Col. 3:1-3). Where we set our mind will determine what reality is in our life. We will either believe in natural reality or Kingdom reality. Setting our minds on the things above will reveal Kingdom reality to a believer. Reality is not the created; it is the Creator who created it. God is more real than what He creates. Kingdom reality will reveal to us that the power to heal the sick comes from God and not us. It is the knowing of truth that sets us free (John 8:32). The truth is that it is God's will to heal us. And it is always God's will to fulfill His will; that's why it is His will.

As this truth reforms our culture, there is an increase of power to heal the body of Christ. This power is not ours; it is God's. It increases as the vessel it flows through becomes less restrictive. I have come to realize that God is not a believer. He didn't write the book because He needed something to believe. God is a creator, and we need to believe He creates. Increase comes by believing. In Prov. 24:5, we are told that knowledge increases power.

FIVE-FOLD MINISTRY

Part of being an apostolic work is understanding the five-fold ministry according to Eph. 4:11-13: *"And He gave some as apostles and some as prophets, and some as evangelists, and some as pastors and teachers, for the equipping of the saints for the work of service, to the building up of the body of Christ; until we all attain to the unity of the faith, and of the knowledge of the Son of*

God, to a mature man, to the measure of the stature which belongs to the fullness of Christ."

This Scripture tells us that we need apostles, prophets, evangelists, pastors and teachers active in the church, until we all attain to a unity of faith to a mature man and to the measure of stature which belongs to the fullness of Christ. In other words, until we are a mature bride, moving in the fullness of Christ, we need the five-fold ministry for the equipping of the saints for the work of the kingdom of God on the earth. Some have said that the work of the early apostles and prophets was enough and we don't need them today.

The early apostles and prophets laid a foundation for the church to build upon according to Eph. 2:20. That foundation had signs, wonders, healings and miracles in it to be built upon. The problem is that today we haven't built up the body of Christ with signs, wonders, healings and miracles as we were supposed to. Now we need modern-day apostles and prophets to re-lay the foundation that was torn down by lack of faith.

As an apostle, leading an apostolic work, we are re-laying the foundation of healing and miracles through Healing Rooms around the world. The household of God is being built up as the saints are equipped and begin to do the work of setting the captives free. Our desire is to work with the local church by equipping and healing the saints, saving the lost and sending them to the church.

ESTABLISHING UNITY

Another aspect of the five-fold ministry is to establish a unity of faith. We accomplish this through Healing Rooms by having our ministry teams made up by people from many churches in each city. For instance, in the Spokane Healing Rooms, there are around 60 churches represented on our team. They attain to a unity of faith because they become a family working together in their destiny with no denominational walls to divide them. They are Kingdom people living in truth, filled with the Holy Spirit and doing the work.

BRINGING THE KINGDOM OF GOD

As an apostolic ministry, we have to bring on earth, the government of God. In Isa. 9:6, it talks about the coming King, who is Jesus, and that, *"the government will rest on His shoulders."* In verse 7, we are told that this government will continue to increase and will have no end. When Jesus was raised and seated at the right hand of God, we became His body (1 Cor. 12:27), and He became our head (1 Cor. 11:3). As His body on earth, we have been given governmental authority to bring His Kingdom upon the earth (Eph. 1:18-23). The government is the Kingdom which Jesus mandated to us in Matt. 6:10: *"Thy Kingdom come, Thy Will be done, On earth as it is in Heaven."*

Our mandate in Healing Rooms Ministries is to bring His Kingdom, as it is in heaven on earth. The key here is that we are not told to bring heaven on earth, but His Kingdom on earth, just as it is in heaven. As an example, if there is not sickness in heaven, then there should not be any on earth. We can move in this governmental authority by the Holy Spirit, who is in us. The Holy Spirit gives us access to the Father for the fulfillment of His will on earth (Eph. 2:18). When our will aligns with His will, then His will can be done on earth through us.

OUR PROVISION

This Healing Rooms work is accomplished by the provision of God's will being fulfilled. The fulfilling of the will of God comes through His Kingdom coming. Jesus said that when we destroy the work of the enemy by signs, wonders, healing and miracles, empowered by the Holy Spirit, that is an indication that the Kingdom of God has arrived on earth (Matt. 12:28). Notice that the Kingdom of God comes by the Holy Spirit. The work of apostles must recognize that the provision of the Kingdom comes by the Holy Spirit, who is available to flow through every believer.

Rom. 14:17 says, *"For the Kingdom of God is not eating and drinking, but righteousness and peace and joy in the Holy Spirit."* The Kingdom of God is in the Holy Spirit and the Holy Spirit is in us (Luke 17:21). Our provision is our inheritance which is His will for us. God not only gives us His will as an inheritance, but He puts His Spirit in us as a guarantee that we receive it. It's a position where we dwell in victory and live in righteousness and peace and joy in the Holy Spirit.

THE SUPERNATURAL

Since the Kingdom we bring is in the Holy Spirit and the Holy Spirit is supernatural, then we must become familiar with the Spirit realm. It doesn't do us any good, as an apostolic ministry, to teach about how to heal the sick and not teach about the supernatural. Without an understanding of the Spirit realm, we will have a tendency to develop formulas for the work. I have discovered that healing is only difficult when I think it comes by my power. It must come by the power of His might (Eph. 6:10). When it's God, it's easy. The key is that we are the vessels God uses. We might say it this way: without God we cannot; without us He will not.

When we become born again, we become a new creature. We are no longer limited to earth or the world's order of things. We become a spirit man, occupied by the Spirit of God. 2 Cor. 5:17-18 says, *"Therefore if any man is in Christ, he is a new creature, the old things passed away; behold, new things have come. Now all these things are from God..."* The Spirit of man now has the capacity of heaven available to him by God. All of the old things, or what was under the curse, have been redeemed through the blood of Jesus. Now all things are new and these new things are from God. The new things come by His will for us as we walk in His Kingdom.

HEALING AND HEALTH

After we had been in Healing Rooms Ministries for 10 years, I began to recognize that the body of Christ was as sick, if not more sick, than when we started. This began to concern me to the point that I began to ask the Holy Spirit about the condition of His body. He began to talk to me about the healing movement, and how it needs to be changed. The revelation that came changed my life. First He said, "You only have one body; you mess it up and we are both out." He said, "Stop destroying my body with poor health. The work of healing," He said, "deals with your condition; the place of being healed deals with your position."

I was led to this scripture (1 Cor. 6:19-20): *"Do you not know that your body is a temple of the Holy Spirit who is in you, whom you have from God. And that you are not your own, for you have been bought with a price; therefore, glorify God in your body."* I realized that my body doesn't belong to me; it was bought with a price and belongs to God. My body is a temple of God's spirit and I am to glorify Him in it.

In other words, I have a responsibility to God to steward my (His) body into good health. If I don't do this then sickness will reign in my body. Either God will reign or sickness will reign. I realized that it must grieve the heart of Jesus to know that His body is bearing the sickness He bore for it. We are not supposed to get healed so that we can get sick again. We have been trying to get healing into sickly bodies and it's not working.

In Gen. 6:3, we are told that our days shall be 120 years. I have a scientific periodical that says, today with proper nutrition and exercise, man should live to be 120 years old. I figured if an unredeemed scientist can agree with God, so can I. After all the Bible does say as a man thinks within himself, so is he. We cannot achieve good health by man's order of diet and exercise. It must be Spirit led. When we partner with the Holy Spirit, He will provide the power to sustain good nutrition and exercise. This is important because we're talking about the house.

Eph. 3:16 says, "...that He would grant you, according to the riches of His Glory, to be strengthened with power through his Spirit in the inner man." This gives us the apostolic authority to take command over our body and steward it into health. My goodness, if we can't move in power over our bodies, then how are we to move in power over the enemy?

Our mind must be renewed to this truth, and all the work of healing points to one thing – a body with no sickness in it. God didn't design us to be sick. There was no sickness in the garden until the fall. Jesus, the last Adam, redeemed us from that curse. Redemption sets us free from the curse. It sets us free for one reason, so we don't have to experience it any more. We have the Holy Spirit in us; therefore, resurrection power can extinguish every fiery dart of sickness.

I am, as of this writing, 67 years old and I work out six days a week and have good, Spirit-led nutrition and am healthier and stronger than I have been in 40 years. I am going for the 120 years in good health and strength.

FINANCING THE VISION

As an apostolic leader, coming from a business background, I realized that the work must grow through a kingdom business plan. Since we are not church based and tithes belong in the church, we had to rely on developing other sources for income. Offerings only would not sustain the growth of the ministry. So, we have developed a resource plan that includes IAHR membership fees, product development and sales, an on-site bookstore, partner program, on-site and web on-line school, conferencing, web streaming and T.V. production. Our goal is to make these resources available to the network of Healing rooms so they will have financial provision.

RELEASING REVELATION

Another aspect of apostolic leadership is releasing revelation. The five-fold ministry is to equip the saints for the work of the Kingdom. Eph. 4:13 also says we are to build up the body of Christ into a mature man, to the measure of the stature which belongs to His fullness. It takes the revelation of the Holy Spirit to grow the body into increase. Yesterday's revelation will not suffice for tomorrow's needs. God has more than we can contain. Moving toward the fullness of Christ puts a demand on us to increase in revelation. The word of God is living and active; therefore, it's creative. It's not creative in a book; it's creative in a believer. We must have revelation to take us to new levels. In 1 Cor. 2:16 it says, we have the mind of Christ. With the mind of Christ we can think according to heaven and not be limited to earth. The Holy Spirit is in us to connect our thoughts to His. Thus, according to 1 Cor. 2:13, we can connect spiritual thoughts to spiritual words. Then, we can confess those things that are not, so that they can be in the natural realm.

FATHERING A MOVEMENT

One of the key qualities of apostles is to bring a fathering to the body of Christ. I am quite often asked, "How do you pastor a work like Healing Rooms Ministries that is worldwide?" I answer that question by saying, "The ministry isn't pastored; it's fathered." The blessing of Fathering is when the kids fall down, you get them up, encourage them that they can do it, and send them out. A father teaches and encourages sons and daughters to move into their destiny. The work of the five-fold is to bring the children of God into a maturity and into the fullness of the Spirit to become a harvesting bride. We are to make ready the people of God.

Luke 1:17 says, *"And it is he who will go as a forerunner before Him in the Spirit and power of Elijah, to turn the hearts of the fathers back to the children, and the disobedient to the attitude of the righteous; so as to make ready a people prepared for the Lord."* Apostolic forerunners are preparing the way for the next generation to arise into all that God has for them.

It's interesting that Spokane is known as "The City of the Father's Heart." This is because Father's Day began in Spokane through a Mrs. Sonora Smart Dodd who proposed it on June 19, 1910.

The work of apostolic leaders is essential in today's climate. Everything that can be shaken is being shaken for one reason, so that what cannot be shaken will remain. We receive a kingdom that cannot be shaken (Heb. 12:26-29). The household of God must be built upon the foundation of God's Kingdom that cannot be shaken. This will move the church from a rapture mentality to a harvest theology.

ABOUT THE AUTHOR

Cal Pierce and his wife Michelle grew up in Redding, Calif. where they were members of Bethel Assembly of God Church. Cal served at Bethel as an elder and board member. He says he was "the most bored board member the church had." For 25 years he was stuck in a form of Christianity that denied God's power. In June, 1996 during a service where God moved powerfully, Cal was changed by the power of God. Cal's life has been changed ever since.

Cal, a Real Estate Developer, felt God draw he and his wife, Michelle, north to Washington State in November 1997. "We sold everything, packed up our furniture and moved to Spokane having never been there before. We were not sure exactly what God wanted us to do, so we continued to seek his direction for ministry." Having studied the revivals, Cal had read about John G. Lake's ministry in Spokane. Cal visited Lake's grave site once each month for over one year to pray.

"On February 28, 1999 I started a 40-day fast. I went to Lake's grave site to pray when I heard God say, 'There is a time to pray, and a time to move.' There was no doubt that

God wanted us to re-dig the generational wells of healing in Spokane." Cal called in intercessors and began training up healing teams. On July 22, 1999 the Spokane Healing Rooms were re-opened in the same location they were 80 years ago, and have since moved to two nearby buildings to accommodate the rapid growth of the ministry. The ministry now has an international impact.

Cal is Director and Michelle is Co-Director of Healing Rooms Ministries. Cal teaches at conferences around the world about the provision Jesus provided in the atonement for our healing. Michelle joins Cal in traveling to conferences. In addition, she is an international speaker bringing forth the encouraging and enlightened Word of God. You may contact them at: Healing Rooms Ministries, 112 E. 1st Ave., Spokane, WA 99202. www.healingrooms.com

CHAPTER SEVENTY-EIGHT

WHERE IN THE WORLD IS THE CHURCH?

DR. TONY DALE

"We evangelicals pride ourselves on our scriptural foundations and sound theology, but time and again we have missed the essence of what the Bible teaches about the most fundamental things. Nowhere in 'The Book' do we find para-church, which means 'beside church' or, in the minds of some, 'not really church.' If para-church describes anything, it is the work of the Holy Spirit, who comes alongside the church! The phrase has been conjured up to keep at bay those who seem to threaten what possessive and sometimes hierarchical church leaders have come to regard as their domain. In God's eyes there's one church; para-church really is church too!"

John Noble, British Pioneer Leader, writing in his book, *The Shaking,* published in the U.K. in February of 2002.

"And when He ascended on high, He gave gifts to men…And his gifts were that some should be apostles…" (Eph. 4:8, 11)

So what is an apostle? I doubt biblically this is defined by what we call ourselves on our business card! Rather, Paul expands on his message by both example and teaching to show us that apostles are the servant leaders, the entrepreneurs, who brave the obscurity and challenge of new frontiers to make sure that Christ is preached where no one else has gone. They are usually viewed by both the world and the church as those *"at the end of the parade, the off-scouring of the world, yes like dung"* (see 1 Cor. 4:9-13), but to God they are his ambassadors (2 Cor. 5:20).

An apostle is literally a "sent one" in the Greek. In Latin and English the Greek word for "Apostle" (*apostolos*) becomes the word we know as "Missionary," or one sent into a place of darkness to show forth the glory of Christ. Apostles are strategic pioneers, planting churches and providing impetus to see *"Christ being formed in you"* (Col. 4:19) in any and every place.

I am looking around the room at those that I share church life with. Bethany is a student at our local state University. I wonder if Jesus is showing up in her among her fellow students? There's Rosaura! She was on welfare a year ago. We didn't know when her son brought her to church that she was also a crack addict of 30 years' standing. Now she is running a cleaning business and seeing transformation in her family. Vic and Shama are from a Hindu background. She is a manager at a big box, national department store chain for one of the name brand cosmetic labels, and he works in a patient advocacy company. Clearly there is no apostolic material here...

NOT! In every case, these people are starting churches, sometimes multiple churches within the environment in which God has placed them. *Apostle* is not a label of having reached the heights of Christian leadership, but is a description of the call of God on certain lives.

I'm a medical doctor by training. Does this mean that the only thing that God can use me for is the practice of medicine? Tell that to Luke! By concentrating power and authority into the hands of a special elite or professional class, usually called "clergy," the church has marginalized and thereby rendered ineffective most of its members.

How well I remember the frustration of being an experienced professional, leading teams of people in my medical practice, and competent to set up conferences for physicians from all over the country, but apparently not competent enough to teach a Sunday school class at the church. Something is wrong with this picture. It is interesting, quoting again from John Noble's book, *The Shaking,* that "by rising up and endorsing His apostolic team as church, Jesus set a precedent for all time, which we have ignored throughout history to our cost. We have marginalized the God-given missionary or growth forces within the church and labeled them para-church."

OUTSIDE THE WALLS

Much of the real impetus for church growth and maturation has come through the so-called "para-church" organizations, because we tend to force the apostolic and prophetic types out of our churches, that for the most part seem to prefer or reflect a "pastor-dominated" form of leadership. The result is vision-depleted churches, tending to the needs of their members, rather than Spirit-inspired assemblies, reaching out to deal with the needs of the world. The reality is that much of the need of the world can be more effectively dealt with outside of the confines of "church," rather than within the walls (or homes) of much of what currently passes as "church."

John and Marion are family doctors. As they listened to the Holy Spirit's prompting, they realized that many elderly patients, among others, were coming out of the hospital to a lonely, empty apartment. So, they began arranging for volunteers from their church to take patients home from their hospital stay, and to assess what further help the person might need now that they were out of the hospital.

Helping those recently discharged from the hospital by doing some shopping or picking them up for church meetings, these volunteers became the church beyond the walls. Over a period of time, the local social services began using John and Marion's volunteers from a wide array of churches to help with most of the discharged patients in that district. This is church in the marketplace.

Another medical friend of ours decided to keep track of all of the patients that he spoke to about the Lord for the first time over the course of a year. At the end of the year, this is what he found: just over 50 patients had actually given their lives to the Lord the first time that he spoke to them about Jesus in his medical office. Another 50 had given their lives to the Lord on a second or subsequent visit during the year of this study. An additional 50 had been spoken to about the Lord, but had not yet responded to the message. This represents over a hundred lives that had been meaningfully and radically touched by God in his office during that year.

This is church at work.

I have a friend named Pam, a skilled nurse, who is also a natural evangelist. She came to my medical practice to stand in for another member of the staff who needed to be on an extended maternity leave. There was a six-week period while Pam was working with me that we saw at least a patient a day give their lives to the Lord. Every day! This is church in the medical practice. It is not that God just wants to raise up "church" in any and every place where He sends His people. He also wants to raise up apostolic and prophetic leadership to demonstrate His divine love and power to a world that is waiting to see God's Word become flesh.

Victor Choudhrie is such an apostolic figure. This highly successful and acclaimed cancer surgeon was also the Dean of one of the best-known medical schools in India. God told him to leave medicine and start planting churches. With no theological background and no church-planting experience, he was forced into the only textbook he knew on the subject, namely, the book of Acts. Now, 20 years later, there are tens of thousands of house churches and more than a million people who are a part of the network that has grown as a result of Victor's obedience to the Holy Spirit. This is apostolic work, the ascended Christ building his church on earth.

Patrick Dixon was a chest physician who found himself caught up in the growing AIDS crisis that hit Britain in the mid '80s. Caring passionately about the patients and about the public health aspects of this emerging crisis, Patrick applied himself to his patients' humanitarian needs and to Britain's apparent blindness to the seriousness of the AIDS problem. Out of this concern grew the largest of the British AIDS charities. But this was not to be the end of Patrick's story. Having seen what happens when one is open to pointing the way to the future, Patrick has developed into one of the best-known lecturers and forecasters of business and economic trends in Britain. He finds himself widely in demand to speak to major corporations across the world to help them understand the times in which we live.

This is prophetic work, Christ speaking into the marketplace.

In our own limited way, my wife Felicity and I have seen the power of Christ in the marketplace of business. Unable to practice medicine in America because our British licensing is not accepted here, we moved into business. A few years ago we started an evangelistic Bible study with some of our business colleagues. We invited 12 friends to join us for a weekly study in the book of Proverbs so we could explore together "what the wisest man who ever lived had to say about wealth and finance." Over the course of the next year, all of these friends found the Lord. That became the foundation of what has since multiplied into a network of house churches whose influence has spread literally all over the world.

MEET THEM WHERE THEY ARE

This is church. This is the risen Christ reaching into people's lives, where they are, and meeting them at their place of need. If you are looking for the apostolic and prophetic people in church, you may be looking in the wrong place. Many, marginalized by their churches, are nevertheless reaching out in ways that only the Holy Spirit could have initiated and are demonstrating how to bring church to the people, rather than people to church. Jesus never told us to go and get the people to come. He told us to "go" (Luke 10:3 and Matt. 28:18-20). As Keith Green so eloquently put it in one of his songs, "Jesus commands us to go; it takes a call to stay." The businessman is as called as the evangelist, the university professor as called as the pastor. And what's more, the businessman and the professor can probably support themselves in the process.

It is an entirely Greek philosophy, which gives rise to the impression that somehow it is more spiritual to be pastoring than to be creating profits. For example, in our own situation over the past years, we could provide not only work for many people, but also the finances for mission trips for ourselves over a three-month period, and for the training programs of hundreds of church planters in other countries. The nature of the apostolic is to be entrepreneurial.

Paul wanted to labor where no one else had gone before. He was not looking to build on another man's foundation or to be supported by another person's labor. For him it was a matter of pride that he could find a way to bring the gospel to people without charge. Many in the business community are an incredible example of what the Rom. 12 ministry of "giving" or "liberality" is all about.

Rich DeVos, the owner of the Orlando Magic basketball team, and co-founder of Amway, not only models how to maturely manage and give away millions of dollars to inner city missions, but also has devoted his time and talents as Chairman of the Board of Gospel Films, helping it reach millions for Christ through film.

Full Gospel Businessmen's Fellowship International (FGBMFI) never viewed itself as anything more than a "para-church" organization. But, its chapters in cities across the world are probably more like New Testament "church" for many people who attend them, than the actual churches that they go to on Sundays. A campus group may not be comfortable calling itself a church, because it may be viewed as competing with the "real" churches off campus. But, does that make it any less church in the Biblical sense? Christ is calling the church to get out of the walls and into the world. Christ is calling his apostles to go to the world, not wait for the world to come to our churches.

As I quoted earlier in this chapter, "Christ gave a command to go." It is time for us to stop asking people to come! Let's go to them.

ABOUT THE AUTHOR

Dr. Tony Dale, Founder of The Karis Group (www.thekarisgroup.com) and of The Health Co-Op (www.thehealthcoop.com), is a church-planting pioneer working with house church movements around the world. Along with his wife, Felicity, they have authored numerous books including *Small Is Big!* and *The Rabbit and the Elephant,* and they are on the board of House 2 House Ministries (www.house2house.com). Tony's current passion is helping the body of Christ see that we have biblical answers to the national health care crisis, and The Health Co-Op is his practical application of these ideas into the marketplace.

Tony is an incurable entrepreneur, always looking for the next adventure in his walk with the Lord, and has helped to start or incubate several Kingdom businesses. He and his wife, Felicity, who is also a physician, trained at the world famous St. Bartholomew's Hospital in London (www.tonyandfelicitydale.com). After practicing medicine and helping develop a Christian ministry to physicians in the U.K., the family moved to the United States in 1987. The Dales have four children and numerous grandchildren. To learn more or to contact Tony, visit his websites or email him at tdale@thekarisgroup.com.

SECTION XII

SUMMARY & CONCLUSION

CHAPTER SEVENTY-NINE

EPILOGUE

DR. BRUCE COOK

Are your ears still ringing? Is your heart still pounding? Is your mind still racing and your spirit still soaring after being exposed to and immersed in an apostolic marathon and download from 70 Kingdom leaders? Wow! You have been exposed to—and likely been infected with—the "apostolic spirit" that is transferrable from apostles, just as the "prophetic spirit" was transferred to Saul in the Old Testament by the company of prophets and he was *"changed into another man"* (1 Sam 10:6). I pray that all who read this anthology be likewise "changed into another man"—the person and nature and character of Jesus Christ himself.

I decree that you, the reader, receive an apostolic impartation and activation, and a transference of the apostolic spirit that is in this apostolic company of authors and elders. I charge you to go forth and to do mighty exploits and great deeds from the place of knowing your God (Dan. 11:32) but more than that, to hide these apostolic precepts, teachings and models in your heart, and to become part of the apostolic movement in the earth today, and part of God's apostolic army in the Seven Mountains of Culture.

Don't try to go it alone, however, as some teach, saying that you and God are enough. While true in principle (Rom. 8:31-39), the context of that is persecution and opposition, so that is a lonely road and a lonely existence and is not the plan of God for your life, unless it is for a special season of preparation or testing or discipline. God is a relational God and we are designed and commanded throughout Scripture to be part of the body, to build each other up in love, to bear one another's burdens, to make our joy complete, to serve one another, to be hospitable and charitable, to not forsake the assembling together of the saints, and to be under authority. Find some others with the same or similar values, spiritual DNA and vision, and join together either formally or informally to build together as an apostolic team, tribe or network and accelerate the process and path you are on. They are out there if you have eyes to see and ears to hear.

Now that the book series has been written, and you the reader have arrived at this point after presumably reading all or part of this apostolic anthology, our journey together here is ending, but the adventure of walking with Jesus and the Holy Spirit living in your heart, and building and expanding His Kingdom with His sons and daughters and ministering angels, continues both now and forever for those who have called upon His name in faith, through all eternity. I pray that you have been encouraged, enlightened and empowered by what you have read, and that you have a new appreciation and respect for and a deeper understanding of the apostolic and apostles.

The apostleship and apostolic dimension is such a rich, broad and vast topic to explore and mine that no one book or anthology can cover all points or address all possible dimensions of this subject, or exhaust all avenues of inquiry—not even this one. Knowing that up front, I prayed and trusted the Holy Spirit to speak to me and to the various contributing authors the things He wanted us to address, write about and focus attention on in these chapters, sections and volumes.

As stated earlier in the Preface of Volume One, this is a work of the Spirit and not a work of man. So, I decree that it finds its way to hungry hearts and to thirsty spirits across the earth and around the globe, both now and in future generations if the Lord tarries, in Jesus' name, amen. May the Lord use this anthology of apostleship for His good pleasure and for His glory to impact the nations, reform the church, mobilize the army of glory, purify His bride, hasten His return, and accelerate the end-time harvest. Thank you.

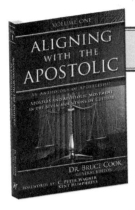

VOLUME ONE

ALIGNING WITH THE APOSTOLIC
A FIVE VOLUME ANTHOLOGY OF
APOSTLESHIP & THE APOSTOLIC MOVEMENT
DR. BRUCE COOK, GENERAL EDITOR

Foreword by C. Peter Wagner
Foreword by Kent Humphreys

Volume One contains the Introduction and Overview to this historic work by 70 authors, written by General Editor, Dr. Bruce Cook. This volume contains an explanation of the research methodology used in compilation of the anthology and an extensive glossary of 80 apostolic terms.

VOLUME ONE

SECTION 1:
Introduction & Overview—
- Coming Into Apostolic Alignment
- What an Apostle Is, and Is Not
- Levels of Maturity and Types of Apostles
- Apostolic Authority: A Two-Edged Sword
- Origins of the Patriarchs & Judaism Are Found in the Marketplace
- Origins of the Church and Christianity Are Found in the Marketplace
- Apostolic Reformers in the Marketplace

www.KingdomHouse.net

KINGDOM HOUSE
P U B L I S H I N G

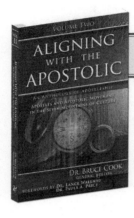

VOLUME TWO

ALIGNING WITH THE APOSTOLIC
A FIVE VOLUME ANTHOLOGY OF
APOSTLESHIP & THE APOSTOLIC MOVEMENT
DR. BRUCE COOK, GENERAL EDITOR

Foreword by Dr. Lance Wallnau
Foreword by Dr. Paula A. Price

VOLUME TWO

SECTION 2:
Apostolic Government

SECTION 3:
Apostolic Foundations

www.KingdomHouse.net

KINGDOM HOUSE
PUBLISHING

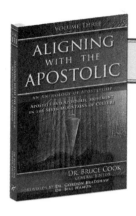

VOLUME THREE

ALIGNING WITH THE APOSTOLIC
A FIVE VOLUME ANTHOLOGY OF
APOSTLESHIP & THE APOSTOLIC MOVEMENT
DR. BRUCE COOK, GENERAL EDITOR

Foreword by Dr. Gordon Bradshaw
Foreword by Dr. Bill Hamon

VOLUME THREE

SECTION 4:
Apostolic Intercession

SECTION 5:
Apostolic Character & Maturity

SECTION 6:
Apostolic Education

www.KingdomHouse.net

KINGDOM HOUSE
PUBLISHING

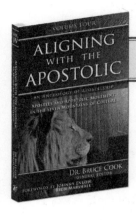

VOLUME FOUR

ALIGNING WITH THE APOSTOLIC
A FIVE VOLUME ANTHOLOGY OF
APOSTLESHIP & THE APOSTOLIC MOVEMENT
DR. BRUCE COOK, GENERAL EDITOR

Foreword by Johnny Enlow
Foreword by Rich Marshall

VOLUME FOUR

SECTION 7:
Apostolic Fathers & Mothers

SECTION 8:
Apostolic Leadership & Teams

SECTION 9:
Apostolic Creativity
& Innovation

www.KingdomHouse.net

KINGDOM HOUSE
PUBLISHING

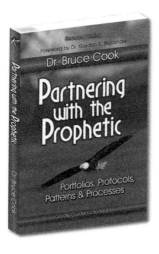

ALSO BY DR. BRUCE COOK

Finally, the one book on the prophetic that I can use both in my graduate level course on 5-Fold Ministry at Regent University, as well as in the equipping ministries in the churches that I oversee. In a time of traveling light, this is the one book on the prophetic that will give you focus and passion for its full restoration.

Dr. Joseph Umidi |
Professor, Overseer, CEO

Partnering with the Prophetic is a resource that every student or minister of the prophetic should have in their library. Bruce skillfully teaches, instructs, and imparts faith for activation in this timely book. I have witnessed the operation of Bruce Cook's prophetic gift and received prophetic blessing and encouragement from God through him. Both Bruce and his gift are authentic—true gifts to the Body of Christ.

Patricia King | Co-Founder of XPmedia

Prophets are not the only ones who need to understand the prophetic. The whole body needs to understand the prophetic and allow the Holy Spirit to move in that way. *Partnering with the Prophetic* will bring clarity and unity to the church. It will give us ... a release, a great understanding to our native people that believe in the prophetic, which they call THE DREAMER.

Dr. Negiel Bigpond | *Morning Star Church of All Nations Co-founder Two Rivers Native American Training Center*

w w w . K i n g d o m H o u s e . n e t

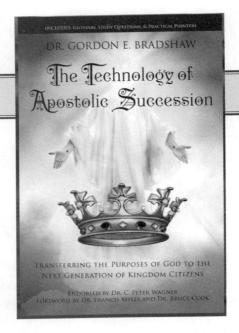

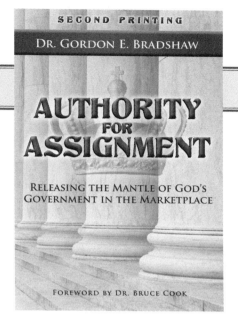

AUTHORITY FOR ASSIGNMENT
RELEASING THE MANTLE OF GOD'S GOVERNMENT IN THE MARKETPLACE
DR. GORDON BRADSHAW

How will "God's Government" affect the marketplace today?

It will come through the restoration of one of God's greatest supernatural technologies ... "The Mantle of Misrah!" Misrah is a Hebrew word that means "government and prevailing power." Inside this powerful mantle we've been given a supernatural problem-solving dynamic that restores the marketplace to its highest level of function for the Kingdom of God!

w w w . K i n g d o m H o u s e . n e t

NOT FOR PRICE OR REWARD
MOTIVES OF THE HEART REGARDING RICHES, WEALTH, AND STEWARDSHIP
DR. BRUCE COOK

If the complexities of economics are not enough, add to the equation the attitudes, motivation, and behaviors of men. The rise and fall of currencies parallels the rise and fall of nations, since money is a creation of man and its use is controlled by men.

Our motives matter to God, and character counts. *Not for Price or Reward* targets the personal level—focusing on motives of the heart related to money, and the subtle ways that Mammon lies to and seduces us. Watch for news of this book's release!

w w w . K i n g d o m H o u s e . n e t